Aukati

MICHALIA ARATHIMOS

AUKATI

m

aukati

[Māori](verb) to dam a stream, to prevent one from passing, to block, to discriminate against;

(noun) border, boundary marking a prohibited area, roadblock, discrimination, justice, line over which one may not pass

© Michalia Arathimos 2017

ISBN 978-0-9941378-5-2

Cover design and illustrations: Sarah Laing
Book design and typesetting: Paul Stewart
Editor: Mary McCallum

Printed in New Zealand by Your Books, Wellington

MĀKARO PRESS

PO BOX 41 032 EASTBOURNE NEW ZEALAND
www.makaropress.co.nz

Aroha και αγάπη, Ira

PRÓLOGOS

This one thinks she is the centre, but she is only a part. The other thinks everything is the centre but himself. She has long hair that falls down her back, hair she can hide inside. When his hair gets long he razors it off, the fine points biting at his palm. She has always been adored. She carries it like a weight. Her shoulders hunch, and she is shamefully aware of it. Don't let yourself sag like that. Stand up. Be proud of who you are. You are the first of us to go to university. You are our hopes and our dreams. He has only ever been needed, which is different from being adored.

Where she is filled with voices, he is empty. He and his mother sit alone, together. Blow out your candles! Blow them out! Big breath! He gasps and gasps for air in the quiet room. In her are old songs. Forty years. To make a better life. He has emptied himself of words. They were mere repetitions, after all. Did I tell you that story about your father? She prefers not to be touched. In bed she wants the snatch and grab, frisson, a hot collision. For it to be felt, and over. He likes tenderness and curation, the body a carefully mapped terrain.

She is filled with her work. Of course there is her voice, the one she keeps quiet because it wasn't practical to use it. And she'd never earn any money. And they said they didn't want her to live on nothing. They said, Do you think that's why your grandparents came here, so you could grow up to live in poverty?

He knows the right people and does photography. It's a living, of sorts. It makes no difference. He photographs trees and snails. It's a talent that he has for seeing the light. He's always loved the bush, though of course he knows its hunger, its fickle generosity. She moves through work and out the other side. There she finds she has used her lover as a flotation device. The family is far away. She cuts free the device, and goes under.

He fights casually, mainly through the documentation of small moments. The answer maybe is in the bush, but people cut it down. It is not a question of the bush's innocence. His pictures attract the wrong sort of attention. *Just because you're not paranoid doesn't mean they're not out to get you.* He makes the best of it, like his mother did. That's what I thought when your father disappeared, she said to him. You're just going to have to make the best of it. You just have to carry on.

All she wants to do is sing. She goes on the road. This is where other people find lost things. This is what you are meant to do. She's not sure what she is looking for: evidence, collectables, things that will make her throat open.

He gets into the car and drives. He knows it's naive, but someone has to try and save the world.

PÁRODOS

Now the long blade of the sun, lying
Level east to west, touches with glory
The gates of Taranaki. On one hand, Mokau
On the other, Whanganui. But watching

Open, unlidded, is the golden eye of day!
O marching light, across the eddy and rush
Of Te Tai-o-Rehua, striking
The white shields of the enemy!

1

The mountain, mantled lightly in snow, was almost too regular in shape, like a child's sketch of a mountain. There was a trace of mist about its peaks. Even though it was cool this early in spring, the sun had hit their tent and Isaiah could no longer stay asleep. He and Sam had driven well into the night, arriving too late to be welcomed. Such focus had been necessary to keep the car on the road, to keep the thin white strip on one side and the car on the other. More than once he'd come to himself, the car drifting gently across the line.

Though the tip of the mountain was shadowed he could tell the cloud would burn off by lunchtime. It would be a good day for walking. But by then he'd be cooped up, in the press of the marae welcome, listening to speeches in a language he didn't understand.

They were camped outside the clearing, away from the other cars. Isaiah pissed into the ditch next to the tent in a long, satisfying stream. As he did he surveyed the place: the dense bush, the wharenui up on the hill, the hills rising bare beyond it. It was smaller than he'd expected, shabbier, dwarfed by the mountain and by the surrounding land.

A man stepped out from behind a tree.

'Mōrena, cousin. He roaroa te wā kua kitea.'

'What the hell?' Isaiah hurried to button himself.

'I said, "He roaroa te wā kua kitea."' The man didn't seem to mind Isaiah's discomfort. 'Now is that any way to greet a cousin?' He was enjoying himself.

'I don't speak te reo,' Isaiah said.

'Ahh,' the man said. He scratched his chin. 'Āe. Well, long time no see, bro.' He dealt Isaiah a great clap on the shoulder. 'Last time I saw you, you were probably three years old.' His father's tangi. 'Go on,' the man said. 'Tell me I don't look a day older than twenty-one!'

He looked more like fifty, but held himself like someone younger. Tattoos covered most of his face and forearms. Those on his arms were clumsy and blurred; prison tatts, Isaiah guessed. But the one on his face was chiselled and sharp, imposing. He wore impeccable camouflage gear from head to toe. There was nothing in his dress to distinguish him from an ordinary soldier but for a small tino rangatiratanga flag stitched to the sleeve of his shirt.

'I'm Rangi,' the man went on. 'I'll be your guide.' He laughed a huge, disarming laugh. 'Nah, jokes, man. You're not a tourist here.' He looked Isaiah over. 'I'm your father's cousin. You're like him. Taller, skinnier though, eh. Got to put some meat on those bones.' His hand went thoughtfully to his chin, which was lightly bearded. 'Bet you never cut up a cow.'

Isaiah shook his head. The man straightened up, with one eye on the mountain, as though it might have something to say.

'Well,' he said, 'reo or not, you've got to come in for the pōwhiri. Your kaumātua want you.' Isaiah must have looked densely at him, because the man sighed. He gestured to the bush, where a faint path led around the main entrance, presumably onto the pā. 'Polly sent me,' Rangi went on. 'Your aunty. Really you should be out at the gate, but considering who you are, we're gonna sneak you in to meet your whānau.' He grabbed at Isaiah, shifting him towards the path in the bush.

'But what about …'

'That chick you were with last night?' said Rangi. Isaiah wasn't sure if he was meant to feel intimidated or not. 'She'll figure it out when she wakes up. She was the one told Bryce, who called and told Matiu who told Polly, that you were all up for getting your language back, your lost culture. Said you wanted to find out all about your dad.'

Isaiah moved quickly into the bush. He could hear the faint sounds of speech behind him, the other protestors waking up. Then they were alone in the dense green. 'How did you even know I was ... me?' Isaiah asked, in a last effort to regain control.

Behind him Rangi laughed his loud, slightly insane laugh. 'Easy as, bro,' he said, and they were out of the bush into the light. The wharenui reared up before Isaiah, much larger than it had seemed from a distance. 'Your own whare tīpuna!' Rangi said, pride in his voice. He seized Isaiah and, pulling him close, gave him a long hongi. 'Nau mai! Haere mai!' His smile enveloped Isaiah. 'Easy as to tell you apart from the others. One, you look like your dad, and two ... didn't you notice?' He laughed uproariously. 'You're the only dude out there who's not white!' He walked away towards the meeting house, leaving Isaiah no other option but to follow.

Isaiah wished he had brought one of his cameras. There were several modest houses and a few buildings that must serve as storage places. Then the ground gathered itself and rose to where the meeting house sat. The panels on its side were intricate, a dark carved wood. The morning light was perfect now, diffuse and soft. It would highlight all the whorls and ridges of the carvings. But he could only take pictures with permission, anyway, and he wasn't sure even then that it would be allowed. His camera bag was back in the car, and Rangi was calling from up ahead.

'Hurry the bloody hell up, cuz!'

Isaiah went on. He'd wanted to meet his father's people and enter his own marae confidently, not like this, feeling rushed and bleary. He was still only wearing a T-shirt and pants, and in the cool air, he would have liked another layer. He rubbed at his face under his glasses.

Rangi's head appeared from the porch of an outlying building as Isaiah rounded the corner. Lying on the table in front of him was the naked carcass of what must have been a steer. Rangi was holding a chainsaw. He revved it in Isaiah's direction. Isaiah supposed the meat would be for the hangi later. He'd never thought much about the mechanics of dissection. Rangi kept up his mad grin, nodding his head towards the porch, where a woman sat, smoking. In one hand she had a potato peeler and in the other, a cigarette in a pearl holder. She glanced at Isaiah and blew out smoke in a delicate stream, as though in front of her was not a bucket of half-peeled potatoes but a tableau from an opera with which she was not entirely impressed.

This must be Polly. Polly featured in his mother's stories of the pā as the aunt closest to Isaiah's father. He'd heard the specifics again and again: Polly was the school teacher, the one who had taught his father piano, the one who'd paid for his education in the city, the one who'd sent him away. Polly who had cut his father out of her life, cleanly and entirely, on the occasion of his marriage to Isaiah's mother. Polly had had plans for Isaiah's father that didn't include him marrying a pākehā, his mother would say. Then she would laugh.

Polly stubbed out her cigarette on the wooden arm of the chair. She must be eighty now, at least. He did not remember her face, but as he approached her chair to greet her, there was something familiar in the movement of her hands. He wasn't prepared to recognise her smell: the dry rasp of smoke mixed with some lavender-like perfume. There was in his memory the fine weave of a long black skirt and himself reaching up, a voice high above his head, a gold ring on a long brown finger.

'Āe,' Polly said. 'Mokopuna. Haere mai.' She stood, small and thin but very upright. The potato peeler fell from her hand into the bucket, but apart from this one concession she seemed composed.

'Kia ora,' Isaiah said, coming forward to meet her. She pressed her nose to his. When they moved apart he felt her tears on his face. She did not acknowledge them. Instead she looked at him with her head to one side.

'Kōrero Māori?'

'No, Aunty.'

She let out a small huff of air. 'Could have taken a class.' He did not know what to say. 'Oh well, no matter. At least you look like your father's boy.' Tears continued to slide down her nose and out of the corners of her eyes. She looked past Isaiah to Rangi, who paused in his sawing as though afraid of the repercussions if he did not. 'You're right, he does look like his dad. Lucky he didn't take after his pōrangi mother, eh? Breastfed you till you were four, she did,' Polly said. 'And picked you up all the time, after every little cry. Some kind of a hōhā city pākehā! Wouldn't have time for that kind of thing out here. Just gave them formula in my day.'

'Aunty,' Rangi said. 'Don't you know what they say these days? The breast is best!'

Isaiah couldn't help laughing. Polly put her hand on his. 'But you are like him, you are,' she said.

His father was famously even-tempered. It wouldn't hurt to let Polly believe he was the same.

'Call me Iz,' Isaiah said.

'Your proper name is Isaiah,' she said. 'It was your father's second name.'

'Isaiah is a Christian pākehā name,' he said. 'The first Isaiahs in our family, they lived in colonial times. I don't want some coloniser's name.'

Polly blew cigarette smoke into his face.

'Yes,' she said. 'Your people were Christian people. Clean. Honest. They went to church.'

'It's not a real Māori name,' Isaiah said.

'Real Māori, real Māori,' Polly said. She ground the cigarette against the pāua ashtray. 'Those pākehā from the city who can't be bothered with your real name? Well, they can call you whatever you like. But I, and everyone here on the marae, will call you Isaiah.'

Isaiah followed Polly to the rear of the wharenui. She walked with small quick steps and held her head very upright. She was starling-like. Her various adornments gleamed in the sun. She carried herself lightly, smoothly, like an aged dancer. All that Isaiah had seen of his father were images in old photographs. He felt a space open up in his chest. She turned and grasped his arm, as if she was aware of it.

The old people had said that Isaiah's father would be an orator, a lawyer, or a politician. His father had been sent to the city to bring something back, though as a child Isaiah could never quite understand what it was the people expected him to retrieve. He'd thought back then that it might have been money, because his mother had told him that the pā was poor. Now he knew it was something else: an elusive and unattainable thing, justice maybe, or mana motuhake, or people: something that would restore the pā to what it had been.

They entered the kitchen at the back of the marae. Polly slammed the door. The room held the opposing smells of fish and some sharp astringent cleaner, and was filled with a crowd of people. There ahead of them was Rangi, who must have gone in to get started on his work. Polly clung to Isaiah. Despite the drama of their entrance, no one looked up. Rangi was muttering. It took Isaiah a moment to realise he wasn't speaking to the people around him but to the line of chickens he was gutting. He greeted each as he picked it up, wielding the knife, almost parentally proud as their innards splattered into the basin. His speech was threaded with English expletives. Polly banged her staff on the floor. Isaiah had not noticed it until now: it was carved and ancient, of pāua and wood.

'Isaiah Tane Mahuta,' she said, addressing the room. 'Son of Tane Isaiah Mahuta. My nephew.'

Rangi went on talking, unimpressed, until a thin youth beside him stood on his foot. All the movement in the room stopped. Carrot graters were held in mid-air, and the tea towels fell still. They all looked at him quietly, until it was comical, until some of the other aunties (he assumed they were his aunties) began to laugh. 'Looks scared to death,' one of them said to Polly.

'What you doing busting in here like that?' one of the others said to Polly. 'Got work to do. No time to muck about.'

Isaiah kept his gaze level and his shoulders back. The younger man next to Rangi stepped forward and cleared his throat.

'We knew that you were coming,' he said. His face was dark and thin and scarred with old acne. He was a little stooped. He stepped towards Isaiah and for a strange moment Isaiah thought he was going to bow and kiss his hand. 'I'm Matiu. I extend welcome for all the whānau –' But here Rangi let out a rude laugh that turned into a cough, cutting Matiu off. A large old woman bustled through the doors.

'Five minutes to the pōwhiri,' she called. 'Five minutes, then you all get yourselves in there to greet. There's not enough of us. You,' she called to Matiu. 'Cat got your tongue? What you looking all po-faced about?' No one answered her. 'What's he looking all po-faced about?' she asked another of the women. Then she saw Isaiah. 'Ahh,' she said. 'Ahh. Well, it makes no difference either way. We've still only got five minutes.' She took Isaiah firmly in her arms, and squeezed him. 'Little Tane,' she said in his ear. 'I would have known you anywhere.' She turned and stared at everyone. 'Get to work, whānau,' she said. 'Last time the tea ran out and the sandwiches were soggy. We're never going to shame ourselves like that again.' She pulled Isaiah towards the exit.

Matiu looked ripped off. He had made a nice speech, after all.

'Why'd she eat so many of them then if they were so bloody soggy?' he said.

'They've waited almost your whole life to see you, they can wait a few more minutes,' the woman said to Isaiah. 'I'm Mary, anyway. I'm your aunty. We need you up front. Hardly any men to greet the manuhiri anymore.'

She sighed and bowled away, calling to the men near the door, figures with carved staffs and canes who were obviously senior.

It was a large wharenui, one of the largest he'd seen, and old. It could have slept two hundred people. The tukutuku panels that told of his ancestry extended all the way up the walls. The rafters were the ribs of the house, of course, and the central post its backbone. It was dim. There was something wrong with his eyes. A woman called outside: a long, devastating cry. He'd expected to be out there, with Sam and the others, as they edged towards the door. He had not anticipated that they would know he was coming, that they would invite him in first.

If he tried very hard, he thought he could feel this wharenui's sacredness. It was as if the building did have a mana of its own. He tried the word out in his mind. One of the older men looked at him. He stood near the photographs, which were mostly black and white. He recognised no one. The poles in the centre of the marae were held by the ancestors beneath them. Their arms overlapped, one sometimes sitting atop another, pāua eyes shining.

The older man gestured wildly, with great, welcoming arcs of his arm. If Isaiah felt anything it was a certain transparency, as though the marae and the people in it were real, and himself a permeable copy. He stood there, Isaiah, Tane Isaiah Mahuta's son. He saw himself at a distance, walking forwards.

After the call, there was quiet. The guests would be beginning their approach. In his mind's eye he could see the small group, shuffling towards the entrance of the marae, and the hosts waiting for them. His people. Who of the guests was meant to go first here, the women or the men? Did his friends even know? A part of him wanted to be out the front with them, to see. But he was tangata whenua now. He would have to ask Sam later.

'Haere mai, haere mai.'

The old man reached out a hand and pulled Isaiah in to share his breath. He came out of the hongi and looked into the old man's eyes. The man held Isaiah's gaze for a long time, then released him. Was he another relative? He wasn't sure how complex the family relationships were here. Perhaps everyone he could see was a relative of some kind, but he didn't think so. The few relatives he'd met after his father's death had always been vague about their exact relationship to him. They were always just an aunty or an uncle. It was not permitted to write his whakapapa down on paper, so he had never seen it.

The old man pulled Isaiah into line beside him. The rise and fall of the karanga beat against his ears. He would resolve not to see ghosts everywhere then. He stood carefully upright. Surely he was too junior to be placed here? The local people started to file in. The space made them slow down and fall quiet. The light made the tukutuku patterns oddly animated. People settled themselves with small adjustments of scarves and skirts.

'Haere mai, haere mai.'

Rangi arrived. He looked from the old man to Isaiah and back, and moved in between them. Isaiah stepped back. He made his breathing slow and regular. He felt slightly dizzy. He seemed to see birds in the rafters, or the shadows of birds. It was hard not to look straight up. The feeling of lightness in his head was increasing. He tried to breathe down into his legs, into his toes, as a grounding measure. He was dimly aware of Rangi snorting softly, and giving him a challenging look, but it was all he could do to stay upright. There. The tukutuku patterns were flickering, as though the patterns of red, black and white were revolving upwards.

'Haere mai, haere mai.'

He turned to Rangi to excuse himself, but the visitors were upon them, and the mihi had started.

Isaiah tried not to catch Sam's eye. His girlfriend stood with the group of pākehā, his friends from the city – Melissa and Kate, others who were familiar to him from past actions, and a few he didn't know. Her hands were clasped in a respectful way. He was concerned that if he looked at her he might smile. It was odd, having woken up beside her in the sleeping bag this morning and then seeing her here, on the other side of the marae.

In the small crowd being welcomed was a man Isaiah knew mainly by reputation. Bryce was an ex of Sam's. His head rose above the others and he alone looked intently at Isaiah, nodding as if in confirmation. Then Bryce launched fluidly into his talk, his whaikōrero. Sam had been using the word for weeks to describe her educational talks, so it floated easily into Isaiah's brain now. She was always dragging te reo into meetings. Isaiah felt that something was expected of him in response, a certain gratitude. Last month, the popular te reo word had been mahi. Everything was about people's mahi. Bryce was speaking quickly and fluently in te reo, outlining their shared purpose. Many of the locals nodded. Isaiah understood mainly the English: environment, pollution, solidarity, fracking, and then the odd te reo word like mahi.

Now the waiata would begin. The pākehā stood quietly and Isaiah suddenly realised: they hadn't decided on a song. They had all arrived at different times and were from disparate groups, and every one of them had assumed that another had sorted it out.

Across the room Polly gave Isaiah a disappointed look. They were his people, after all. The silence lengthened. Then Melissa and Kate were pushing a woman to the front of the group. She was darker skinned than the others, with long black hair worn loose down her back. She wore crisp jeans and no political patches and looked altogether too ordinary, like a misplaced government worker. He saw that the others had taken her for Māori, but she looked as lost as Isaiah felt. She was slightly gawky-looking, her features too sharp to be pretty. She had thick, strong eyebrows and a serious expression that made him concerned for her. Perhaps she was Middle Eastern, or Italian. But he was fairly sure she wasn't Māori. And even if she was, like him, that was no guarantee that she knew what she was meant to do.

The woman opened her mouth to sing, but no words came out. Someone gave her a little pat from behind.

'Pōkarekare ana …'

Her voice was good, and her accent wasn't that bad, but Isaiah could not suppress a slight physical flinch. Rangi stirred beside him. Then the other pākehā joined in, lifting their voices with palpable relief, fading out during some of the trickier bits. Isaiah watched as the woman's face turned a deep, satisfying red. The best faces were the ones that were imperfect; the ones that were slightly asymmetrical, or had a too large nose. Perhaps he would ask to draw her.

Then the visitors were filing past him. It was the moment of contact, the moment he had feared. The flickering of the panels had subsided. He greeted each new person nervously, hoping he was doing it right. But no one pointed him out as an interloper and demanded that he stop. He had a brief warm feeling. Maybe he'd been right to come.

Bryce passed him. Melissa passed. Kate hongied Isaiah. He'd sat in meetings with them, eaten with them, schemed with them. But now they looked at him with a certain pride. He wanted to object, to say, look, it's just me, Isaiah, but he saw that to them he was a kind of talisman. Sam came past and hongied him enthusiastically. Further down the line the woman who had sung approached, still blushing.

2

The mood in the camp near the outskirts of the pā was tense and held, like the moment before heavy rain. Alexia had dressed in the tent lying down, pulling on her jeans and shirt awkwardly and trying to ignore the creases. Now she was in the small crowd of activists awaiting the invitation onto the land, and balking at having to make conversation without having had her morning coffee. It was almost cool enough for her to need her jacket, but not quite. The air coming down from the mountain was fresh. Alexia was still surprised not to have woken up in her apartment in the city where the seasons didn't matter so much. Her transition from city dweller to traveller had been so swift. She marvelled at these people, at their apparent cheerfulness and their ability to form coherent sentences so early in the day. Many of them seemed to know each other and spoke in low voices as they waited. She sat with Aidan and Hannah, the people she was travelling with, and hugged her arms to her body. The air had a hint of the mountain's snow in it.

The structures of warfare were still evident: the crests and defensive bumps green and furzed over now with grass, but still there. The deep cut of a river wove through a scattering of small, modest houses, batch-like and close together, all in varied states of repair. Outside the boundaries of the pā was a sudden flattening out of bush and hill. Cattle-grazing land stretched away on either side, pleasant, easy grassed plains, all the way to the mountain. Her eyes caught again and again on the carving at the pinnacle of the marae. She was too far away to see the details, but the sun kept lighting on a bright thing there, maybe inlaid pāua in the eyes of the figurehead. It glinted intermittently, blinding her.

'They'll call us when they're ready,' Aidan said. He strummed his guitar, which she recognised as an extension of his body, even though she'd only known him a little while. His partner Hannah started singing softly. Aidan was Irish, with long blond dreadlocks and tattered clothes. Hannah was fragile-looking and kind to everyone.

'Coffee!' yelled one of the men in the clearing. Alexia felt a surge of gratitude. He came around and offered her a tin cup, which she accepted. He poured elaborately from a kettle, lifting it so high that for a moment she was afraid she would be burned. He grinned and she noticed his pale blue eyes before he moved on. The coffee in the cup was almost tarry.

'That's Bryce,' Hannah whispered, pointing at the coffee pourer. 'You're going to want to watch out for him.'

'What do you mean?'

Hannah looked into her cup, her long blonde hair brushing her lap. 'I guess he's a bit of a character, that's all. That's his wife over there.' She flicked her eyes at a woman much younger than Bryce. 'And that's her girlfriend there, beside her. It's all out in the open. Bryce has other partners too. Like, a lot of them,' she said, grinning at Alexia. 'He's kind of a famous activist. He's been around a while.'

A woman was standing in front of Alexia, holding out an envelope.

'For koha,' she said. She smiled, revealing a set of even, healthy-looking teeth, like a fine mare's. She was stocky and wholesome.

'Hi, Sam,' Hannah said.

'Sam,' Aidan said. He drew a wad of notes from his pocket and put it in the envelope. 'That's for me and Hannah, for starters.' His voice took on a certain gruffness.

Alexia had not thought about koha. She had only twenty dollars in her pocket. Hurriedly she thrust this at Sam. Sam did a thing where she pretended not to look at the money but actually looked. Then she gazed at Alexia's dark jeans, her new sneakers, the ruffled white shirt she had last worn at a law school presentation, and turned wordlessly away.

'Aidan's ex,' Hannah whispered. 'Makes him nervous.' She started to roll a pair of cigarettes. Aidan began tuning his guitar. But Alexia could hear that the instrument was already in tune.

Then she heard the call. The long, drawn-out karanga cut through the clean air and hit her low in her stomach. It was a bodily feeling, as though she were crying out herself, or weeping. It pierced the chatter and made the people go still. She saw the notes as lights, one long, peaked heartbeat of red and gold. The next notes wrung the air and pulled the manuhiri in. They began to straighten and move towards the entrance place. Alexia stood, her body clenched as though it wanted to run, a feeling in her throat like a suppressed series of notes, like an answer.

The visitors moved towards the marae. Their approach was magnetic: inevitable, almost delicious. It was as though they were being drawn in by the karanga and at the same time repelled by it.

'Closer together,' the blue-eyed man Bryce said, up near the front. They passed through the carved entrance posts and onto the ground before the house. The marae ātea, Alexia remembered, from her compulsory course at law school. She'd resented being made to learn a language other than her own; would have rather spent her time studying Greek. She'd skipped as many classes as she could.

'Get closer. That's right. It's the women first in these parts.' Bryce's voice was authoritative. They moved as instructed till they were arranged in a wedge with the men at the back. The kuia standing ahead of them called out, her voice clear and her body bent and small. Aidan and Hannah were to Alexia's left and Sam was on her right. Aidan turned towards her.

'When am I meant to take off me boots again?' he whispered.

'Shh,' Sam said, turning and glaring. 'The time for kōrero is later.' She faced the front again, a vague smile recovering itself on her lips, as though nothing had been said. They were close enough now to see the kuia's long black skirts, her large pounamu, the feathers she wore in her hair. Alexia took a breath and let the music in again. It was a visual luxury, a celebration of bursting lights.

The marae was large. Its ribs rose up to meet the ancestor carved at its head. The porch was already covered with shoes. The pāua in the eyes of the figure on the central post gleamed. The kuia was flanked by other women, but despite her stature she held them all, visitors and guests, in her thrall.

Then they were filing slowly onto the porch. Sam looked up from where she'd placed her practical boots and smiled benevolently at Alexia. Perhaps she smiled at everyone, all the time.

Three kuia were lined up near the door. There was a complex interchange of looks and smiles as people entered. Bryce strode forward confidently, and Sam went on beside him. There was the dense bush on either side, the barren hills, the great blue dome of the sky. It was possible to feel that even the air was observing her. A kuia near the door shifted and smiled pointedly at Alexia, as if in recognition.

Entering the dim space was disorientating. There seemed to be many people present, but not nearly as many as the wharenui could hold. The activists were gathered in a tight group near the middle. Bryce's head rose above the others. His face said he was enjoying all this immensely. Good stuff, he seemed be thinking, with each smile and nod. Good stuff!

After the speeches and acknowledgements came a moment of silence. The waiata! Now they were all meant to sing. Alexia felt an elbow in her ribs and saw one of the female activists nodding at her. She pushed Alexia forwards until she stood at the front of the group. The marae was filled with polite shuffles and throat clearings. There was a pat on her back. She heard Bryce whispering encouragement.

God, they thought she was Māori, and they expected her to lead the singing. As pākehā they were deferring to her. She tried to shake her head, but the people around her didn't notice. This had happened a couple of times before. Once when she'd changed schools, and once at the start of her university degree, when the Māori receiving her at the marae had given her special looks of recognition. She tried to resist the hands that were pushing her forwards now. She didn't know any appropriate songs!

Now everyone in the marae was looking at her, waiting. In her panic she scrabbled in her mind for lyrics. Cross your legs. Cross your arms. Sit up straight. Here are the poi we have made out of plastic bags and plaited wool. Here are the harakeke windmills. Move in time, hands on your waists. But people were staring now and her face was getting hot and all that was running in her head was a nursery rhyme in Greek, which was the wrong language altogether.

> *Fengaraki mou lambro*
> *My little shining moon*
> *light my way so I can walk*
> *to go to school ...*

Instead, she clasped her hands in front of her, and launched into another song, sounding the vowels as best she could. They were similar to those in Greek, after all.

> *Pōkarekare ana ...*

Alexia went somewhere else when she was singing. It wasn't a comfortable place, exactly. And it wasn't really a place. It was more that she went somewhere else, which was sometimes preferable to being where she was.

Then it was over, and Alexia felt the visitors relax. The hosts formed a long line and the guests began to file past and hongi. Alexia was always challenged by the intimacy of the practice. She felt guilty for not mastering it. Greeks kissed on the cheek; one, two, three kisses if they were being emphatic. But this sharing of breath was so direct, it was all she could do not to duck her head and shy away.

A man grasped her hand. The wrinkles on his face fell down in folds. He drew her towards him. She leaned in, trying to hold herself still, her face warm from her performance. She glimpsed the man's eyes: dark, teary, brimming with warmth, before they closed and his nose approached hers. But she missed! Her own nose swept to the side and onto his cheek, and then everything was lost in awkwardness.

Alexia was passed along to another man. At the last moment, sensing her discomfort, he changed the hongi into a kiss. Then she was standing in front of a man in camo gear, who pulled her in quickly. Centimetres from her face, he stopped and looked at her. Was he wondering, too, if she was Māori, or a relative? All at once she wanted out; to run out into the air and breathe unencumbered, to walk freely towards the mountain. He leaned in and hongied her, and then as if to say, there, all done, handed her on to the next person.

Her immediate thought was that she recognised this man. They stood eye to eye, gazes almost aligned. He stood very upright, hand reached formally towards her. But she did not know him. He was slender and about her age. He had black hair cut neatly short. His clothes were generic: an earthy-coloured T-shirt and plain green pants. He had dark-rimmed glasses frames that weren't quite thick enough to be fashionable. The hand he had extended was long-fingered. The skin on his face was stretched taut across the bones. There was no excess on him, nothing wasted. He could have been in an ad for an outdoor adventure company or some expensive multifunctional watch, the kind that told you your physical co-ordinates. His skin was quite light, a tan colour, and his eyes were flecked with green, like her own. That was it: he looked Greek to her.

They moved forwards at the same time. His hand was unpleasantly sweaty, but then so was hers. She leaned forward too quickly. She thought he'd go for a hongi but he moved his head jerkily towards her cheek. His lips grazed the corner of her mouth. They straightened up, and his face creased as he studied her. He was still holding her hand with disarming gentleness, his eyes moving quickly behind the glasses. The sturdy man beside them made a sound and Alexia let go. The touch of his lips had been quick, light, entirely accidental.

Stephen had been firm and practical with his kisses. Alexia, unlike most of the women she knew, had always preferred to skip the preliminaries and go straight for the full body contact: the ungentle hold, the rough push and pull. It was what she liked. It was what she had thought she liked.

3

Here was his river. Here was his maunga. Here was the mountain, still clad almost halfway down its slopes in snow from the winter, overlooking the lands like a guardian, which he supposed was what the locals thought it was. Here, also, were his people: Rangi in his camouflage gear, which after a few days Isaiah had learned was his customary outfit; Matiu, friendly and deferential; Polly, as hard and pared back as some artefact in a museum. Isaiah spent the first week in rapture at the actual beauty of it: the lands, rolling towards the coast on one side and towards the mountain's slopes on the other. He spent the second week in a flurry of activity, writing and deploying letters to the council in opposition to the fracking. He was finally here, and he was with Sam and his friends, and there was a good fight to fight. Every morning he began to wake naturally with the early spring light. He would leave the comfortable bed where Polly had housed him in a building near the wharenui and go outside, just to breathe the sharp air.

He knew everyone from the city, mostly. He trusted them. The only mystery was this Alexia. He'd asked Aidan about her. Who knew Alexia, who could vouch for her, where did they meet? But aside from having met her at a few gigs in the city, Aidan didn't know much about this woman. He said she'd hit it off with Hannah, and that she could sing, so they'd invited her along on their tour as a back-up vocalist. When they'd heard the pānui to come and support people in their protest they'd postponed the tour, and Alexia had come along.

By the end of the second week the council hadn't responded to any of their emails or phone calls. None of their media releases had been picked up. They had put in calls to radio stations and wrangled a list of media contacts from a source, but no one was interested. Isaiah and Sam and some others proposed that a small group go to the council building and request a dialogue with the counsellors. Polly and the locals approved the plan.

Alexia was not included in the group. It had emerged that she was a law student. She seemed happy to remain behind and investigate possible legal routes for future action.

Isaiah hadn't known what Sam was planning to do.

He and Sam and a few others were outside the council house. They had gone in and asked about their letters and been given a list of other people to contact. They had asked for a particular counsellor by name – the one who was pro-fracking – but were told he was at lunch. Now they were outside in the square, drinking coffee, watching the workers mill about. Isaiah kept trying to steer the group back to the car, but each time, Sam would start a new conversation, and they would be delayed. She was carrying a courier bag that she'd made out of old shopping bags.

A man came towards them with a small group of others. They were all dressed in suits. Sam seemed to fixate on them. Then she approached, calling the pro-fracking counsellor's name. He didn't answer immediately. Sam went on, calling the name of the people and the fracking location, asking him what he was planning to do about their letters. The man had brown hair and glasses and was lean and fit-looking, not at all like Isaiah's idea of a bureaucrat. Now the man raised his hand, palm outwards.

'I don't know anything about it,' he said. 'If you'd direct your correspondence to my secretary …'

That was when Sam threw black paint. Isaiah guessed it was a simulation of oil. The man bent his head and seemed to collapse under the weight of his surprise. There was enough paint that it flooded his face, making channels around his eyebrows and dripping onto his suit. Sam had concealed it in her bag in some kind of bottle. Another man ran past them and into the building and came out with a security guard. He pinned Sam to the ground.

Isaiah felt the guard's hands as if they were on his own body. But he and his friends just stood there and watched. It would not do Isaiah in particular any good to get involved.

'Shame,' Sam chanted, lying on the ground. 'Shame.' The counsellor swore and was helped to his feet. The guard was pressing Sam down harshly onto the pavement, but there was a wild kind of joy on her face. All around them lunching workers stopped drinking their coffee and eating their sandwiches and stared. Sam met Isaiah's eyes over the security guard's shoulder, and he nearly laughed. Sam had no fear.

The police were very nearly called, but after some discussion the counsellor declined to press charges. It was just what that girl wanted, he said. He wouldn't give her the satisfaction.

Sam returned to Isaiah, smiling, as if she had won a prize.

He was sceptical about the efficacy of such an action. He was also sceptical about whether the others at the marae would approve. But on the long drive home, he kept this to himself.

4

It was a relief for her to sit with her notebook and laptop in the makeshift library room off the wharenui, sifting through legal papers. If the place and the people and the processes here were all new to her, at least this wasn't, this taking of legalese and bending it to her will, these small acts of translation. This was the secret Alexia had discovered about the law: it was really only another language, merely a series of agreed-upon rules. You could take these rules and re-interpret them, or use them as a scaffolding for new ideas. But for the most part the practice of the law was about adhering to a script. And she had always been good at adhering to the rules, until recently.

When Rangi put his head through the doorway she jumped. She knew so few people with full moko that it was difficult not to stare.

'Meeting in five minutes, sis,' he said.

The woman she had learned was Sam stood to lead the discussion. The room was slightly stuffy, and a local man with a stooped frame went around opening windows to let in the spring air. There were maybe thirty people present, and a couple of the others whom Alexia was becoming familiar with were setting up a projector: Kate and Melissa. They and Sam always seemed to move as a group. All the locals were there, and the tall man Bryce, who was fussing with his laptop. There was the man she had greeted clumsily on the first day, slim, dark-haired, sitting easily in his chair. She had learned his name too: Isaiah.

She noticed with a jolt that everyone had naturally sat together with the people they knew, and that this meant one side of the room was Māori and the other white. It reminded her of her church, where she had, recently, tried not to weep out loud. They maintained an old tradition of seating women on one side and men on the other. The rule was not strictly obeyed, but when people followed it the church looked just like this. At the last moment she sat with the Māori side, on a chair near the wall.

'Kia ora,' Sam said. 'Thanks everyone for bringing your ideas to the meetings earlier this week, and thanks for your support around our little demo.' It was clear she was addressing the locals. 'I thought we could use this session to do some education around fracking, and maybe talk through some possible strategies for stopping it. Bryce?'

Alexia marvelled at this woman's ease. Now Bryce opened a document on the laptop, and rose.

'Fracking is a word for hydraulic fracturing, a method that companies use to locate natural gas or oil, and extract it from the rock.' He pulled up a diagram showing a metal structure at the top of a deep cross-section of a well. Rangi cleared his throat. 'In your area,' Bryce went on, 'the wells they are intending to bore will most certainly be in search of natural gas. Some not far from here have already passed the exploratory stage, so there's a good chance they'll put in quite a few working wells. They've only recently passed an Act that means the location of these wells must be disclosed to the public, but that involves a lengthy series of requests.' Bryce flicked into another screen and Rangi cracked his knuckles. 'Once they bore a well, they pump fracking solution into it, mixed with sand and chemicals. The idea is that the fluid literally fractures the earth horizontally, releasing the gas that may be trapped in the fissures in coal seams so it can be channelled to the surface.'

Matiu shifted loudly, and Rangi coughed. Polly let out a protracted sigh.

'Of course, there are often problems as a result,' Bryce went on. 'Earthquakes, air pollution, water pollution. The environmental impacts of fracking are many and various. It's outlawed in much of Europe, and they're talking about banning it in Canada. They can't ensure the wells don't leak run-off, for one thing. And they have to get the sand and water for the fracking fluid from somewhere, so they'll be mining the land and collecting thousands, maybe millions of litres of water from your river. And, when the frack fluid comes up again from the ground, they have to do something with the toxic waste. Landfarming is one way they'll try to deal with it. They scrape the grass and topsoil off a field, and lay the waste down. Then they just put the grass back on top of it, like a lid.' He flicked over to a shot of an immense pond. 'Or they'll store water in pools like this, lined with plastic. Often the frack water leaches out into the earth. This has implications for cattle health, for farms, for local water sources ...'

'For God's sake, man!' Rangi was suddenly beside Bryce, huge and furious in his camo gear, closing the laptop. 'Stop wasting our time.'

'Rangi!' Matiu tried to shush his cousin, but Rangi went on.

'Nah,' he said. 'I'm not putting up with it anymore.' He turned to the group. 'We've been patient for weeks. Let them do it their way, we thought. But then he comes in here and tells us everything we already know? Where do yous get off?'

Alexia was embarrassed. She'd not known any of the information Bryce had covered, and had been interested in the presentation.

'We do have the internet here,' Matiu said. He seemed almost apologetic. 'All the info's out there. There's even documentaries on it.'

'Of course we know the risks,' Polly said. 'We wouldn't have put out the pānui for help if we didn't know how dangerous it was.'

'Come in and educate the natives,' said Rangi. 'Who do you

think you guys are – missionaries?'

Bryce sat down, and was gracious enough to apologise. There was an awkward silence. Then Kate spoke.

'Let's try to get this meeting going again,' she said. Her hands twitched, so she clasped them together in her lap. 'I'd like to start with a round.' The hands were small and claw-like. 'I feel that following the action outside the council buildings, we might need to debrief.' As though she was passing a talking stick, she turned to Sam. 'We all admire your commitment to the cause, Sam, and I know you've had some trauma as a result of being attacked by the guard yesterday. I thought we all might like to hear about how you're processing your experience.'

Processing. As though Sam's infraction with the police had been some kind of food, and Sam had taken it in and was grinding it all, slowly, to pieces; the black oil against the shirt of the politician, the space that would have opened around the scuffle on the street, the crowd's rapt attention. Alexia hadn't seen it but she'd heard about it. Sam bore no visible marks of violence. Her face was impassive underneath her short, blunt-cut fringe and cropped hair.

Melissa let out a sob. 'I'm sorry,' she said. The expression on Sam's face was almost holy. There was a compelling internal and external healthiness to her, like if you stuck with this woman she'd feed you on ethical food and take you for bush walks. Melissa sniffed, a sniff outrageous in length and magnitude.

Polly could control herself no longer. Her waiata cut through Melissa's sniff and brought the world outside the room into focus. Alexia could hear birdsong outside, children talking, distant bulldozers at work. Polly sang low and full, a welcome song, but there was a hardness to her voice that no one could mistake. The tune looked to Alexia like rough waves on the sea, all sharp points rising. She quelled it. Polly was wholly still, formed like a tight fist around her voice. Melissa fell quiet.

'That is how you open a hui,' Polly said. 'In these parts.' She sat back in her chair, her staff in one hand. Rangi leaned forwards and put his hands on his knees.

'We are here by the grace of our ancestors, who guarded and protected this land,' he said. 'Who gave their lives for it. Now they want to make it barren. There will be nothing left here for our children. All these facts and figures and sharing of feelings and all that, we don't have time for it. Or, all due respect,' he said, looking at Sam, 'for one-person acts of bravery.'

Sam blushed.

'We want to make one thing clear,' Polly said. 'So far we have kept within the rules. We have not endangered the people of this place by breaking the law. Some of our iwi are working on the fracking site. They have mouths to feed, and they can't afford to turn down the work. They are people from here, connected to this land. We don't approve of their choices but, in the end, we will all be buried in the same place. We want no violence between us. It's not them but the fracking company that we take issue with.'

Rangi smiled a charming, quite unbalanced smile. 'So,' he said. 'What are we going to do to shut the dirty bastards down?'

The ideas were various and enthusiastic. At the end of the meeting Alexia stood near the door. It was too late to go back to her papers, and the campsite she was sharing with Aidan and Hannah the musicians was unappealing. She told herself she wasn't really waiting, but when the man with dark hair passed her she smiled and fell into step next to him. He smiled back at her.

Before they had a chance to speak she heard a low whistle. Sam had come up behind them and was touching Isaiah's hand. It was a familiar touch.

'Really put my foot in that one, didn't I?' she said. 'God, what a stupid thing to do. I didn't think they would mind my action. I can't believe we haven't come up with a collective kaupapa yet.' She rolled her eyes at herself. She reached into her pocket and pulled out a handful of something and offered it to Isaiah, and then reached out and offered whatever it was to Alexia, too. Sunflower seeds.

'We need to have a good kōrero about decision-making processes.' Sam had started out speaking to both of them, but now she and Isaiah were intent upon each other as they walked out into the hall, and Alexia was on the outside.

'We need to let the iwi take the lead in meetings,' Isaiah said quietly. 'We'll have a talk about strategy amongst ourselves.'

How had Alexia not seen it? They'd had several meetings and she'd never before linked Sam and Isaiah. But the way Sam had touched his hand made Alexia certain. If they were a couple, though, they were an odd one; they'd seemed so independent until now. She looked at the sunflower seeds in her hand. She didn't fancy eating them from Sam's pocket.

'Sam, can I ask you a question?' Isaiah said. Alexia was eavesdropping now. 'How did the locals know I was coming? You were the one in who was touch with them about our expected numbers.'

Sam's voice, when it came, was efficient.

'It was only practical to tell them, Isaiah. I thought they'd want to know.' There was a pause. 'Sorry if you felt ambushed. Did you have some romantic idea you were going to sweep in and surprise them all?'

Alexia heard Isaiah laugh.

'You know me so well, Sam,' he said.

5

They were bent over their breakfasts when Isaiah realised it. Sam must have gone onto the fracking site in the night. The fact of her betrayal opened out in him like a wound. Since they had got here they'd been sleeping in different rooms. Polly had put him in his own room, and Sam and Melissa and Kate were sharing another. He had not felt like arguing at the time. Now, the three women were whispering to each other. It could only mean one thing. Sam was an excellent politician, but sometimes a less than tactful girlfriend. It would have been for practical reasons, though, that he had been excluded. Relationships with the pā were still delicate, and it paid to keep Isaiah blameless in the eyes of the local hapu. After the last meeting Polly had again expressed her desire that no one should act on behalf of the group, and that included night-time expeditions.

Isaiah sat beside Alexia, the woman who seemed so out of place with her shirts and feminine skirts. Sam was on the other side of the table, with Kate and Melissa and their bowls of oats and soymilk. Melissa seemed upset, but that didn't necessarily mean anything; Melissa was often upset.

'Devastation,' Kate said.

'Annihilation,' Sam said.

'Total destruction,' Melissa said.

'Like the earth is wounded,' Kate said. Isaiah wondered if she ever realised how melodramatic she sounded sometimes. He knew she was being sincere. Kate was an older activist, rendered waif-like by years of what she thought of as 'the struggle'. She noticed him staring and stared back with her red-rimmed eyes. She didn't return his smile.

'Hey, Isaiah, you'll like this one!' Isaiah had the sense of needing to almost physically inflate to deal with Rangi. 'A Buddhist horse walks into a bar,' Rangi said, 'and the bartender asks what he'll have. The Buddhist horse, he says, "I'm not a big drinker, but can you make me one with what is?"' People laughed, the group from the city joining in slowly. 'Get it, cuz? What, Iz?'

Isaiah declined to answer. He was distracted by Alexia and Sam both: Sam might be imparting information he wanted to know, and Alexia was all pink cheeks and dark hair. He made a mental note to ask if he could draw her. Matiu was asking Rangi if he thought they should plant the gardens the old way, following the cycles of the moon, or whether it was all actually bollocks. Matiu said they'd be stupid to turn their backs on the knowledge of the kaumātua. The whole time he was speaking he was offering people things: passing the butter along, offering milk to Alexia, making sure the children had more bread, working automatically without looking at what he was doing.

'But who's got time to find out about all that now?' Rangi said. 'We've got to get the kūmara in soon. It's spring. Best one to ask is your aunty, but she's back up the coast and she never answers her phone.'

Sam, Kate and Melissa's whispering grew stagey. Isaiah resisted the idea that this was partly for his benefit.

'The bulldozers,' Melissa said. 'The scale of it. The toxic effluent.'

'The old ones,' Matiu was saying grandly. 'They knew the way. My koro, he knew everything, how to smoke the eels, cure the fish, everything. But especially he knew about the gardens.'

'Well, why didn't you bloody write it down then?' Rangi asked.

'So poisoned, so ugly,' Melissa said. Then there, at the long wooden breakfast table, she began to cry. A look of concern passed across Alexia's face. Melissa was a pale woman, frail and wet-looking even when she wasn't crying. She meant well, Isaiah wanted to say to Alexia, feeling oddly implicated.

'Are you all right?' Alexia asked.

Melissa looked accusingly at Alexia's bowl through her tears. Isaiah was familiar with the hierarchy that existed amongst his friends of vegan vs. other. It was best to be vegan, but vegetarians were highly thought of too. The locals would escape Melissa's judgement because of their pastoral setting, and also they were the victims of colonisation, which in her world view trumped everything else. Isaiah himself sneaked into acceptability on a lower rung, as a freegan, which meant he would eat whatever he was given.

'Why didn't *you* write it down?' Matiu asked.

'Thought you were the top talent round here, bro,' said Rangi. 'Aren't you our resident bush philosopher? Wouldn't want to step on your toes.'

'Melissa's fine,' Kate said. She put an arm around Melissa's shoulders. 'She's just crying for Papa-tū-ā-nuku.'

'The earth mother?' Alexia asked. She began, helplessly, to laugh, snorting softly through her nose, the colour rising in her face. Isaiah was so close to her that their shoulders were almost touching, and he could feel the heat coming off her through her shirt. She was so undiplomatic in her reactions that he was a little shocked. But it was refreshing, too. She picked up her bowl and left the table.

Rangi frowned at her fleeing back, but Matiu drew him again into conversation.

'She wouldn't understand,' Kate said to the table as a whole.

Isaiah was often frustrated with his friends and their inherent tribalism. But when you were trying to achieve the things they as a group wanted to achieve you had to be a special sort of person. You had to be strong in your convictions. It wouldn't make a difference if he defended Alexia, so he didn't.

'You know they didn't like things to be written down, anyway,' Matiu said.

'That's an old rule, and only for whakapapa anyway,' Rangi said.

'It's not like I'm the only one around here with a pen.'

Rangi turned brightly to Bryce, who was holding forth on the dangers of chemical fertiliser. 'How's it going? You ready to fight the frackers?'

Bryce smiled broadly. 'Down with the capitalist oppressors,' he said, with absolute sincerity.

'What did you see on the site, Melissa?' Isaiah asked. Melissa looked at her breakfast. 'What did you see?' he asked again, louder this time. There was a note in his voice he couldn't quite keep under control. But Melissa looked at Kate, and Kate looked at Sam. The three women bent over their bowls without speaking.

Well, fine. He would corner Sam later and get her to tell him everything. He caught her eye. She stared at him, her expression as open as ever. He watched a tear drip down Melissa's long face and fall into her soymilk. Melissa had been eroded by years of unsuccessful actions. He had never seen her cry over anything personal, but she cried easily and often over the state of the earth.

Sam's betrayal wasn't worth being upset about. But still, it was a bad start to the day. He took his plate through to the sink where Alexia was washing dishes. She took it from him. She wasn't laughing now. Instead, she seemed vaguely embarassed.

'Did they go onto the frack site?' she asked. 'Already?'

'Seems like they did,' Isaiah said. If it was this obvious to Alexia then the whole table could have picked up on it.

'But that's so disrespectful,' Alexia said, with a primness he did not like. 'Surely we should wait till the elders okay that sort of thing?' Then suddenly she laughed. 'But listen to those three … tears of the bloody earth!' She bent forward at the waist, her mouth wide. He should be offended by Alexia's laughter, which was culturally incorrect after all, but instead he found himself laughing too, hoping he wouldn't be heard. 'I'm sorry, Isaiah,' she said, straightening up at last. 'I know you're Māori. I didn't mean to be insensitive.'

'Oh,' he said. 'The Papa-tū-ā-nuku thing? Don't worry. I'm not –' he began to say, but then he couldn't think what it was that he wasn't. Through the open doorway they could see Melissa still crying as Sam whispered to her. Suddenly Isaiah found himself laughing more freely, until – holding his hand over his mouth – he had to leave the room.

In the ablutions block he leaned into a stall and continued to laugh, soundlessly, pressed against the cold metal door. His mother had always had a thing for deep questions, for getting in touch with everybody else's emotions. She would ask him how he was feeling. He would answer that he was okay. She would inquire again; no, how was he feeling really? He was fine, he would say, growing increasingly annoyed. Because she would leap on any nuance of his expression or tone, he had learned to maintain ambiguity. He had taught himself to withdraw to his bedroom if he needed to be sad or happy. He was a master of silent rage, and silent laughter too. Like now.

He wanted to learn what Sam knew, to grill her for details. What did the site look like? Was the pollution visible? Was there run-off apparent already? Could it be photographed? These were serious questions. But his body laughed.

When he went to wash his face at the basin, though, his reflection appeared to be crying. His tear ducts had opened as if released from a long damming. It was an entirely physical thing. He watched, astonished, as the fat drops darkened the concrete floor in great, ragged spots. There was a sick feeling in the pit of his stomach. He went into a stall and sat for a while, his face dripping water and tears.

When Isaiah turned twenty-one his mother had given him his father's pounamu. He never wore it. Beautiful and cold, it was too heavy to be comfortable. It was a toki, an adze, so dark green it didn't reflect the light, almost large enough to seem like the tool it once would have been. Unlike the smaller pounamu his mother had given him, it did not warm against his skin. 'You'll need this one day,' his mother had said to him. 'When you go back home.'

To her his trajectory should have been straightforward: she would give him the upbringing and the skills, and his father had given him the background. In her mind he was meant to become some kind of peace warrior, fighting for people's rights.

In some of his earliest memories he was attending protests with his mother. There were the pictures of him on her shoulders, with his dark curls, his mother's fair hair flowing past her shoulders. She would always be holding some banner or other, and her mouth was inevitably open. He'd learnt to shout 'fascist' at the police, and he'd learnt to stay back from the police line after he shouted it. He'd overheard many words at his mother's kitchen table. His mother's friends would begin speaking quietly but always end up shouting: *racism feminism fascism liberalism anarchy resistance revolution*. He'd understood that his mother was part of a great, ongoing war; that there were terrible things happening in the world and that it was up to them to fix them. There would be a special feeling in his mother's kitchen then, late at night when they had forgotten to send Isaiah to bed. Some man, usually with a beard and a plaid shirt, would put down his glass of beer and conclude a long speech. The feeling would be there in the quality of the silence: a feeling of zealous conviction.

Many years later he would think of how warm he had felt, how peaceful and sure, underneath that table. If he could hold the feeling in his hands it would look like an arrow: clean, white, aimed directly at the enemy. His mother and her friends were the good people, the people who cared. But by then he had ceased to think of his mother as good, and thought of her instead as deluded. It was clear to him now that there were still enemies. What was unclear was if the good people existed, or if they ever really had.

Someone came into the bathroom. Isaiah wiped his face with his hands, making sure to keep his head low. It was Aidan, the musician. Isaiah pretended to be washing his hands alongside him.

'If only we could just firebomb them,' Aidan said. 'The frackers.'

'It's hard to even say who "they" are, though,' Isaiah said. He didn't like the weakness in his voice.

Aidan took in a dramatic gulp of air, and let it out slowly. 'You're right,' he said. 'Puppets in the place of puppets is all we've got to fight.'

'Better invest in some quality scissors, then,' Isaiah said. 'Only thing is, I'm not quite sure how far some of these people want to go.'

Aidan nodded slowly.

Isaiah's father's pounamu sat at the bottom of his pack, wrapped carefully in tissue.

6

S omeone was strumming a guitar in a back paddock and singing in a low, sonorous voice, words Alexia couldn't understand. Voices came from inside. The light was almost preternaturally bright, turning the grass a vivid green and the clouds fluorescent white. A small boy called Tama was sitting beside her on the step. Tama was seven and had adopted her as his pet visitor. Children were often intrigued by Alexia. It was as if they could sense her secret world of lights and notes. She was wearing leggings with a galaxy print. They were her exercise leggings and, she sensed, way too fancy for around the marae, but she was low on clean clothes and beginning not to care. Tama wore cut-off shorts and a white T-shirt and a backwards-facing cap. He was methodically pulling at her leg, watching the print stretch, and then shrink when he released it.

Beside them the urupā was shaded by surrounding bush. Whenever she walked past it on her way to the campsite she felt it pulling at her. Again, there were the slight, firework-like lights that came with the chinks and twangs of the guitar. For a moment she slipped into it, the notes moving and dancing freely in front of her eyes, then she pulled herself out. She was grateful for Tama's presence. The evenings were difficult. She was friendly with Aidan and Hannah, of course, but she couldn't spend all her time with them. They were a couple after all – and while some of the others had warmed to her, she didn't have any real friends here to hang out with.

It was in her early teens that she'd started seeing the lights.

They had been so otherworldly, those first small flashes and latticed trails in the air that others could not see. The lights were like those drawing her in now: small scribbles in the air. For a while she had avoided telling her parents. But the lights were always there, at their strongest in music class and when she would lie on her bed after school and put on headphones and lose herself in the emerging patterns.

Her world closed down to the four walls of her bedroom with their gold wallpaper, her David Bowie poster, and the duvet shielding her from the outside world. She would play tapes on her small tape player, watch the lights dance and write furiously in her diary: 'I think I might be going crazy. They're not ghosts. They seem to like the music.' It all went together, this conviction that something was wrong with her and the way boys began to look at her at school and the warm new array of feelings she had available, especially in her lower body. She knew the other things were normal, more or less. But the lights were hers alone.

She waited till she was sure, so that when she did tell her parents and was taken to a specialist she could say yes, the lights followed the beat of the music and yes, different colours corresponded to different notes and yes, she could actually see the bars unfolding in the air, not recognisable as a musical score but intelligible to her: each song a distinct series of flares and bursts. When it was decided that she had music synaesthesia she was both immensely relieved and embarrassed at having her secret exposed.

Alexia had to learn how to manage the lights so that she would not be distracted by them. She had mastered, eventually, the art of intentional suppression, but the music from the back paddock, which was atonal and oddly dirge-like, eluded her defences. She could see the flashes now, faint but sharp over the urupā. She began to go there, into that place. The knowledge that what she saw was not real – 'only a quirk of perception', as the specialist had put it – was replaced by rapture.

Tama's bare shoulder brushed her knee, and she jolted out. No more lights.

He followed her gaze to the graveyard.

'One of my nannies is in there,' he said. He turned the baseball cap he wore around to the front, and then turned it backwards again. She heard a small meow. Tama called the cat to him without looking at it. It leapt up and settled itself on his lap, a grey tabby. 'They're only dead people. You shouldn't be scared of them. Once, though,' he said, 'Nanny came in the night, and told me off. I took my brother's kete. His was better than mine.' He looked defiantly at Alexia. 'She said if I didn't give the kete back, she would lean on me.'

'What do you mean?'

'Lean on me,' he said. 'Like this.' He turned to Alexia and laid his head against her. 'When it happens, you can't breathe.' He backed away and looked at her from beneath his thick eyelashes. 'And she said I had to give back my sister's iPod, too, from where I hid it under the bed.'

'What if she hears you talking to me?' she asked.

Tama laughed. 'She won't care!' Alexia could still feel the imprint of his head against her. 'She won't mind about you.' Alexia wondered why; was it because she was kind, or because she was unimportant?

'Anyway, I don't take people's stuff anymore,' Tama went on. 'Only sometimes apples, but they're from Taylor's farm and once that was all our land so it belongs to us anyway.' He regarded Alexia along the bridge of his nose. 'That's not really stealing, but you wouldn't understand.'

He leaned towards her again and pulled at her galaxy leggings. The fabric smacked her skin.

'Why are you doing that, Tama?'

He looked up into the night sky, which was obscured by clouds.

'Everyone's so worried about this fracking. Fracking, blah blah blah!' Tama threw his arms around wildly. 'Don't they know the universe is always expanding?'

She looked at the stars on her leg, the supernova rendered in bright green.

He dashed away down the path, running barefoot, with no apparent pain, on the river stones. She avoided looking back at the urupā, where she knew the lights would be dancing again, the notes too weird and random for her to read.

That night she sang quietly to herself as she did the dishes. The sparks danced over the knives, only for her. She felt her voice loosen here in a way that it had not in the city. Even in the crowded kitchen, she was unafraid.

She felt a hand on her back, a quick warmth landing and then passing away. She jumped, hands sliding in the suds-filled sink. Her fingers grazed a knife's edge.

'You!' she said. Isaiah grinned madly.

'Keep going,' he said. 'Your voice. It's unbelievable.' As soon as he said it he stopped smiling. Alexia's hand was bleeding into the water. She would have to do the dishes all over again. 'I'm sorry!' Isaiah said. 'Wait, I'll get …' He grabbed for a cloth and her hand at the same time. She couldn't help laughing, at him, the situation, his ineptness.

'Let me do it.' She took the cloth from where he was fumbling at the cut and wrapped it firmly. He reached out to put pressure on it. His eyes had fine lines at the corners. His eyebrows were black like hers, and he had unfairly long lashes and high cheekbones. His mouth was a contradiction: the lips full and cynical at the same time.

'I'm sorry,' he said again, meeting her eyes.

'Shut up,' she said. 'It doesn't hurt.' She became aware that he was still holding onto her hand.

'Alexia,' Isaiah said. 'I was wondering if I could draw you sometime?'

What a line! But she had seen him sitting at the edges of the field near her camp with his journal and one of his ever-present cameras. No one had asked to draw her before. She could hardly bear to think about trying to sit still under his eyes.

Sam had come in through the door. She stood there, taking everything in. By the time Isaiah noticed her and smiled, she had her features in order. But Alexia had seen things that weren't intended for him twist across her face. She pulled back, clutching her bleeding hand, reminding herself of what Aidan had told her about Isaiah and Sam's relationship. Apparently, like Bryce and his wife's, it was an 'open' one. But maybe that was just a line that Isaiah gave out? Maybe that wasn't how Sam saw it at all?

Sam's face was neutral again. Alexia was reminded of an old word: fetching.

'Alexia's cut herself,' Isaiah said. Relief flickered over Sam's face. And just as suddenly as Isaiah had moved away, Sam was next to her, tutting, looking into the sink full of blood.

'Let me see,' she said, and Alexia found herself offering her finger up almost gladly. 'This needs a bandage.' Sam nodded at Isaiah. 'You want to finish up these dishes? I'll take Alexia to the first-aid cupboard.' It wasn't a question. Alexia found herself being led away.

Outside, they walked side by side in silence. Blood dripped off Alexia's fingers onto the soil. After the light of the kitchen everything seemed too bright.

'So where do you whakapapa back to?' Sam asked.

Alexia looked at the woman, at her slightly upturned nose, her pug face. Their feet kicked up red dust.

'The capital,' Alexia said.

'Oh,' Sam said. 'I meant, your iwi.'

'I'm Greek,' Alexia said. After they'd realised she wasn't Māori, people always wanted to know what part of Greece she was from, and whether she'd been back, and tell her how great it must be to be part of a culture with real 'roots'. They never seemed to realise that they themselves were also part of the great tide and wash of culture; passengers from somewhere headed somewhere else, even if they could not see it.

'Sorry. I thought you were Māori,' Sam said. Then she shrugged, as if that was the end of her interest in the subject. Her eyes were a wide, innocent blue. 'So you're like me, just pākehā.'

And that was Alexia's sore point. She didn't want to put be in the same basket as Sam, collected like flotsam into an amorphous cultureless group. Alexia was pākehā but she was also Greek. At times, she was mainly Greek: it depended on the context.

'I'm Greek,' she said again.

Sam smiled an impenetrable smile. 'The Greeks aren't doing too well at the moment, are they?' she said mildly. 'But you are only pākehā, anyway,' she went on. 'Your people were colonisers too. They just came later. I wondered why you didn't know the tikanga, why you forgot to have koha ready. "Pōkarekare ana"! I should have known. You're just a whitey after all!'

This was a speech that Sam had been working up to for some time. She gave Alexia's arm a hard, joking punch, and laughed, a single laugh that Alexia did not echo. They arrived at the toilet block.

'My mother's generation were punished alongside the Māori kids at their school. They weren't allowed to speak their language.' The hue of Isaiah's skin came into Alexia's mind, coffee-coloured, absurdly similar to her own, as if they were related. 'They were tolerated, not welcomed.' She knew as she was speaking that it would not make a difference. She was speaking of a complexity that Sam did not wish to understand, an ambiguity in her system of inherited blame.

Sam threw open the cabinet door and pointed to the bandages.

'I mean, of course I'm also white –' Alexia went on, a little desperately.

But, elaborately, Sam turned away. Halfway out the door she called back over her shoulder.

'Sorry, sister! Can't chat! I've got some work to do before

the meeting!' Her face was filled with a kind of restrained joy. Then she was gone, leaving Alexia in the toilets with blood on her hands.

7

The meeting was being held in a small room off the kitchen. Isaiah thought Sam looked tired as she handed around cups of tea. Isaiah took one, though he wasn't in the habit of drinking caffeine. The feeling of optimism they all had started with was still present, but there had been delays and complications with their legal applications. They'd had one success: a local paper had come out to the marae to do some interviews and published a story, but it had been buried on the seventh page.

'The story in the paper looked really good,' Matiu said. He was upbeat, despite the rain that lashed the window and the sodden muddy ground that they had waded through on their way here. The spring rains had started. Isaiah supposed he was used to it.

Following the article's publication they'd received several calls from the press. But Isaiah was sceptical. They'd been here more than a month now. He'd spent more time than he would have liked being polite to aunties and charming to cousins, and listening dutifully to Polly's tales about his father. He was suspicious of anything that looked like forward movement. They were already running out of money. There were vague plans to hold a concert, which would need to raise a certain amount to sustain the numbers staying at the pā. There were now about forty visitors in addition to the local hapu. Only a few people lived here all year round, but relatives had been arriving steadily from the cities. The article had been promising, but what was a token show of interest from a rural paper? He wanted documentaries, political debates on the national news, international calls for solidarity.

Adding to his frustration he had, out of deference to the locals, not yet ventured onto the fracking site. It remained a sore point between him and Sam. She'd tried once to tease him about how he was being uncharacteristically well behaved, and he'd nearly yelled at her. She'd backtracked quickly, seeing the look on his face. His apparent neutrality had always been part of the game plan after all. But it galled him she had seen what they were up against and he hadn't. It was like his early days as an activist when he'd tried to 'fight capitalism'. His battle with capitalism had been like firing rocks into a void with a slingshot, without ever sighting the target.

Isaiah had kept his father's pounamu in reserve. But today he had decided to wear it. There was one photograph of his father in which you could see the toki, a deep green against the white business shirt that he wore. His mother had told him his father never took it off – except that after he had gone she'd found it packed carefully away in a drawer.

Polly came into the meeting late, without apologising. Her eyes lit upon his neck. Rangi, too, had noticed. Polly said nothing. She sat, put a pre-rolled cigarette into her pearl holder and blew her cigarette smoke up and away.

'It's not enough to get one article in the paper,' Isaiah said. Sam nodded, and surprisingly, so did Rangi. Alexia was absent, going over some information needed for correspondence with the council. She would probably have disagreed with him if she had been there. 'We need to do something proactive. We need to strike.'

'What is this "strike"?' Polly asked. 'That sounds like fighting talk to me. Your father, he wasn't a fighter.'

'If what you say is true, Aunty, your water is already showing signs of contamination. Your gardens are beginning to die.' Isaiah shook his head. 'You think a few words published in a small-town paper are going to change that? We've got people here, momentum. We need to use it.'

'To do what?' Her eyes were watery. If it wasn't Polly, he would have guessed she was afraid.

Racism feminism fascism anarchism resistance revolution. At university Isaiah had chosen political papers, though he was sceptical about what he could learn within the institution. But to his great surprise he'd found that he was being given a series of codes. The codes were the keys to the conversations he had grown up inside. He began to enjoy the work. The university became a refuge from his cold flat. He would go to the library in the evenings and lock himself into a bathroom stall. He used no literature, no magazines. He would touch himself, mechanically, hastily, spending everything against the tissue. Then he'd go out to where his bag sat slumped against a desk in a dark aisle and read political texts. The feeling would flow through him again, that old feeling of rightness, of absolute conviction. But now he was learning the language of it. He had a feeling too of perceiving the enemy, of seeing them, without being seen.

Isaiah had become involved in various groups. At one anti-mining meeting the rights of Māori had come up. Did anyone know what tribe the land had belonged to? Did Māori oppose the mining? Could someone contact them? The group had turned to Isaiah, waiting for him to speak, as though he had a direct line of communication to that particular tribe.

He saw that if he stepped into this role he would access a particular form of influence. Isaiah took his time. Then he told them he would contact the local iwi on their behalf. He said he was sure they would oppose the mining. He spoke of tūrangawaewae, of mana motuhake, of the unification of groups with common agendas. The faces of the attendees had shown a new deference. Afterwards a girl had pulled him aside, and told him she liked what he had said. It was Sam.

'There are actions we can take to undermine the fracking

company,' Isaiah said now. 'At a certain point the legality of these actions might become an issue. But our legal actions seem to be going nowhere. They're not going to stop the mining exploration. There's too much money in it. We have to show them that we're not powerless, as a people.' He smiled, looking at Matiu, Rangi and Polly, who were his relatives after all. His blood.

'You're not like your father,' Polly said. She rammed her cigarette into a saucer. 'Your father would never put his own people at risk.'

'You think you can walk in here and we'll listen to you, above our elders, because of who you are?' Matiu said. 'You think we're going to fall at your feet because of some old stone around your neck?'

Isaiah felt the pounamu for what it was: a cold, unwieldy presence.

After the meeting he fetched his sketchbook and walked towards the wall of bush. But Sam caught up with him. The bush shielded them from where the fracking machinery continued its work, already stripping the earth back.

'Didn't go so well for you in there.' She eyed the pounamu. 'I guess the secret weapon didn't work out as well as you had hoped.'

He was so grateful that he took her hand. She squeezed it, and then let it go.

'I just wanted to talk to you about Alexia. I want you to know I don't have a problem with her.' Sam looked as sunny as ever. Isaiah realised he had stopped walking. He moved forwards again.

'Why would you have a problem with her?'

'Well …' Sam said, and she closed her mouth. Sam generally so straightforward that any hesitancy was not a good thing.

'What?'

'Other people do. Have a problem.'

'What's that supposed to mean?'

'Nothing. It's just that we have to be careful.' They walked a little way. Sam stumbled on a bump in the ground; Isaiah did not help her. She hated any overt signs of chivalry.

'You mean you think she's a spy?'

'Don't you?' The bush line was darkened by the imminent dusk.

'I don't think anything of her, particularly.'

'Have you asked to draw her yet?' Sam regarded him in that way that she had, as if he was someone she was fond of, an aquaintance in need of advice.

'I have, actually. She hasn't agreed.' There was defensiveness in his voice. Sam laughed.

'Anyway, I don't have a problem with Alexia, myself. I just thought I'd let you know.' She smiled at him, and took his hand again. 'It's all up to you.'

8

Alexia had been asked to do some emailing, the equivalent of cold calling. She was going though the contacts on a list of media outlets, crossing them off one by one. It was strangely satisfying work. It was good to have structure and a purpose. She ran out of printer paper, and went to the cupboard to find a new ream. But there was nothing in it but an old guitar. Its surface had been buffed smooth by the hands that had played it. There was the slope and swoop of it, the dull patina, a scar where it must have been dropped. On inquiry it appeared that no one minded if she used it.

When she played music she thought of her grandfather, his fingers moving fluently across the strings of the bouzouki. All she had were odd lyrics and scraps of tune, not Greek songs but her own variation on them. For him there had only been the one kind of music.

That night, after a day's worth of emailing, she decided to play. There was a nice heft to the guitar. She warmed up, running through some finger exercises, and played a couple of tunes. She wasn't composing, only working on building strength after being so long away. It felt like the music was a place and she had gone away from it, as if it was the constant and she the uncertain element, coming and going like the weather. The music held still. It was a relief to be there, fingering out the notes, seeing the lights burst and fade.

She saw a vision come up across the field. The sky was grey, against which her lights were all the more bright. She shaded her eyes, cutting out the flares, and found that the vision was real. It was Ana, one of the children, who was perhaps twelve. She had an eel over one arm and was stroking it. It was almost as big as she was, its mouth open in an uncanny grin. It had milky blue eyes that Alexia could discern even from a distance. Ana's brothers Tama and Maitai came galloping after her, a hysterical edge to their voices. Tama's cat was not with them.

'You three up to something?' Alexia called. Ana petted the eel with long, slow strokes. She seemed almost crushed under the weight of it, but unafraid. The eel remained placid.

'What's it to ya?' Ana called. 'This is my eel, so there!'

The eel's tail swept around suddenly and hit Tama. The movement was slick and serpentine, and Alexia felt the fright ring deep in her body. Tama began to run. By the time he reached Alexia he was in tears.

'She's not supposed to!' he said. 'They told us to leave them in the river! Mako always comes when she calls but she shouldn't take him out.'

Ana disappeared down the bank with Mako. When she came back he was gone. She approached sulkily. 'He's my eel,' she said.

'He likes it better in the river though, doesn't he?' Alexia asked.

'He loves me,' Ana said, stubbornly.

'She makes him come to her with kai!' Tama said. 'She puts food in a sock and his teeth get caught and then she gets him out!'

'So what?' Ana put her hands on her hips.

Alexia picked up the guitar and began to strum. 'Don't mind me,' she said, addressing herself to the air. The children began to listen, and she felt suddenly shy.

'Awesome,' said Ana. She'd forgotten her rage. 'You could play at the concert.'

'What concert?' Alexia asked.

'We're gonna have a concert,' Maitai said. 'To raise money. You should play!'

'I'm not very good.' They watched her fingers move along the frets.

'You're a liar,' Maitai said. Alexia made to get up and leave, but he grabbed her arm. 'Don't you care about the tūī Ana found, and that dead pīwakawaka by the gate, and all those bees?' he asked. The bees had been found most recently: a sad black rain that had fallen in the clearing by the river. Isaiah was worried. Bees were very sensitive, he said. The state of bees was always a quantifiable indication of an eco-system's health. 'What if our eels get sick?' Maitai went on. 'They've been here for ages, our eels.'

'Stupid,' Tama said. 'Not just for ages. Forever. They been here since before the people came. It's in the old stories. They say a eel showed us where to go, when we had to move from down by the coast. They say it was a queen eel. She came and got the chief in the night and she took him up the stream, and there were all the kai tuna in the moonlight, just waiting. And she showed him this place. So we came here.'

'Far out!' said Maitai. He seemed genuinely impressed. 'You think Mako's a king eel? But who told you that, anyway? You're only seven. People don't know anything when they're seven.'

Tama's special cat arrived and wound about his legs. It was an ugly cat, and very attached to Tama, who was fiddling with his cap.

'Nanny told me, and so did Polly. Some of our eels are so old they probably even remember when we moved. Maybe one of them's the queen.' He flung his arm out towards the bridge. 'They're special eels, Rangi said. They live in the land water and the sea water. They're magic.'

'Shut up,' Maitai said, but mildly.

'They live on Papa-tū-ā-nuku and in Tangaroa too, so they gotta be magic. That Mako, he's more than a hundred years old. Polly knew him from when she was a girl. She says he's got the same scratches as he had then, on his head.'

'She told me that too,' said Ana.

'I don't know about all that,' said Maitai. 'But I know one thing. They're dangered.'

'What's dangered?' Tama asked.

'He doesn't know anything,' Maitai said sadly. 'People don't know anything when they're seven. Dangered means there's only a few left. So you gonna play guitar? To raise money to help save the eels?'

He was good, she had to give him that. To distract them Alexia started to play and to sing: silly rhyming lyrics about an eel and his lover. Maitai and Tama laughed, but Ana crossed her arms and made her toughest face.

'That Mako he loved Ana, loved her like fish and chips, and up out of the creek he came and kissed her on the lips!' Alexia sang. Ana hit Alexia lightly on the arm, but she was laughing too. The lights fired and fell. Alexia kept them at one remove in the way that she had learned to do, with her breath.

Then Isaiah was there, looking at Alexia over his glasses in a scholarly way, as if studying a scientific specimen.

'Isaiah,' Ana yelled. 'Alexia's being stink, Isaiah!' She ran to where he stood at the bottom of the wooden porch. Alexia stopped playing.

'Why'd you stop?' Isaiah asked. The lights faded.

'She was hassling me!' Ana said.

'She said Old Mako would kiss her on the lips!' Tama said. They were falling over each other laughing. Ana was still hanging on Isaiah's arm.

'Who's Mako?'

'A eel,' said Tama. 'A eel who loves Ana.'

'Go on then, play,' Isaiah said.

Alexia strummed loudly, surprising herself.

She'd run into Aidan and Hannah in a bar in the city the night after she'd split from Stephen, and on the strength of her drunken singing they'd offered for her to tour with them. She didn't know them well, but it was just what she needed, to be away from her old apartment and the university, to be free from anyone she knew. Alexia had been travelling with them for a couple of weeks when they'd changed their course, and had not yet gathered the confidence to perform. She'd been aware of the awkwardness of her position, the third wheel in the van built for two. Coming here was almost a relief, an escape from Aidan and Hannah's unrelenting cheerfulness and hospitality, and from the threat of doing what she had always wanted to do: playing music.

Already, her law degree was receding as if it had been a dream. She wasn't sure what had come first; her disillusionment with her work or the realisation that Stephen was a different sort of person from herself entirely. Her family thought she was spinning out of control, rebelling. Perhaps she was.

Isaiah stood in front of her expectantly. She would play as if he wasn't here, as if she was only playing for the kids, or the no one that had filled the field before they arrived. But here, the emptiness was never really emptiness. She often saw odd gold notes on the grass, sound markers without exact origin. Only upon listening very closely could she discern distant music, more like tinkling water than an organised tune. Under the sound of the wind was a strange distilled quiet like the overlaid memories of older silences. The land was not uninhabited.

She began to sing. She was playing a Latin American ballad. For a moment she gave herself over and entered into it, the bursts of pink and red. She increased the tempo. Isaiah folded his arms.

Alexia had taken advanced classes in music at school. She had been taught classical and flamenco and knew how to play twelve-string guitar. But when she'd got to law school she had given up. The demands on her time were too great. And studying music had been against the wishes of her family. 'It makes your synaesthesia worse,' her mother had said. 'It makes you lose touch.'

Her father's concerns had been more practical. 'You want to live in poverty?' he'd ask. 'You want to take the opportunities your grandfather gave you and throw them in his face?'

Her music had become a secret thing, a shameful thing. She had not played in front of anyone for years.

She finished the song. Isaiah nodded.

'We can use you in the fundraiser,' he said and started to walk off.

'No. I can't. I'm sorry,' Alexia said. Isaiah stopped. The children were quiet.

'Then why are you here?' he asked her. 'What are you doing here, coming to meetings, camping on the land, scabbing off these people, if you don't want to help?' His eyes had gone cool and remote.

'Scabbing?' she asked. He hadn't even smiled at her performance. He hadn't even tapped his foot. 'I'm probably the only person here who's not on the dole. You're the ones leeching off these people. I don't think I'm the worst interloper here.'

Ana stared. Tama was kneeling on the grass, his baseball cap in his hands. Maitai seemed confused. Too late she remembered the pōwhiri: herself being welcomed on one side, and Isaiah on the other. He had seemed so entrenched in the group of pākehā activists from the city that she'd simply forgotten.

'Well, they told me you were studying to be a lawyer,' he said, slowly. 'But I didn't believe it until just now.' It was meant as an insult. 'Actually, I'm from here,' he went on. 'This is my land. I'm not just some pākehā do-gooder jumping in on the fight.'

Alexia could not bring herself to formulate an apology. He waited for one, too righteously, she thought.

'I don't perform,' she said.

Maitai suddenly lost patience with her.

'You don't care about our eels!' he yelled. The cat mewed loudly. 'You don't care about our river and our bees and our land! You're just dumb! A stupid dumb pākehā!' He ran away, pulling Tama after him.

with grandfather reverent and show them in his face. Chief must had been...

9

The fracking site lay before them. It had once all been pā land, but had long ago become a series of farms. During the wars the new settlers had put up their fences. Then the soldiers had come with stronger weapons: starvation, guns, worse things. The people resisted but they lost the land anyway, Polly'd said, and finally their chief had been killed. All Isaiah could see now would once have been shared land. Isaiah's land.

'There,' Polly had said, pointing over the fields. 'All the way up there, as far as the river, then right up through the bush to the mountain. That's how big our lands were. But they took them, all the way back to the aukati.' Isaiah rolled this new word over in his mind: the boundary line. Though Sam was with them Polly spoke exclusively to Isaiah. Beside them the bush formed a wedge between the urupā and Taylor's place.

'Aukati lines were not our way of setting boundaries. Lines in general were not our way. The Crown made us draw the line. The land, it's that Taylor's now, and he's doing what he wants with it.' Her string of pearls was knotted artfully against her scarf, and her long white hair was plaited carefully into place. The words twisted at her mouth and pushed tears into the corners of her eyes.

The bush had been allowed to grow up over the aukati line, as if to obscure it. It wasn't spoken of. But Isaiah had become aware of an odd mannerism the locals had. He had thought at first they were doing it out of respect for the urupā, or for some finer point of tikanga he had not yet grasped. They would point to the mountain or gesture to the far bush. They would raise their eyes unshielded to the sun. But whenever they looked in the direction of the line their eyes would skip quickly past it. Polly had looked directly at the aukati while she was talking, and it was this that caused her to stop. Her old brown fingers were clenched, strangely similar in shape to his own.

Now the old pā land was in front of him and the moon hung full and low. Isaiah crouched at the edge of the wedge of bush, which was in fact only a thin veil between the pā and the land being used by the company. Stalled at the edge of the wide, bare space, he could hear very little, only his own breath and Sam's, ragged from their walk. They had talked about the prospects for holding a fundraiser. They had musicians here, after all: Aidan and Hannah and Alexia, though Alexia had said in some kind of fit that she would not play. He was sure he could talk her around. They were still attracting protestors, and the money would help to fund further actions.

Sam came and knelt behind him. She wore a black bandanna over the lower part of her face, like himself, to foil the security cameras. His breathing changed as he saw it. Where he supposed there had been open farmland was a swathe of bare clay that stretched far over the land for many kilometres. In the moonlight the earth's surface showed up almost daylight clear, but cratered, broken. It was a land torn open to the sky. As they crouched in the ditch between the bush and the exposed earth it seemed they knelt between completely unconnected landscapes, as though a piece of desert had been picked up and dropped into the middle of the rich green land.

Isaiah became aware of two scents. There was Sam beside him, of course – the cloying scent of some oil she always wore, and her musky body odour. She was so close he could have had her right there, pushed her into the bush like he had done on reconnaissance missions before. That was half of the attraction of Sam – her adventurousness, her readiness, the boyish way she would tackle him in the dark. But her smell was overwhelmed by another – the reek of the pit before them. The fumes took him by the throat. There was nothing romantic about this reccie, nothing mischievous. They were crouched on the edge of a pit.

The land was levelled like a cup of flour someone had scraped a knife across. The clay was wet and slick, the kind of clay that would be a harsh yellow in the sun. Where the rim of the cup would be, the surrounding paddocks rose up on either side, five feet above the level of the shorn field. It would be a pit but was too large to be a pit, extending towards the mountain. At the edges of the depression were temporary fences made of orange plastic mesh. Beyond these were vague shapes off in the distance: Taylor's herds, now relocated.

There were three or four tanker trucks in Isaiah's immediate view, and further away, still more: huge cylindrical shapes in the darkness, arranged haphazardly, like outsized, mechanical cattle. From the trucks ran fat tubes which Isaiah knew from his reading must carry the frack fluid – the waste water and chemicals and oil that escaped up out of the ground containing hundreds of toxic compounds. There was a black pool in front of him.

'Landfarming,' Sam whispered beside him. 'It's happening already.' This was what he hadn't been able to imagine, not on this massive scale. The company had rolled back grass and topsoil into scrolls. They were dumping waste fluid, millions of tons of it, into the open earth. When they were done they would roll back the grass on top. Taylor would be given back the field, and his cattle would graze in it, and people would eventually eat the cattle. The river entered the bush behind where they were crouched, their breaths still short.

'You can smell it,' Isaiah whispered. It was like turpentine. But there was more to it, something rotten and animal-like, as though there were dead bodies in the ground. He coughed as quietly as he could.

'I told you,' Sam said. 'I tried to tell you how bad it was.' She was furious. In the face of small wounded things, Sam would go mad with rage. Confronted with pollution she became savage. She was very black and white. She separated the world into good and bad. And the fracking site was bad. Isaiah had not seen anything to compare it to: not the open coal mines on the West Coast, or the vast quarries in the north.

Sam grabbed his hand. 'Come on,' she said. 'We have to move. Security will be round at ten.' She had spent many nights hidden in the bush, tracking the movements of the guards: the specific times they patrolled, the shift changes. There were five pods consisting of two guards each. They rotated the watch every two hours. Right now they were between shifts and on the lazy side of the tea break. The guards didn't carry anything with them except radios. For all their uniforms, they seemed fairly harmless.

The balaclavas Sam and Isaiah wore over their faces could be pulled down to be worn as scarves. In a hidden pocket Isaiah had a monopod for his lightest camera. It telescoped inside itself till it was only centimetres long. They had left a bag of their normal clothes in the bush in case they needed to change quickly. They'd walked through the river on the way here, a route that would confound dogs if they were chased. Their black clothes were chosen to appear casual, and Sam carried a dog leash. If they were caught they'd say they were out walking their dog and that it had run away. He pulled it out, watching the horizon and the security towers for movement, but there was none.

He and Sam crawled down the bank to the water. In his shirt pocket the camera was set to night exposure so that he could take pictures without a flash. It would take a long time, a minute maybe, to get any good images. He'd need to keep still, even with the monopod. Sam stood, shielding him from the one visible security camera, while he bent down as if to tie his shoe. He eased the camera lens out, covering the pilot light with his hand. He fitted it to the monopod and raised it, framing the expanse in the viewfinder.

Across the dark pond came a series of howls. Dogs. Damn. Sam and Isaiah did not waste time. As she began to run, he slid the camera back under his shirt. He followed her as she scrambled up the bank, catching her boot heel and pushing it up when it slid in the wet clay. As they gained the top she bent her head towards him and indicated the path back through the bush. He was dismissed. He was the one carrying the gear – the camera and the monopod, the sample test tubes, the containers for collecting contaminated soil. They had arranged that he would be the one to slip away should they be threatened with capture. It was a logical decision to split up if they needed to run. He was taller and faster, and Sam was better at small deceptions. She would be safer without him, more likely to talk herself out of whatever trouble she was in.

She ran away from him along the mouth of the pit, pulling a steel whistle from the neck of her jacket, her other hand yanking down the balaclava so that her head was naked to the sky. As he ran towards the bush, she sounded the whistle. Briefly the dogs were silenced, then they started again, apparently heading for Sam.

'Toby!' she was calling. 'Toby!' She pulled a dog lead out of her pocket, unfurling it like a flag. 'Here, boy!'

Sam would see Isaiah failing to escape as a cowardly act, one that threatened the whole operation. But there she was, silhouetted against the open pit, waving a leash and sounding the whistle madly, her jacket hood down, the shorn back of her neck white and vulnerable in the moonlight. Fuck their code of honour.

Isaiah ran towards her, his breath coming in painful gasps, the gas from the pit dry in his throat. He yanked at his own balaclava, stumbling up from his crouch into a half-run, swearing and tripping and almost falling. The dogs were upon them now, their howls tripping off a panic switch in his body.

There were four, five animals – snarling, lips pulled back

from their teeth. Sam hadn't seen Isaiah. He was facing the security camera. There was movement at the security tower. A tall figure coming up behind the dogs. The man was whistling and calling as he came. He wore no uniform.

As Isaiah reached for Sam, she leaned down towards the foremost dog and then knelt, opening her arms. He grabbed the dog by the collar, but realised that it was licking Sam's face and fawning at her hands. Sam was good with animals, but not that good. The collar in his fist was decorative, with diamantes on it. The other dogs who surrounded them seemed motley and varied in breed. These were not the security guards' dogs. He let go.

He had time to see anger cross Sam's face before the dog, frightened by Isaiah's sudden movement, turned and snapped at his fingers. He leapt back, and another dog grabbed him from behind, the teeth tearing through his thin pants and into his leg. He felt a strange, pain-free pop, and then the dog had him. Pain followed, in a hot needling rush. Then Isaiah was on the ground and it seemed they were all on him: Sam's dog with its paws on Isaiah's chest and another one ripping at his leg and one more coming at his face from the side, and Sam was yelling.

Isaiah was released. He stood up, breathless, aware of his blood pounding and the slick wetness at the back of his knee and the horrible proximity of the dogs, who were whining now, but under some kind of control.

The man knelt by the dog that had wooed Sam, holding it back by its collar, speaking in a low, soothing voice.

'Bloody idiot,' he said to Isaiah. 'What did you think you were doing, attacking my girl like that?' He stroked the dog under the chin.

Isaiah took a step back. Sam stood at his side. He sensed her nervousness. He'd changed the plan. If they messed this up now, it was his fault. He faced the man and did his best to smile.

'Sorry,' he said, putting an arm around Sam. 'Thought she was going for my wife.'

The man stood slowly, studying Isaiah's glasses through his own silver frames. Isaiah could feel the monopod cold against his chest, the test tubes in his pants pocket. Luckily the tear in his leg hadn't hit any gear.

'She wasn't going for your "wife",' the man said. 'Seems like she had things under control till you grabbed Fran.' The dog let out a sudden howl. 'Down, Francesca,' the man said. The name was so unlikely Isaiah wanted to laugh.

'Did you see a border collie?' Sam shook the lead out and put her other arm round Isaiah. 'We've lost Toby,' she said plaintively, her eyes lowered. Before the man could answer, she turned to Isaiah, 'Well, hon, we should head off. Maybe Toby's just gone back to the camper?' She had put on a vaguely American accent, as though to impersonate a tourist.

The man began to laugh. It was a strange, desolate sound. All at once Isaiah was assaulted by the smell of the gas and the frack fluid, the sight of the dark water beside them.

'Toby, my arse,' the man said. 'I should set my dogs on you. You're coming with me.' He made a low whistling sound. Sam gripped Isaiah as the dogs, smoothly and with a practised ease, surrounded them.

From the nearby tower came two figures with torches. Isaiah reminded himself of his rights. He was trespassing, but security guards didn't have the powers of the police. They couldn't legally search him. If they did choose to, however, he was concerned about his equipment. One of the men spoke into his radio.

The dog man sighed. He had short, fine hair and a sensitive face. He peered myopically at Isaiah.

'Well, bugger me. You two just keep your traps shut. All right?'

Then the guards were there.

'Caught myself a couple of tourists,' the dog man called.

'Is that right?' One of the guards was Māori. Perhaps he was from around here, perhaps from Isaiah's own iwi. 'Sure you haven't caught yourself a couple of ... explorers? Maybe from that place over there?' He jerked his head towards the pā.

'We were looking for our dog, Toby.' Sam gestured with the leash.

'Right.' The Māori guard drew the word out. His companion remained silent, his hand resting on his radio as though it were the holster of a gun.

'I found them, fellas. I'll escort them out,' the man said. 'My dogs will find their Toby, easy as.'

The dog that had licked Sam's face started a low whining, sniffing at Sam's hands. Suddenly Sam blew the steel whistle, shocking even the wooden-faced guard.

'Toby!' she yelled. 'Toby!' Her accent had got thicker, and she acted as though she was close to tears. 'I'm sorry, hon,' she said to Isaiah. 'I'm just so worried about our dog! He's about so high,' she said to the guards, 'and he has a cute little jacket on. It's red. I knitted it. If he's fallen into this huge pool ...'

'If the embassy finds out you've been holding us, your government won't know what hit them,' Isaiah said, in his best approximation of an American accent. 'My wife and I came here for some relaxation, not to be held like criminals. I'd think twice if I were you. You don't know who it is you're dealing with.'

The Māori guard's face twitched.

'Oh, I think I know who I'm dealing with,' he said. He turned to the dog man. 'They're trespassing,' he said. 'We could have them arrested.'

'This is still my land,' the man said. 'I own it, even if you lot are leasing the rights.'

'Fine.' The Māori guard held his hands palm outwards into the air. 'Take them. But I don't want to catch you here again. They're all yours, Taylor. But kua whakatūpato koe.' He was speaking to Isaiah particularly. The guards departed.

'Thanks.' Sam had dropped the accent.

Taylor was surprisingly young, maybe in his mid-thirties. He drew himself up with a sigh. 'I feel like I'm in hell. Come on, Francesca. Come on, Petal, Rose, Petunia. Come on, Daphne. Come on, you two sorry bastards.' Evidently they were going directly back through the bush. It was obvious that Taylor knew they were from the pā.

What had the guard said? Isaiah had long ago come to terms with his lack of language knowledge. It wasn't his fault that he hadn't grown up speaking te reo. His mother had always urged him to study it. Of course she wanted some kind of spokesperson for a son, some campaigning, justice-seeking hero. Suddenly he saw the irony of it: Polly had wanted this for his father, too. And his mother thought she was so different from Polly. He had responded by not learning te reo, by demonstrating a lack of interest in all things Māori. It hadn't been a conscious decision. It had never truly bothered him, his lack of understanding. But it was a horrible feeling not under-standing the words as he moved about his own land.

'Why'd you help us?' Isaiah said. The words sounded angrier than he would have liked. Taylor ignored him.

'Blasted fools,' he was saying.

'What do you mean, you're in hell?' Sam asked.

Taylor ignored that too. Instead, he looked at the lead she was trailing in the mud.

'That's seen just about as much use as a prayer mat at a piss-up,' he said. 'Two "tourists" in the wops in the middle of the night by this pool of filth. Honestly – heel, Petunia – what did you buggers think you were doing?'

'What did you think *you* were doing out here, Taylor?' Isaiah asked. They'd reached the bush. 'Did you want to see exactly how much damage you've already caused?'

'This is my land,' Taylor said. 'If I want to walk around it, that's my business. What do you think it is I'm doing here? I'm up the boohai shooting pokakas, son, what do you think?' Now Isaiah could hear the faint accent behind his words. He was Dutch, maybe, Swiss, Germanic anyway. The boohai, the pokakas, the buggers, all of it was an affectation – Kiwi slang Taylor had picked up. Taylor laughed. 'No,' he said. 'I'm just here because of the pā kids,' Taylor said. He leaned down and petted Francesca softly. 'They come out here to see. Caught one of them the other day, down by the water. Well, they say it's partly water.' He glared at them suddenly. 'The adults came first, now suddenly it's the thing to do. This kid, he could have fallen in. There's pits everywhere. They've undermined the land.' He swore, some of the words foreign. 'I didn't want to do it,' he said. 'They came in with teams of lawyers, threw money at me. Said if I didn't agree, they'd sue. I couldn't afford to fight it. You think I'd want to do this to my own land?'

Stolen land, Isaiah thought. The blood had congealed at the back of his leg and the pain had lessened to a dull throb. Sam pulled at his arm.

'Take that meat out of your pocket, love, and give it to Francesca,' Taylor said. Sam drew a bag of raw meat from her pocket and fed it to the dog. Isaiah admired her. She found meat repulsive, but she would set even that aside for the cause.

Then he remembered Sam's silhouette against the sky, as she whistled and called out, almost as though she wished to be found. Of course she had wanted to draw attention away from him and from the gear, but he'd seen odd things happen to activists before. The hopelessness and frustration of the work could take people over, until they welcomed contact with the authorities, until getting caught was a kind of relief. It had happened to him when he was very young. He'd assumed that Sam had worked all that out years ago. But there had been confrontation in her stance: an eagerness, a way of standing that you would sooner see on a stage.

'I'm Isaiah.' He extended his hand to Taylor. 'I'd like to talk to you sometime soon.' Taylor's hand was unusually soft for a farmer's.

'Haven't seen you around the pā before,' Taylor said. 'Come along, Petunia, Francesca, Petal, Daphne, Rose. Welcome to paradise.' And he left them at the edge of the bush.

'That is the most depressed farmer I've ever met,' Sam said.

Together they went into the trees and the smell of the open pit dissipated. Isaiah flicked on his mag torch, which he'd hung on a cord in his sleeve. The landscape behind them suddenly seemed unreal. In the bush the birds rustled and called, and he could hear water running. He turned to Sam with a smile on his face.

'So what the hell was all that about, you breaking our protocol?' she said.

10

There was so much time to think when you didn't have a television set. Alexia and Stephen had got into a habit of watching documentaries every night, coming home from their respective days too exhausted to speak. If it wasn't the TV, it was the internet, or their phones. It was so much easier to sit and surf. When had it begun, this mindless erosion of her time? She couldn't remember. She lay in the tent in her sleeping bag and pulled off her socks. It was definitely growing milder: she could no longer see her breath in the mornings. She had reading material, a law book she was meant to be studying, but she couldn't stomach opening it. Instead, she lay there and remembered. Sometimes she remembered when she didn't want to.

Alexia was five when her grandfather had had his first heart attack.

'He almost died,' her mother had come to tell her. Papou was in the hospital. Her mother wept helplessly. Alexia patted her back as it heaved. After a while Mama rose, and they went into the bedroom and knelt by the large icona. The Virgin's face peeking solemnly out of the metal.

Alexia's mother prostrated herself. 'I will give something up,' she said, 'if you keep him alive.' She pulled Alexia down beside her. 'What will *you* give up?' she asked. What could Alexia confess? But Mama was preoccupied with her own bargaining. 'I will be a good wife, a better wife,' and she began to recite the Lord's Prayer. Alexia, on her knees, watched as snot crept down her mother's face, tracing paths through her make-up. Just when she thought she was safe, her mother grabbed her.

'You have to sacrifice something. The doctors say that he has a chance.'

Death was a thing that Alexia had no experience of. Death was a location, somewhere cold and empty. She could not imagine her grandfather going there. He was too real to vanish so easily.

Mama would pull Alexia's crimes from her body ... Alexia stilled herself. She could continue to appear present even when she wasn't really there. She kept her face blank and her eyes unfocused. When she surfaced in her place the sun was shining. There was a field and beyond that wilderness. She had built a hut in the trees. There were things in there that she liked: a wooden clog, a windmill with Greek patterns that Papou had kept in his shed, a small hammer. If she tried hard she could see the individual pebbles in the riverbed, and each perfect stalk of grass.

Her mother had turned back to the Virgin and her ululation. Alexia was not required to catalogue her faults. There were a dozen that she would prefer not to have to voice: selfishness, pride, forgetfulness, sinning in her thoughts against her parents.

'Pray with me, Alexia'

Alexia understood God as a collection of stories. But maybe if she wished very hard, her grandfather would live. Maybe God was just a concentration of people's wishes.

'Páter imón, o en tís ouranís.'

They stopped only to pull themselves up and do their crosses, three times over their hearts in an anti-clockwise direction. Alexia's knees grew sore. She tried to get up to go to the bathroom but her mother pulled her down.

Alexia prayed. She swore that she would be good if God allowed Papou to live. She knelt, and the wish grew larger and stronger, until it encompassed her completely. That time, it had worked. Papou had been released from hospital. And it worked, too, a few years later, when he'd had another heart attack. Alexia had fallen into the habit of believing in the power of the family's prayers. She had fallen into the habit of being good.

But now he was gone and no amount of being good would change anything anymore. She turned over in the tent and tried to sleep.

11

It was a rainy, messy day, cloudy and wet in turns. Isaiah didn't usually feel the cold, but the damp bothered him. They had all agreed that a party must be sent to try and convince Taylor, the farmer, to help them. Alexia had volunteered to prepare an educational pamphlet, so she was staying behind. Isaiah wondered how much of this was to do with Sam being included in the visiting party. The two women didn't avoid each other exactly, but he had noticed Alexia affecting a kind of blankness when Sam was around. It was possible to observe it. When Sam spoke in a meeting, Alexia wouldn't respond. It was as if she was afraid of offending her. But Sam didn't care about personal tension. She leapt on Alexia's suggestions with the same enthusiasm she had for everyone's ideas, although it seemed like Sam had to try especially hard with Alexia to overlook certain things.

What things? The way Alexia's long hair brushed against her shoulders, which were often bare, displayed in an expensive blouse. How she pursed her lips in thought, without knowing it was cute, or put her finger on her nose when they were all in debate. The way this all contrasted with everything Sam was about.

But it was Sam who was here beside him now, reaching her hand up to guide him over the farm stile. It was Sam who was always here.

'Isaiah!' Tama was following them, running full tilt, a cat in his arms. Ana was behind him, and behind her, Maitai, who was splashing through puddles in his bare feet. For a moment Isaiah envied them growing up here. Then he remembered what they were all going off to do and the feeling stopped. The beauty of this place and its liveability were finite.

'Isaiah!' called Tama. 'We want to come too!'

The small group stopped on the other side of the fence. Isaiah and Sam, Rangi and Bryce. Tama was already climbing the stile. The scrawny cat gave Isaiah a long-suffering look.

'No way,' Isaiah said. 'You three have to head home.'

'Aw, why?' Tama said.

Maitai's face fell. 'Told yous,' Ana said, tugging at Tama.

'It's inappropriate for children to come,' Isaiah said.

This seemed to drive them away, Tama muttering about there being nothing interesting to do round here, ever.

'"It's inappropriate for children,"' Rangi mimicked. 'Can you even hear yourself? They're only kids. That Alexia, she hangs out with them. Gives them the time of day. You're so caught up in your head, you don't even see how much they want to spend time with you. You might not have had rellies growing up, but you have them now.'

'You're an uncle now, Isaiah,' Bryce said. Because of his height he leaned down towards Isaiah as he spoke. Isaiah stepped back involuntarily, as if Bryce's apparent kindliness could be physically avoided.

As they approached Taylor's farm the closeness of the bush dropped away. Bryce and Rangi strode ahead, talking about something that was causing Rangi to wave his arms around a lot, and Sam reached out and slipped her hand into Isaiah's. They hadn't spent any personal time together lately but, oddly, their political chemistry had increased. They spoke often: on the way to meetings, in the kitchens, at lunch, always about the campaign. Sam would talk about direct action and he would be drawn in. The space that had been their relationship had given way to larger issues. She seemed as enraged as he was about what was happening to the land and about their shared helplessness. It made Isaiah question the time he allotted Sam and Alexia in his mind, as if such concerns were petty and base. Perhaps Alexia felt a similar fury about the cause but she didn't express it in discussions about strategy. Isaiah stumbled and his hand shook loose from Sam's. He used the stumble as an excuse not to keep holding on.

Taylor's house was a functional box. Around it there were kennels, a chicken coop, a terrain buggy, a ute. A woman opened the door. She was stringy and weathered. A dog barked.

'Shut up!' she yelled.

The woman ushered them into the lounge, where Taylor was standing by a packed bookshelf, patting at his dogs. The room smelled strongly of canine. A pile of climbing equipment lay in a corner. Taylor greeted Rangi as if he was an old friend, then gestured for them all to sit on the couches, which were thick with dog hair. The bookshelf was filled with books by surprising authors: Camus, De Beauvoir, Spinoza.

Taylor expressed his sincere gratitude for their visit and then left the room to make tea. One of the dogs came over and sat at Isaiah's feet. She gave a low growl. He offered her his palm and she snapped at it, but stayed close to him. He removed a manila folder from his bag and placed it on his knee.

'Was that his wife?' Sam whispered. 'And is that his climbing gear?'

'She's probably just a farm hand,' Rangi said. 'I think Taylor used to climb, for sport.'

'How come you two are on such good terms?' Sam asked.

The dog thrust her nose between Isaiah's legs.

'He's our neighbour,' Rangi said. 'Of course I know him. If someone gets in an accident out here, you have to call on each other.'

Taylor entered carrying a silver tea tray with china cups on it.

'Come away now, Petunia,' he said. The dog left Isaiah reluctantly.

Rangi sniffed at his tea. 'You trying to poison me?' he asked.

'Peppermint,' Taylor said. 'It's good for the digestion.' The dogs set up a low collective howl. 'Come, Daphne. Come on, Francesca. Come on, Rose,' he said.

Isaiah laid the manila folder on the table. 'We've come to ask for your support,' he said. 'We're going to the council to request they make the fracking land into a reserve.'

Taylor was incredulous. 'But that's my land,' he said. 'If it turns into a reserve, who's going to compensate me? Besides, I've already signed all the documents. Sugar?' Rangi nodded and stirred his tea with great concentration.

'Whether it's your land or not is arguable,' Bryce said. He stood up. 'Whether it's salvageable is not.' He looked at Taylor's bookshelf. 'There's still a chance that we can save it. I see you're a well-read man. It appears you've given some thought to philosophy, to ethics.' He picked up the folder and placed it in Taylor's hands. 'Here we have a possible solution,' he said. Isaiah was almost impressed.

Petunia had snuck back to Isaiah's side. When he put his hand on her head, though, she growled again.

'Those aren't my books,' Taylor said, sadly. 'They were my wife's. My sheila's.' His accent was stronger today. Definitely Dutch, Isaiah thought. 'When she up and left me I thought she was pulling my leg. I was arse over tit in love with her.' He crossed the room and stroked a book spine: *Anna Karenina*. 'Now I'm alone,' he said, with a complete absence of irony.

Petunia's teeth sank into Isaiah's hand – not hard, just enough to hold on. Isaiah tried to pull it away but the dog held firm. When she let go there were deep indentations. He tried not to let his eyes tear up with the pain. He regained his composure enough to speak.

'Just give it a read,' he said to Taylor. 'If we had your support it would make a difference.'

'Nothing will make a difference now,' Taylor said. It was unclear if he was discussing the fracking or his wife.

'A man's life cannot be ruled by ladies alone,' Rangi said.

Isaiah stroked the red marks on his hand. 'That's your gear, right?' He pointed to the climbing equipment on the floor. 'You must love the bush.'

Petunia went to Taylor and crouched near him, panting.

'My father used to take me on climbing trips,' Taylor said. 'Moved us here when I was ten. He loved the forest. He taught me survival skills, that sort of thing. He was a bit of a *dag*, I'd say. But his heart was as good as gold.' He eyed Sam with a vague longing. She was sitting close to Isaiah. Sam had small, fine whorls of blonde hair by her ears; Isaiah had forgotten how he'd loved that. 'Ever find that Toby, Sam?' She didn't answer. 'Yes, I like to go up into my hills and climb.'

Isaiah's father had died in this particular swathe of bush. He had, like Taylor's father, known bush lore. But along with the usual training he'd also had his inherited knowledge, the older skills that he'd wished to test. He'd gone in, Isaiah's mother had told him, without food or water, up behind the pā. He had wanted to try and 'live Māori' – to live off the land for a couple of weeks, eating ferns and grubs, just to see if he could do it. It was the same bush he'd played in as a child. It didn't occur to anyone that he might not come out.

Some people thought he had fallen into a cave or a ravine far up the mountain. Others said it must have been a flash flood. Others thought he might have tried to climb a rocky abutment and simply fallen down.

Taylor was speaking to Isaiah as though he was the only person in the room.

'He taught me to fish and hunt, my father,' he said. 'Guess you didn't have that when you were growing up.'

Sam suddenly stood up. Isaiah put his hand on her arm and pulled her down. He knew she wanted to protect him, but pissing Taylor off wasn't in the plan.

'Lucky you,' Isaiah said, keeping his voice as even as he could. Ever since he'd started school, he had pushed himself to learn all he could about survival – dad or no dad. He had elected to go on every outdoor activity, on every camp or course, to attend any workshop that could develop his skills. He had learned to climb, to abseil and belay, to anchor and knot, to crimp his hands onto holds almost too small to see.

'Shoulda known better than to think you'd help,' said Rangi.

'I found out about you,' Taylor said, still talking to Isaiah. 'Guess you think you're going to come here and save this place.' He chucked Petunia under the chin. 'Guess you think you're going to ride in here on your white horse and save the pā. Chip off the old block, eh?' he said. 'Isn't that what you Kiwis say?'

The dog smell in the room seemed to crest and rise. Rangi put his half-drunk tea on the table.

'Not drinking any more of that weasel piss,' he said. He grabbed Isaiah's arm and steered him towards the door. 'Don't worry about this dumbshit pākehā sell-out,' he said. 'He thinks with his bank book and he's ruled by the ladies. Can't even control his own dogs.'

'You keep that,' Bryce said indicating the folder in Taylor's lap, 'for when you're ready. All the environmental data we've collected is at the back.'

Before Rangi manhandled him through the lounge door, Isaiah caught a glimpse of Taylor's vacant eyes, one hand on the folder, the other resting on Petunia's head.

As a boy Isaiah had loved to learn anything he could about his father. Later, though, he had grown uncomfortable with his mother's stories. Eventually he'd stopped asking altogether. Now when she spoke of his father he'd tune her out. It was in the end the finite nature of the stories, the unbearable repetition. She told and re-told, and always he was expected to act amused and interested at the right times. There was no ignoring the fact that some time long ago his mother had run out of charming tales.

When his mother told these stories her face emptied of all

of its customary expressions and assumed a bland innocence. She'd speak faster, more eagerly, confused about why he didn't want to hear. 'Oh, and he loved you,' she'd always say, at the end. 'How he loved his little boy.'

By the time he was eight Isaiah had formed a habit of biting his nails.

'If you could see the way he'd look at you, before we lost him ...' She would cry sometimes, messily, scattering apologies and tears. He would fetch tissues. 'You were his only child,' his mother would say, laughing and taking another sip of wine. She would bite her nails too, but coyly, only the thumbnail, and only when she was drinking. In her it was an endearing habit, a quirk that went along with her flying hands and her many rings and her perfume and her scarves. 'He always said he wanted sixteen children,' she would say. 'Before he disappeared.'

By the time he was a teenager Isaiah bit his nails until they bled.

On the other side of the farm stile the group seemed unsure where to go. Since they'd left Taylor's yard they hadn't spoken. But they had to face their failure. They would have to take the news back to Polly, and to the others. Isaiah was familiar with these small moments of dissappointment, the sense of deflation. It wasn't as if he'd held much hope that Taylor would support them. It wouldn't make financial sense for him to do that.

Now his nails were cut neatly short, and unbitten. He had started weaning himself off the nail-biting when he started taking photos. It had taken a long time: until he was twenty-five, only a couple of years ago.

'Onwards, to the next action!' Bryce said, his fist in the air. Sam rolled her eyes, but began to follow him towards the wharenui. There was a sudden blow to his shoulders. Rangi was in his face, grinning his cracked, lopsided grin. In the overcast light the patterns on his skin were a deep green.

'Don't let him get to you, cuz!' he said. 'He's not all there in the head. Like the prophet says, "Onwards!"' And he started to whistle comically, walking away from Isaiah and checking to see if he was following. Isaiah caught him up in a hurry.

'Rangi, can I ask you what something means?'

'What?'

'Kua whakatūpato koe.' Isaiah sounded the words carefully, worried he might have memorised them wrong. Rangi stopped walking.

'It's a warning, bro.' He smiled. 'Now what could you have been doing to make someone give you a warning?'

Isaiah did not answer, but Rangi seemed a little bit impressed.

12

H er nights in the tent were growing more real than her days. The people she visited in her mind were people she knew, unlike those she was trying to help. Here was the thing people here didn't know, the thing Alexia was holding back: a part of her had died. It wasn't the part that had loved Stephen. A week before she met Aidan and Hannah, she'd been at her grandfather's funeral.

She replayed it again and again: the phone call, how she had borrowed a car from her friend and went at once, how she'd stood, unmoving, at the front gate. Her grandparents' house was bland, unassuming, another well-groomed house on a tidy street. It was impossible to believe that Papou had gone, entirely, that he would not be coming back here. What the house had to tell passers-by was nothing interesting – that the people inside subscribed to *TV Guide* and that they liked carnations with their sharp cinnamon scents. The house held for Alexia a thousand other stories. This was the first house Papou had ever owned. Inside it were all the things that made up Alexia's memories: all the meals cooked and all the coffee that had been drunk. Each child had been raised and fed and had gone to school, everyone had been clothed and the babies bought presents.

Her borrowed car was shameful beside the other cars. Now she was seeing it with her Greek eyes, it voiced its politics clamorously, bumper stickers predicting an imminent oil crisis, plaintively requesting there be *No Asset Sales*, declaring the moral choice of vegetarianism in the face of animal cruelty. Alexia was not vegetarian now, but she had been once. She had given it up one Christmas, when Yiayia had wept wildly over her refusal to eat the lamb. For hadn't Papou come here and worked in a fish shop for forty years so as to provide the family not only with education and better housing but also with proper food? To make a better life? And her Greek eyes told her that her flimsy top was immodest, her sandals too casual for this day. Alexia had come immediately when she'd heard. Yiayia would already be wearing the black clothes of mourning, packing away her patterned house dresses forever, but Alexia hadn't even thought to pull her hair away from her face.

There was the small olive tree on the verge. She leaned against the trunk. This was one story about Papou's home that would be obvious to anyone standing on the street: someone here had considered the New Zealand native planted by the council a waste of space. It had been ripped out and replaced with an olive tree, a more practical tree, capable of bearing fruit and providing olives and oil. But the tree was stunted. It was still unclear at this point whether it would grow in the clay.

The front door of the house opened. A wail came from inside. It was grief as pure sound. In front of her eyes, the lights started. She was surprised to see that Yiayia's grief was a white sheet that was draped over everything, one smooth simultaneous blanket of notes. She blocked it.

Suddenly she was running through the gate to the front door, unclear as to why she had lingered there, standing on the street like a stranger. Her grandfather was dead. Then she was inside and they were all around her, in their black clothes and gold chains and crosses, carrying the smell of candles. Their hands were on her and they were holding her and she was crying and saying in Greek, I'm sorry, signomi, forgive me, and Yiayia was saying why and she was saying because I wasn't here.

Inside the house Katherine alone was sitting down, her

bright dress contrasting with eveyone else's clothes. Alexia greeted her. There was relief on her sister's face. Now Alexia would do the talking. As the eldest, it was her job to fetch and carry, and to listen. Alexia had grown up in the centre of a circle of relatives. It was her job to understand them. She put down her keys on the telephone table in the hall and wiped her face and asked how it had happened.

Every morning when Alexia woke in her tent beside the pā, the first thing that she thought was: Papou is dead. The second thing she thought of was Yiayia's wail, and the light rising and falling, going white across her vision. White and white and white.

It was another muddy spring day. There were lambs in the fields: people went to see them. She was uninterested.

There were more meetings. Alexia stayed quiet throughout, though Isaiah always tried to catch her eye. Hannah and Aidan played music around their campfire well into the night. She went into her tent and lay there, thinking, listening to Aidan, 'The Irish', teaching Hannah Gaelic songs.

She had done everything right. She had played the good Greek girl.

She had gone to the funeral home. She had needed to see it for herself, to prove that it was real. She had been offended by the ugliness of the undertaker. His forehead was high and pale and seemed quietly alarmed at the forwardness of his nose, which was a fleshy bulb. Alexia had tried not to look at his exploded blood vessels. There was a moment of awkwardness while the undertaker bobbed, his hand flailing for the correct hand to press. Finally he settled on Yiayia's, which was willing to be held.

Everything was hushed as if under glass. The undertaker took them through to the room with the waxwork in it. His hands, which Alexia had avoided, were horrid; long and white and capable of things. Alexia watched her feet move forwards in their black ballet slippers, one, two, one, two, like a swing that cannot stop of its own accord. Then they were in the room, bunched close together by the door, and the white-handed man left them. There was an enormous arrangement of flowers, a heavy velvet curtain and a coffin. The coffin seemed small from a distance, a toy boat sailing in the sea of the room.

Yiayia held Alexia's hand. She walked forward eagerly in spite of her arthritic knees, and the family followed. Around them was the feeling of hung silk. Apart from the rustle of people's clothes, there was no sound.

Papou's body was a fake. He had been shrunk to two-thirds of his size. His skin was awfully perfect, pallid and taut and preserved. It wasn't Papou but rather some replica of him, some smaller scale model that had been produced as a mockery and dressed in his clothes. Alexia hummed a clear C, quietly, and watched the green flash rise and fall. She had never been to a funeral with an open casket. She'd expected it to be less tidy, perhaps. She'd expected him to be here.

She would rather he had appeared as they'd described him on his death bed: in his familiar pyjamas. They'd told her he'd died beautifully, a beautiful death. She'd imagined him with his hands placed just so, on the coverlet. His head resting against the pillow slightly sideways, and his face relaxed. She hadn't known how clear the image that she'd made up was until this moment, when she faced this travesty in Papou's suit. Her father pressed her forwards, toward the doll.

'No, Baba,' said Alexia.

'He looks beautiful,' Mama said.

'So beautiful,' Yiayia said. She began a low keening.

'But he's so small!' said Katherine. 'The suit we bought him doesn't even fit!' Her sister had never seen a dead body either. Alexia leaned against the cool side of the coffin. A body.

There was a smell: embalming fluid. The room was over-heated. Yiayia was crying. On one side Mama supported her and on the other Alexia's uncle stroked her arm. Now Alexia's uncle started to cry and Baba sobbed. She felt she wasn't in the room at all but rather suspended above it in the air, where Papou supposedly would be if he was present. She couldn't sense him in the room. He would be doing something funny if he was: knocking over the hideous flower arrangement for Alexia's amusement, or rustling the impenetrable heavy curtain. But the room remained quiet. He wasn't here. In his place was this imposter, this duplicate they'd paid someone to create.

If he was watching them, he'd think it all overly dramatic. Her Papou had been an understated Greek. He'd be laughing at the silly suit, the waxen flowers, the weeping. She wasn't sure he'd believed in God, though he'd given money to the church all his life. She could see Baba's shoulders heaving as he cried as though he was being dragged physically into the coffin.

13

What kind of space does the absence of a person leave in a life? It was Isaiah's opinion that the shape of the space was up to the person left behind. You could allow it to be a defining thing, like a scar on your skin or a patch on your sleeve. You could allow it to undermine you invisibly at unexpected moments, as when the sand drops off suddenly under your feet in the surf. Or you could allow the space to eat you, like some kind of viral nothingness. The size of the wound was up to you.

In the days that followed their visit to the frack site, Sam had withdrawn. Isaiah dealt with this as he usually dealt with difficulties between them: by not talking about it. It was what she always claimed she wanted: total independence and autonomy. They were in favour of open communication, especially about other potential partners. But their set-up required a large amount of self-moderation. If he had feelings about her or anyone else, he would keep them to himself, seeking to let go of whatever he was feeling instead of making it her responsibility. When had this permeated all other situations they encountered together though? He couldn't quite remember. Sam needed privacy, even from him. Anything else she experienced as an imposition. He suspected sometimes this was more a matter of pride.

He could detect a certain coolness, though, not only in Sam's dealings with him, but in Kate and Melissa's as well. This meant she wasn't processing things entirely internally, after all. He tried to be patient with her.

When they were first together, Sam had asked him endless questions about his whakapapa. In that way she was no different from half a dozen women he had been with: nice, middle-class women who seemed enamoured of his background. The truth was that Isaiah's upbringing, aside from his mother's left-wing activities, closely resembled Sam's. Her father was some kind of public servant and her mother taught at kindergarten. Sam would ask about his marae, about his people. She would ask about his father. It was attractive to be thought so fascinating, but it was a long time before Isaiah admitted this to himself.

His father had gone missing, he'd told Sam, and had never been seen again. They had waited a few months, and then held a memorial service. The police had decided to assume he was dead. The rescue services could find no trace of him where he had disappeared. Isaiah had a vague sense of this time: raised voices in the night, his mother's knuckles white around the cord of the phone, lots of food on the table in plastic wrap, the feeling of lying in the dark and being unable to sleep.

He remembered something of his father too: not his face, not his voice, but his form. The dark hair, the oddly upright posture, a tall figure bending down. But here was the great secret that Isaiah eventually told Sam: there was nothing for Isaiah to miss. Having grown up never really knowing his father, he didn't understand what he should be missing.

Sam always professed at this point in the conversation that she didn't believe him. She was convinced he was the bearer of some terribly romantic, incurable wound. She would ask further questions: did he ever dream of his father? Surely the loss affected his relationship with his mother? Had his mother ever thought of taking another partner? Why not?

Isaiah would respond as monosyllabically as possible. Of course it affected their relationship, and no, his mother hadn't ever seemed interested in other men. He knew that Sam was after something he couldn't give her: a description of a sharply delineated space, a meaningful memory that showed him to be bereft or tragically orphaned, a phrase that would reveal him as she truly seemed to think he was, tattooed with the mark of early loss. It was a matter of pride not to give her any of these things, but the truth was, there really wasn't much to give. His mother had been shaped by what had happened, and so too, to some extent, he must have been shaped. But he had met people with more tragic stories who remembered every moment of them. Isaiah believed there was nothing from which he needed to recover. He had a slightly neurotic mother, and a space in his memory that wasn't really a space at all.

Sam's father was a raging conservative. He voted with an eye to making sure that lazy people didn't get handouts. He was well-off by the time Sam was at university but would not have considered helping her out financially. He said she needed to make her own way in the world. The one time Isaiah met him, he'd told Sam that she'd better put her head down and pull her finger out if she was to get anywhere. He'd said that he had owned a house by the time he was Sam's age, and that people used to have a sense of responsibility. All this without once seeming to notice Isaiah, who sat beside Sam on the tacky brown couch, clinging sweatily to her hand. Throughout the conversation the TV blared and Sam's father sipped from consecutive cans of beer. By the time they left he had drunk at least six, and was a little bleary-eyed. That was nothing, Sam had told Isaiah afterwards. That was just a weeknight.

Isaiah thought he understood her a little better after this. Sam's father, while he was a drinker, was never an out-of-control drunk. While he was critical, he was never horribly abusive. He never hit Sam or her mother. He never dissolved into his rage. Sam told him these things with an odd kind of longing. Perhaps if Sam was in possession of a more clearly defined wound, like she thought Isaiah was, she would feel more validated. Perhaps that was what all the women really wanted, in their sidling up to him, in their commonly held fascination: to be in possession of a kind of definite inherited grief.

Isaiah told Sam the barest of essentials. His father was popular, he was kind to animals and children, old ladies loved him, he was a great talker, and he had plans for the future of his homeland. But no, Isaiah told her. He didn't really remember, he didn't remember, he didn't remember.

But it didn't matter what he said. In those days she still treated him as if he was the bearer of an invisible code. It was not that she wished her father dead; of course not. But how much of a relief would it be if instead of despising your parents in a tiresome way, in a dispirited, disappointed, listless way, as she did, you had the complete absence of a parent, a proper absence, that you could properly mourn?

'Oh, but you must miss him,' she would say. 'Even if you don't know it, some part of you misses him. He's with you, whether you remember him or not.' She would look at him with soft eyes. He'd turn away, or kiss her, whatever.

'I suppose I must miss him,' he'd said once. But he knew this was a lie. Isaiah's father was an echo. Whatever Sam was talking about was not really there. There was a discrepancy between the Isaiah Sam saw and the one he knew to exist. Sure, he was angry sometimes at things he couldn't name. And his mother – his mother.

But Sam had stopped looking at him in that way quite some time ago.

It was surprising that the absence of an absence had been such a presence in his life.

14

Melissa handed her a sheaf of papers to photocopy. Kate handed her an updated media list. Sam smiled a broad, sunshiney smile. Alexia took the papers and a coffee and went into her makeshift workspace. Some days she didn't mind helping. She had ended up here. And if she was here, she could help. But that didn't mean she wanted to be around people. People could be so fickle, after all.

She had been raised with the idea that blood was thicker than water. She was raised with the idea that she was a part of the Family. She was the Family. The Family! Her mother had wanted her to be a lawyer. Her father had wanted her to be an accountant. Her grandfather had said she could be anything she wanted to be.

The third day after the death they held a memorial service.

'Kolliva,' Yiayia said. 'To celebrate the spirit of the dead.' Yiayia had been crying constantly since Alexia had arrived, till it seemed like nothing out of the ordinary, like light rain falling on a garden.

'There's a special way that it must be done,' said Mama. They were cramped into Yiayia's tiny kitchen.

'The kolliva is like his body,' Yiayia said. 'It is grains, like we put in the earth to grow. When we finish it we go to the church and we light a candle. The priest comes and blesses it. And when the people they leave the church we give them a little bag of it, and a tsoureki bread, to take home and remember him.'

Alexia had the ingredients she'd collected from all over town, working from her mother's list. She'd been to the Italian shop, the Lebanese shop, the Iranian shop. She had whole wheat, barley, icing sugar, walnuts, cinnamon, whole cloves, sugared almonds, raisins, and silver nonpareils with which to spell out Papou's initials. Her mother pointed to various packets with one red manicured fingernail.

'This is for the cycle of resurrection,' she said. 'And this is for fertility. This is for remembrance. This is for abundance, and this is for the sweetness of life. You must have a balance of each.'

Alexia fought the urge to write the specifics down. But this was not how it was done. She would be expected to know these things inherently when the time came for her parents, or, if not, to make discreet inquiries. Katherine would not be expected to know. Once mixed, the kolliva did resemble crumbs of earth. What happened to the waxwork, after the viewing? They probably had him out the back of the funeral home, somewhere beyond the curtain. She mixed too fast and some of the mixture spilled.

'Alexia!' Mama said. She took the bowl and snatched away the wooden spoon.

'No,' Yiayia said. She took the spoon and elbowed Mama aside. 'When you make the kolliva it is ee skepsi that is important.'

'The thought?' Mama said.

'You must think of the one you love,' Yiayia said. 'You stir in the memories, the good things in that person's life.' Alexia suspected Yiayia had made this up in order to maintain control of the process.

'I've never heard that before,' Mama said.

'There are a lot of things you don't know,' Yiayia said. 'The old ways.'

Katherine came inside with a card. She gave it to Alexia and put her arms around her briefly before she walked away. The card was minimalistic and tasteful, like everything that Stephen did. Mama read over her shoulder. She and Baba had thought Alexia lucky to have found a man like Stephen; clean-cut, with respectably short hair, who was working towards a marketing degree. Stephen would cook when her parents visited. When he left the room they would exclaim. 'Smart and rich and a good cook too,' Mama would say. 'What more could a woman want?'

'Why don't you get back together with him?' Mama asked as they made the kolliva. 'I just don't understand it. He would have given you a good future.' Alexia didn't respond.

They shaped the mixture into a mound on a round tray and covered it with icing sugar, smoothing the surface with butter knives. It was like the burial site of a king. Yiayia drove the action, and Alexia and her mother were permitted to help. Then from the lounge came the sound of the TV programme changing. Yiayia had the TV on ceaselessly, day and night. It's noise was a constant backdrop to family life. Yiayia patted the kolliva.

'You do the rest,' she said briskly, and removed herself to the other room. Alexia recognised the music: pastel rounded flashes jumped across her vision.

'It's her soap opera,' she whispered to Mama. All at once they were laughing, soundlessly.

'You in there,' Yiayia called out in Greek. 'Get on with it.'

'I thought this was all meant to be sacred,' Alexia whispered.

'I guess everyone has their priorities,' Mama said.

Finally the small sugared mound sat between them: a frivolous thing, a crude child's creation, like a mud pie decorated with berries. Mama arranged Papou's initials on top. Until this moment it had seemed like they were all playing at an elaborate game. Some part of Alexia had thought that Papou would walk out of the workshop, hammer or saw in hand, and pinch her roughly on the cheek. But there, unarguably, in Greek letters, were his initials.

Alexia's mother held her back so that she didn't get tears

on the kolliva. At last she had come down into herself, Alexia thought. At last, she had come back.

Matiu knocked on the door, came in, and placed a cup of tea on her desk. Her head was resting on her hands and she had been staring into space. She thanked him, and he left. Outside the grasses swayed in the constant wind.

But she was back at the church for the funeral.

Wherever she went, she would always be called back, to the sonorous drone and the clink of metal ornaments and the smell of wax. The priest bowed his head and went towards the nave. Alexia had spent much of the service looking up into the dome so as not to be overwhelmed by the lights. The rise and fall of the liturgia was dark yellow and gold, and laid over the elaborate interior – the gilt icons and stained glass and the many gold accessories – the flashes made her feel sick. Finally it was over, and she took up the box that held the fake Papou, and helped carry it out. There had been some controversy about female pallbearers, but money had changed hands, and all had been resolved.

'What are they all saying?' Katherine whispered.

'O Theos na tón anapáfsi,' she said. 'May God rest his soul.'

The mourners came down the steps from the church, kissing the Family's cheeks, pressing their hands. Most would visit the house over the course of the day. They would come for days afterwards, too.

Digestives, insipid tea, no real coffee. Alexia made cup after cup of instant coffee for people on the marae. She moved about like a sleepwalker, which was what she was.

No one had told her grief could strip you out and lay you bare until you didn't know yourself. No one had told her there were other ways of being haunted, aside from seeing ghosts.

The day Alexia broke up with Stephen was the day after Papou's funeral. All that day she had allowed herself to be patted and held. They smelled like her grandfather, the visitors, like clean linen and Greek coffee and the aniseed they used in their baking. They pressed dishes into her hands: feta platters, stuffed tomatoes, dolmades, legs of lamb. Moving softly in her good shoes, she carried the trays of offerings: the icing sugar-powdered kourambiethes she had helped her mother bake the night before, the hard koulourakia, the sweet tsoureki bread. She collected cups. She slowed her steps and bent her head. She didn't see any lights.

In a rare break in the flow of visitors she went to the attic to find more chairs. The ladder was at the back of the house. She experienced a moment of complete absurdity on the roof, almost over-balancing in her small heels and formal skirt. There was a high wind. But it was bright up here, free of voices and condolences and requests. One great wrench of the attic window and she was into the detritus of the Family's life. An old cot, piles of papers, suitcases, faded curtains, one or two serviceable chairs. She stepped rafter to rafter, ducking her head. The bouzouki was propped against the wall of the attic. It still had all its strings. It was painted gold and red. The key-patterned strap was still attached. It was tiny, much smaller than a guitar.

It all came down on her at once. Papou's calloused hands. The twanging sound of the bouzouki, playing rembetiko. Cigarette smoke filling the lounge, and every Sunday, the men drinking coffee and ouzo and yelling about politics. Papou winking at her as his fingers moved over the strings, the men around him playing backgammon and chess, yelling, swearing softly. The sound of the music, plaintive and wry. She had not seen the lights, then. It was before the lights.

They needed her downstairs. She went at speed, flinging the old chairs out the door and down the ladder into a bush below. Then she was back inside and her hand was on the instrument's neck. She stepped out with it and was briefly blinded. A gust of wind pushed at her and she stumbled, then righted herself, her hands holding the bouzouki across her body, the air scraping her hair back off her face. Stephen was walking down the front path towards her. He was empty-handed, dressed in sneakers and jeans, in a bright shirt. Of course, she should have briefed him on the formality of the proceedings. He was wearing his usual look of stoic cheerfulness.

The door of the attic blew shut behind her, and caught his attention. There was Stephen and here she was, on the roof, clutching Papou's bouzouki like a totem. He smiled uncertainly. Then she was down the ladder and in his arms and laughing, the instrument hanging between them.

'Welcome to my big fat Greek whatever,' she said.

'You sure know how to roll out a welcome,' he said. 'How'd you know to get up there on the roof? Is that the way you Greeks always do it?' He looked quizzically at the chairs beside them, askew in the rose bush.

'Welcome to my big fat Greek … funeral,' she said this time, and began to cry.

He patted her on the back, but awkwardly, although of course he had seen her cry before. Stephen, with his normal, pākehā family, his presentable and reasonable parents, the distant grand-parents who sent him cards at Christmas. Perhaps this was not what he had expected? He wiped the tears off her face and suggested they go inside. He seemed almost embarrassed for her.

'You don't understand,' she said, terribly aware that her voice was breaking, out of her control. 'He was like my father. He was more my father than my father is.'

Stephen smiled, as he would smile at a client, his white teeth shining in his mouth.

'It's okay, sweetheart,' he said. 'Let's go inside. You're just worn out by all this Greek drama.' He gestured round the yard, at Papou's carefully weeded vegetables, the chairs astride the bushes, the house, which Alexia did not think looked particularly dramatic at all.

She could have punched him in the face.

15

The day was a thing of fits and starts and truncated impulses. The day was a mystery. It had started awkwardly and seemed good and then got away from Isaiah, like a taniwha writhing underwater.

The awkwardness had started at breakfast, when Alexia had told him that he could draw her. She'd mentioned this offhandedly, as they cleared dishes together. He'd asked when, quickly. He thought she might retract the invitation. She kept her eyes on the plates.

'Now, if you like,' she said.

They went out to a far paddock. They had an hour or two. He carried his sketchbook, a weighty thing with thick pages, and his good pencils. In the time between their leaving the kitchen and getting to the distant hillock he had his eye on, he managed to get sweaty and nervous.

'Beautiful, isn't it?'

'It is.'

The silence was beyond awkward. What could he say? Maybe he should suggest that she wasn't really comfortable doing this?

'How many people have you drawn?'

Her question took him by surprise. He was thinking about his feet moving alongside hers, them walking together. He was wishing that he'd had a shower, that he was wearing the cleaner shirt.

'I don't know,' he said. 'More than I can count. I took life drawing classes,' he said, to assuage her apparant alarm.

They reached the small hill and settled on a rock. There was a small patch of bush here that shielded them. Were they visible from the marae? He made sure they were not. She took the sketchbook from his hands.

'Can I see?'

His hand was still on the cover. He made himself take it away. He'd prefer that she didn't look, though what was there to be ashamed of? It was only the human form.

She opened it. He watched her hands moving through the pages: image upon image of women, in various states of undress. Most of them had been life models, but many of them had been sexual partners too. She touched some of the images with her long brown fingers, as if reading them through touch.

Suddenly he wanted to ask her what she was doing here. Who was she? Why did she seem so serious all the time? He was about to speak when she pointed to an image.

'That's Sam,' she said. He had drawn Sam on a bed, half clothed. He nodded. 'And that's her again,' she said, turning the pages. 'And again.'

'Yes.' How was he to get this started? 'You don't have to take your clothes off, if you don't want to.'

'Can I ask you a question?' Again, he nodded. 'Do you see anything wrong with you doing this?'

'Of course not. It's just part of the way I process the world. I'm a visual person.' He was half deciding he shouldn't draw her after all. Had she brought him out here just to have a weird conversation?

'I guess these woman all felt flattered at your attention.'

He was filled with impatience. 'It's art, Alexia.'

She smiled. There was a dangerous thing in her smile.

'You asked if you could draw me. Would you ask Rangi? Would you ask Polly?'

'No. But that's beside the ...'

'Why not?' The smile was still there. She seemed grimly pleased, as though she had had her worst fears confirmed.

'It just wouldn't feel right.'

She closed the sketchbook with a snap. He shouldn't have asked her. He shouldn't have trusted her with his work.

'I don't think I'll be posing for you.'

He was shocked at how hurt he felt. She had brought him out here to interrogate him.

'Every one of those women I drew was completely comfortable with it.'

'I'm sure they thought they were – at the time.' She spoke lightly, as if it didn't matter to her one way or the other.

They headed back through the trees. But before they came out he stopped her. She flinched at his hand on her back: he noted this, and took his hand away.

'Alexia,' he asked. 'Are you … all right?' He had meant to be more confrontational than this, but the flinch had thrown him. 'I've noticed you in meetings just staring at the wall. I don't know you very well, but it seems to me like sometimes you're not really here.'

'I lost someone very close to me,' Alexia said. 'I lost my grandfather. You wouldn't understand.'

He wanted, so badly, to tell her he would understand. But she had known her grandfather. He supposed she was right.

'I'm sorry, Alexia. Are you sure you want to be here? Are you sure you want to be involved in all this?'

'There's something here for me,' she said. 'I'm not quite sure what it is, yet. But you're right, half the time I'm here. Half the time I just keep thinking about him, about his funeral. I can't believe he's gone.' It was remarkable. A second ago he was justifying himself to her. And now he was wanting to comfort her.

'Well, there's certainly work to be done.' He wanted to hold her, but he didn't think she'd accept it. He stood straighter and made for the marae. She followed him.

'Isaiah,' she said, 'your drawings – they're pretty good.' He waited. He was sure there was a 'but' coming. 'It's just that it's kind of like a stamp collection, isn't it? A gallery of women's bodies.' There it was, the attack. He watched the response flare and rise in him. He tried to control it. 'I'm not keen on being part of a collection, that's all.'

By the time they reached the kitchen again, he was glad to be rid of her.

16

She took the mail to town, picked up groceries and drove back alone, relishing the quiet. She avoided the muddy pot-holes on the road, though the spring rains had cleared. It was heating up.

Alexia wondered if anyone other than Isaiah had noticed that she wasn't really here. She hadn't told him the whole truth. The thing she really didn't want to think about had happened a week after the funeral. In retrospect she should have seen it coming. In retrospect it was easy to see that Alexia and the Family had been going in different directions for years. Did that mean it was right, that their paths had diverged?

Alexia was back at Papou's, slumped on a chair in the lounge, holding a small china cup with a silver rim. The coffee was strong and bitter. The moon was rising and no one had shut the curtains against the dusk. Katherine passed by Baba and was playfully seized. He pulled her onto his lap where she sat, apparently comfortable. There was a knife in the cabinet next to Alexia. It was long, and curved, encased in a richly embroidered sheath. She saw the colour of the blade in her mind's eye: a dark blue steel. Papou's father had brought it back from Turkey, where he'd been taken during the occupation. When she'd tried the blade as a child it had made a mark on her finger: a crescent shape, yellow edged with white.

'We need to talk, Alexia,' Baba said.

'It's about your study,' Mama said.

'It's about your lack of study, actually,' Baba said.

How did they know? Stephen had been concerned about her failure to make a dent in her revision for the bar exam. Perhaps he had taken them aside, before she had finished with him, and had a quiet word?

'The Family have decided what you should do,' Mama said. She spoke as though the Family was a collective intelligence suspended above their heads, contributing in an advisory capacity.

'The Family!' Uncle Steve cuffed Alexia's cheek as he sat down. 'What is this, *The Godfather?*'

The knife in its sheath was still, unchanging. Its edge was smooth and uncomplicated, a remorseless moon.

'We need to discuss your law degree,' Baba said. Katherine was still perched on his lap like an oversized doll. She raised one eyebrow at Alexia as if to say, 'I have not been party to any of this.'

'It's obvious you're not going to pass your qualifying exam at this rate,' said Mama. 'And you've broken up with Stephen. And there's a need here now, at home.'

'There is a need,' said Uncle Steve.

'It would be the logical choice,' Mama said.

Yiayia's crying had taken on a subdued quality, presumably so she could hear the conversation better. What were they all on about? Alexia felt like a cornered animal.

'Logica is a Greek word. You know that?' Yiayia turned to Katherine. 'When we come here, we have nothing. But always, we always have the language.' Katherine nodded.

'We want you to move in with Yiayia,' Baba said to Alexia. Katherine's mouth fell open.

'She won't be able to manage here, alone,' Mama said.

'Traditionally, someone would come and stay after a death,' Uncle Steve said. 'But none of us is in a position to move in right now. I've got a business to run.'

'And I'm working,' Mama said. 'Baba, too. You would have time to study, and Yiayia would have someone here.' Mama passed a critical eye over Alexia. Her hands, which had been flying about effusively, rested on Yiayia's arm.

They wanted to keep an eye on her. They didn't trust her to complete her exam. They thought she was going off the rails. And the weird, sick excitement they were speaking with, all of them; at the heart of it was guilt. They felt guilty they didn't want to move in, and they wanted her to be the solution.

Yiayia had crumpled into a smaller version of herself. In Alexia's earliest memories Yiayia always featured as the lower half of her body: thick legs covered in cotton, brusque shoes, bejewelled hands reaching down, patting and smoothing, her lap available for Alexia to be held upon.

'I'm not sure I …' she said.

'Ela, koritsimou,' Yiayia said. 'Come home with me, my girl.'

'She'll cook for you!' Alexia's mother said, and laughed: a high, cut-glass giggle. 'It'll be like staying in a hotel!'

'It will be good for you both,' Baba said. He leaned forward, crushing Katherine's dress.

'I don't think I can do it,' Alexia said. The knife hung to the left of her vision.

'What will happen to me?' Yiayia asked, in Greek.

'Why not?' Uncle Steve asked.

Alexia saw that everyone had been won over by this idea. Yiayia looked at her with mild disapproval. A tremble went through Alexia's body and into the cabinet next to her. It shook, very slightly, the glass shelf with the knife on it.

'Yiayia,' Alexia said, 'I can't.' She spoke in Greek. All the important things they were saying were in Greek. The lesser things they said in English, for Katherine's benefit.

Now they began to speak over the top of one another, in Greek again.

'The Family will give you some pocket money, of course,' said Mama.

'It's in all of our interests,' said Steve.

'It's in all of your interests,' Alexia said. The shock flared across Yiayia's face. Katherine might not understand the language, but she appeared to understand this.

'We can make it a generous allowance,' Mama said. Oh, Mama's special coldness. How Alexia would forget to do her chores, and everything would become her fault.

'I will not do it,' Alexia said.

Katherine sat up very straight in Baba's arms. When the knife was pulled from its case Alexia knew from memory it made a ringing sound, a cool sound. An unsheathing sound. Baba laughed.

'What would your Papou think, if he could hear you saying these things to us? Here's a Greek word, for you. Themocracia.' Baba was back to English. 'See? Democracy. The seat of civilisation it was, Ancient Greece. Light-years ahead of its time. Let's decide this democratically then, as a family.'

None of them, bar Katherine, really thought Alexia was serious. She couldn't believe it. They thought she would so easily come to heel. She was twenty-six, not seventeen. But now she thought of it, none of her elders had left home until they were married or well into their twenties. She'd had to fight to be permitted to go flatting with her friends.

'All in favour of Alexia moving to Yiayia's, raise your hand,' Baba said. They all raised their hands, except for Katherine and Alexia. 'So,' Baba said, 'through the process of themocracia, the Family has decided.' There was a shifting in the room, a settling down.

'It will be good for your study,' Uncle Steve said, as if Alexia had agreed wholeheartedly.

'It's the least you can do for us,' Mama said. 'After all the Family has done for you.'

Several things happened at once. Alexia stood up. Yiayia started to talk about dinner. Her uncle started to clear plates.

'What the Family has done for me?' Alexia said. 'What the Family has done!' And now she was yelling, spinning recklessly in Yiayia's neat front room – in the house Papou had lived in till he died. Papou, a good man. 'What this Family has done!' Her elbow hit the glass cabinet, but she couldn't feel it, so she hit it again, and the glass scattered into shards, and the knife with the blue crescent blade fell onto the carpet.

'What this Family has done,' she said.

From behind her came the tinkle of other knick-knacks falling: the water wheel with the farmer in village dress, the decorative lighter and ashtray set, the red and black amphora. 'I will not stay here, Yiayia,' she said. 'I cannot. I cannot stay. The Family!' she yelled, though now she wished to stop. 'What a great joke! The Family! You know the truth about the original democracy in Greece? It didn't apply to the women or the slaves. You've upheld its principles beautifully.'

Alexia moved past Baba and towards the front door. Katherine stood to follow her.

'You can't take your sister,' Baba said. But Katherine had already left the room. When she returned she was carrying her and Alexia's bags.

'You don't have to come with me,' Alexia said. But her sister ignored her. They walked down the path to the front gate, Alexia almost stumbling. 'I won't blame you if you don't come,' she tried again. Katherine glanced over her shoulder at the house. Then she swore horribly, in Greek and English, a long string of expletives leaving her sweet, lipsticked mouth.

Alexia took a couple of steps down the path before she realised it: she was out. There was the house on an island in Greece, which she had always intended to renovate, with its olive grove. There would be no land, no renovation, no going 'home' to Greece, no red eggs at Easter, no souvlaki at Christmas, no Saint's Day phone calls. There would be no 'the Family' for Alexia, ever again.

17

One night as Isaiah was settling into sleep Sam came in and gave him a hug. He was not sure why, but he welcomed it.

'Been chatting to our new friend?' she asked, gesturing towards the kitchen, where Alexia and he had just been cleaning up. Sam was smiling her most winning smile.

'I think I get her now,' he said. 'She told me she's lost someone. A grandfather.' He spoke in a rush, as if Sam's smile had extracted the words from him. 'She's grieving, I guess.' Sam nodded slowly.

'That's a good story,' she said. Then she left, as suddenly as she had arrived.

It was Sam, not Isaiah, who had met someone first. For a year after they'd had their conversation about autonomy and ownership, about independence and honesty, he and Sam had been officially non-monogamous. But in truth nothing had really happened that was extra-curricular, for either of them. Their relationship was less restrictive than most he saw around him, and he was happy with that. If, for example, there had been a post-meeting hang-out with their friends, Isaiah would not assume that Sam would go home with him. They often made plans to meet up later, of course, and they often did go home together, but their rules were clear: each was their own free agent, and both of them, Isaiah believed, enjoyed the freedom this allowed. So when he wanted to stay late, for example, and do the dishes in the community house where they often had meetings, apparently washing up but actually talking to a

German traveller who was staying there, he didn't feel guilty, and he presumed that Sam was fine with it. She'd smiled, after all, as she left – her usual open beam – and afterwards she didn't treat him any differently. If anything, she seemed to go out of her way to act more kindly towards him.

Nothing had happened with that woman, or with the French one after that who camped for a week on the couch of the environmental centre, or with the woman from down south who was into animal rights, or with his old friend Bridget, whom he had always had a soft spot for and who stayed for a few days in his bed. Before they had talked openly about it, Isaiah had begun to desire other women with a disquieting regularity. He would be out at a bar or watching a performance or in a café when he'd be rendered breathless, halted by the curve of a neck or breasts. He had always thought of himself as non-materialistic, as unsuperficial, but during this time he would have slept with anyone. Anyone: the waitress who smiled as she passed him the coffee, the tutor of his political studies class, any one of his and Sam's friends.

After they'd decided to be non-monogamous – 'It just makes sense,' Sam had said. 'It's a natural biological urge. No one should be made to live a lie' – the longings dissipated. He wouldn't have been averse to an encounter. At first he had felt like he was wielding some great blunt instrument, this latent desire, which might, now unleashed, strike people down. But after the first few possibilities came and then passed, his desire settled into the background, striking only now and then, but not commanding him with any urgency. Freedom took the pressure off. He had the luxury of choice, and so it was all the more convenient to keep choosing Sam, to choose Sam almost by default. She had very few expectations of him after all.

He didn't know if it had been the same for her. But one day his friend told him that Sam had gone home with someone. The man she'd been with was a person they both knew, passing through on his way to a hui, a fellow environmentalist. Isaiah considered him a sell-out, and there had been rumours of his being a little too popular with women.

'Why didn't you tell me?' he'd asked her the next day.

She seemed tired. 'I was going to,' she said. 'I just didn't have the chance.' It was shocking how much this bothered him. She seemed a little bemused at his response. Was there an edge of enjoyment in her reaction?

It bothered him that for the visiting environmentalist his girlfriend was just another in a series of conquests. It bothered him to think of her moving up and down on his body. The next time he visited her room he wondered whether the sheets had been changed. It bothered him, mostly, that it bothered him.

'We need to set rules about this,' he told her later. 'We need to have clearer communication.' This was as vicious as he would permit himself to be. He would not be possessive; he would not be jealous. Anything he felt just needed to be let go of. It was merely a process, like leaching poison from a wound.

'Absolutely!' Sam said, as positively as ever. 'Clear communication I can do.' And she actually high-fived him.

They had developed from there a nuanced and detailed manifesto for their relationship. Nothing was written down. But it helped, eventually, to offset the guilt that ambushed him when he did cash in on his freedom. They would communicate; they would make sure the other had no reservations about the person involved; they would make sure the other person knew in advance, so as to avoid any awkward revelations.

When he did sleep with someone else it was a casual affair. It was with a tourist, this time from Italy. She was musky and didn't shave her armpits and had several dreadlocks. She had a heavy accent and a healthy, olive-skinned face. She was straightforward and approached him first. Both of them knew she would be off on the ferry in the morning. Afterwards, as they wrapped themselves in the layer of sleeping bags that covered his bed, she rolled a cigarette out of a pouch and paid him what he believed was a compliment. Isaiah enjoyed being someone else's travel fling immensely. Sam, even, seemed to enjoy it, from a distance, as if this woman's attraction to him was a vote of confidence.

'You do it like you really mean it,' the woman had said, blowing smoke upwards in a lazy way. 'You do it like you haven't been fucked properly in years, like you're looking at a woman's body for the first time.'

Did he think of Sam primarily as a woman, or as a friend and comrade? In the beginning he had thought of Sam as his lover. After he began sleeping with other women he realised he thought of Sam as his complete equal, an invulnerable partner in crime. That was how Sam wanted to be thought of too. The other women he found attractive usually had long hair, and were more stereotypically feminine than Sam. But then, most women presented as more feminine than Sam; it just wasn't a priority for her. It wasn't that he had a specific type. He didn't go for women who were flimsy or disempowered. The only people who would sleep with him, he found, after they knew he was in an open relationship, were women who seemed firmly in control of their own choices.

After his first encounter with the Italian, Isaiah had been a better lover to Sam for a time. The knowledge that he had held another body gave him encouragement when faced with her familiar expanse of skin. As he touched Sam, he would think of the angles of the other, the slopes and curves shifting as she moved. It always seemed an innocent thing, his mind following the function of his body. The images of the two women, mingled, were more charged than if he had allowed himself to think of Sam alone. It was only afterwards that he would lie in bed, and doubt himself, while she fell asleep. He would think that he should keep it simple for a while, focus on Sam. But before long the needed edge would fall out of their love-making, that necessary rapt level of attention. And then Isaiah's eye would be drawn away. And then, after the next one, he would be a better lover again.

18

She told herself that she was here, doing important work, with people who liked her. She told herself she might even have met someone, though she wasn't yet sure. She got herself up and out of bed each morning. It was what she could think of to do. She got herself to meetings on time.

Alexia had made herself a strong coffee this morning. She needed it. There they all were, the protestors. There was Isaiah, his dark hair and strangely familiar eyes. They filed into a small room off the kitchen and sat. It was a surprise to see a woman dressed in bubblegum-pink jeans and T-shirt, who Alexia had never seen before.

'Te Kahurangi, Isaiah, Isaiah, Te Kahurangi. You two are cousins, but not by blood,' Polly said. Her eyes skipped over Alexia. Isaiah hongied the girl.

'Te Kahurangi is in her first year of university,' Polly went on. 'She finished school early and got a scholarship. She is studying politics. She will be aiding us in the campaign.' The young woman was lovely: almost as tall as Alexia, but darker. She wasn't awkward, however, or gawky, or slump-shouldered. She was about seventeen. 'Te Kahurangi is fluent in te reo,' Polly added. 'She was raised on the marae.'

Te Kahurangi kissed Isaiah on the cheek.

A meeting followed, in which everything Alexia said was sidelined or ignored. Was she making this up? Halfway through the meeting she tested her theory. 'We should send a delegation to the environmental courts,' she said.

'Te Kahurangi has a friend who works for the radio,' Polly said. 'Maybe she can get us an interview.'

'We should send a delegation ...' Alexia tried again.

'We should write that down, about Te Kahurangi's contact,' Polly said.

After the meeting, Te Kahurangi went to sit on the porch. As Alexia went past she patted the wooden step. Alexia sat. Te Kahurangi's breath smelled of gum.

'You're Alexia,' she said. Alexia nodded. 'Dunno what they're all on about,' Te Kahurangi went on. 'You're not all that.' She turned the corners of her mouth down, assessing Alexia.

'All what?' Alexia said.

'All *that.*' Then Te Kahurangi smiled. 'Nah, just jokes.' A tattoo snaked out of her sleeve. Wasn't she too young to be tattooed? 'You're not Māori though, eh?'

'Greek,' Alexia said.

'Don't worry about Aunty,' Te Kahurangi said. 'She'll come round. She's just got some funny ideas. I keep telling her I've got a girlfriend, but it's like she thinks if she finds me some fine young Māori guy ... Not that he's so young,' she said, gesturing to Isaiah, who had gone into the kitchen. 'Oh, I just mean he's more like your age, I guess?'

Alexia nodded.

'He's big news on the pā, you know. They think they need more men. Everyone's gone away to the city. There's no one here to do the work anymore. But see, you're big news now, too. And chicks are more useful than men anyway, don't you reckon?' She winked.

Alexia suddenly liked her very much.

The next day, at her and Aidan and Hannah's camp, Alexia opted for a cup of real coffee made by 'The Irish' in his billy over the campfire. The three of them had been asked to come and stay closer to the marae but had decided to stay put. You never knew when more visitors might need housing, and they were hoping to recruit more activists soon. She sat with the cup in her hands, looking at the mountain. She could see Papou's hands in her mind, playing the old songs over and over. She could see the smoke rising from his cigarette. There was the mountain, she told herself. There was the bush. Here was the spring cold seeping through her sneakers. Here was a cup of coffee, strong and black.

'But do you actually like practising law?' Aidan was questioning her. Hannah had gone to help with breakfast.

'I'm not enjoying it right now, no. Because I'm not doing it,' she said. 'It doesn't seem real here.'

'What are you going to do when you take the test then, if you're not studying? You going to just turn up and play them a tune?'

'It's just that –' she said. But she couldn't think of anything to say.

'Isaiah thinks you're our great legal hope,' Aidan said. 'The one who's going to save our arses when the shit goes down.'

'But I'm not even licensed to practise. All I want to do is play music,' Alexia said.

Rangi broke into the clearing. He was huffing and red, his eyebrows raised high up on his forehead.

'You want to see a calf being born?' he asked.

'Yeah!' Aidan said. 'That'd blow our city slicker minds.'

'She's in the high field by the reservoir,' Rangi said. 'She's close. Matiu's there. Calving's late this year. It's this global warming. Screws everything up.' He stared at Alexia as though he expected her to contest this.

'I'd like to come,' she said.

They walked the perimeter of the pā lands on a path worn into the grass. The track followed the fence line between the wharenui and Taylor's land. The bush was on one side. On the other the land stretched out into a leisurely green plain. Aidan went ahead on the path. The mountain's peaks were barred by clouds.

Rangi barrelled along in his camouflage gear, carrying a

bucket and a rubber glove. He shook the glove and turned his mad gaze on Alexia. 'Just in case,' he said. All at once he stopped. 'Sis,' he said. Then, unexpectedly, he swept in and hongied her, so quickly she didn't have time to be nervous. He kissed her on her cheek. He rubbed her back. 'We heard about your loss, sis,' he said. 'Kia kaha.' She felt the tears well up. A couple of them spilled over. 'It's okay. It's natural,' he said. 'Now come along. This will do you good.'

Some of the kids had come: Ana and Maitai and Tama and some of their cousins. Isaiah stood at the back end of the cow, who heaved and bellowed. Her coat was amber and her eyes were blank with pain. She shuddered and lowed. Up close she was huge, much larger than Alexia had remembered cows to be. The other cows had retreated to a respectful distance. Isaiah seemed not to notice her. She hoped he'd put that whole incident with the drawing to one side, her refusal. Until she'd seen the pictures, she had thought she might do it.

'Bout time you buggers got here.' Matiu was rubbing the side of the cow soothingly. He saw Alexia and came forwards, and kissed her quickly on one cheek. 'I'm sorry for your loss,' he said. Then each of the children came to her, in quick succession, Ana, Maitai, Tama, and kissed her on the cheek, for which she had to bend down. She clenched her teeth to keep from crying.

'Sorry, Alexia.'

'Sorry.'

'We're sorry.' They were so formal and so sweet that she could hardly bear it. Isaiah was watching her, guiltily. It was he of course who had spread this news. But she felt only relief.

'What's happening, then?' Aidan asked. Ana went to him and whispered. 'Ahh,' he said. He studied Alexia a moment and then came over and awkwardly shook her hand, though his eyes were very warm. 'Why didn't you bloody say anything, then?' he asked, and shook his head. 'Poor lass.'

The cow mooed.

'Got your audience, then, cuz,' Matiu said to Isaiah. 'You going to keep them waiting?'

The cow screamed.

Matiu sidled up to Alexia. His long frame was bent slightly at the waist. He got about the place curved like a fish hook. It made every conversation with him seem intimate, as if he was about to tell you a secret. The child Maitai discreetly took her hand.

'This is her first,' Matiu said. 'They often get stuck with their first.' His voice held immeasurable compassion. 'Is you iz or is you aint my baby?' he sang, to Isaiah.

'Here he iz,' said Rangi. 'Iz. The man with the plan. The man with the glove today, bro, the man with the long, white glove.' He handed it to Isaiah.

'But iz he man enough for the job?' Matiu said. 'Iz he, or iz he not the chosen one, as Polly seems to think? Is he a just mild-mannered photographer, or is he really a super-hero in disguise?' Alexia could not tell if Isaiah was angry.

'Aww, leave him alone,' Rangi said. 'Man's got a big job ahead of him.' He patted the cow. 'Relationship problems, too.' He cast an eye at Alexia. 'Pressures you and I don't understand, secret missions to make in the night …'

'Shut up, Rangi,' said Matiu.

'And besides,' Rangi went on. 'Of course he iz your baby.'

Isaiah narrowed his eyes at them. Rangi backed away dramatically. 'What do you expect, cuz, coming back home with a dumb-arse name like that?'

The cow mooed loudly.

'Let's not forget the real issue here,' Alexia said.

'The real issue,' said Matiu. 'Ha!' But he pointed to the cow's tail, where the issue at hand was emerging. Isaiah put on the glove. The kids nudged each other.

'Quiet, you lot, or you can go back home to your aunties,' Matiu said. The kids obeyed him at once, which was unusual. There was sweat running down the cow's sides. She seemed close to exhaustion. Rangi began to speak quietly in Isaiah's ear. Now he was serious, his words emphatic. Matiu started to speak under his breath, a long, fluid stream of te reo which Alexia assumed was a prayer.

'Now, cuz,' Rangi said. Isaiah did as he was told.

Alexia had expected it to be quick, but instead there was an interval of speech and movement that lasted some time. The cow stamped. Isaiah adjusted his stance and in that moment looked directly at Alexia, but did not see her. She was erased. He was sick with the responsibility of it.

'I can't …' he said. 'It's stuck.'

'Pull harder,' Rangi said.

Alexia wasn't really here. Even with Maitai's hand in hers, her two feet in her sandals there against the green pasture, the scent of cow sweat in her nostrils, she wasn't really a part of this. If she was absent it would be some other woman on Isaiah's mind. The exam was a doorway to a life she'd already envisioned in her mind. She would be an independent professional, a lawyer, a traveller. She would have a couple more relationships maybe, with men who made her laugh. Upward mobility. No children. The cow was moaning almost beautifully. She should go home and study for her qualifying exam.

But her home was packed up and dissolved, the couches given away, her record collection sold, the rest of her things in boxes in her parents' basement. She'd left it all so suddenly – Stephen, her family – the bad parts, the good parts. Alexia's life had had nothing wrong with it, on the surface. But she'd always known that Stephen, with his spectacular cooking and his diplomacy, his supportiveness, his unfailing commitment to reason, was never really hers.

What would he be doing now? He had been planning a holiday, she knew that. They had been intending to go to South East Asia together, saving like crazy. He was probably on a beach on an island somewhere right now, drinking mohitos with a crowd of tourists. She imagined the scene: Stephen, newly tanned, tragically slim from grieving Alexia, ready to confide his story. There would be any number of women willing to listen. She imagined someone lithe and tall, in a batik wrap, possibly blonde, adorned with charming accessories bought from the locals.

And Alexia was here on a grassy hill as a man she was strangely attracted to tried to pull a calf out of a cow without throwing up.

'No,' Isaiah said. 'I can't.' He seemed suddenly livid.

Stephen would have gone in with joking confidence and backed off when he was not capable, unashamed. Maybe that was why she had always been convinced, somewhere in a part of herself she didn't want to face, that Stephen was not meant for her. He was so nice, so unerringly affable. Everything was too bloody easy for him.

Matiu jolted towards Isaiah. The calf's hooves were intertwined with Isaiah's gloved fingers, its blood on the white knuckles.

'Enough,' Matiu said. 'She's in trouble, can't you see?' But Rangi said nothing. Isaiah's gaze was fixed away from Alexia. It would be a lot of work to decode all the silences. He pulled suddenly. The men stepped back and the cow baulked and stomped. She seemed to breathe in and then contract, and Isaiah was pulling a mess of blood and membrane from her. The calf fell to the ground. It was wrapped in what looked like a thin white sheet. Alexia remembered an old word, somehow mysterious: the caul.

'Is it dead?' Tama asked. But Rangi and Matiu were working.

'Get the knife,' Rangi said.

The twisted rope of the umbilical cord was still attached to the mother. The cow turned to her calf and brought her face up to the slick bundle. The calf moved, just a little. Here was a thing that had not yet learned to breathe. Rangi slashed at the caul and pulled it away, revealing the calf's face. It was covered in blood and mucus and surprisingly perfect. It opened its eyes. Rangi cut the cord and tied it.

Isaiah stopped panting, and closed his mouth. His face was a picture of absurd triumph. Suddenly Alexia was purely glad.

'Gross!' Ana said.

'Nah, it's awesome,' Maitai said.

Ana scratched in the dirt with her toe. 'But look at the mum!' she said. 'It's eating the whenua.'

'It's good for the animal,' Rangi said. 'The placenta makes it strong.'

Isaiah came to stand beside Alexia.

'I think it's disgusting,' Alexia said.

'It is,' Isaiah said. 'Utterly disgusting.' He laughed.

The calf shifted, got up on its spindly legs and then fell down again. Rangi surprised Isaiah by pulling him in for a hongi. Then all the kids hongied him as well, as though this were a welcoming ceremony for Isaiah and not for the calf, who staggered towards its mother.

'It's good it's not dead, Uncle,' Tama said.

Isaiah smiled, his eyes crinkling behind his glasses. 'It is,' he said. The cow had got onto its side on the ground and was eating ungracefully. Isaiah turned to Alexia. He'd embraced the rest of them; it would seem odd for them not to touch. He squinted slightly, as if to really try and see her, but didn't move.

The caul lay off to the side, a clammy remnant of the calf's last barrier to life. Alexia supposed the cow would eat this as well.

19

Perhaps he had been wrong to tell Sam. She'd told Melissa, who, it seemed, had told everyone. Isaiah watched the news about Alexia's grandfather go out and form a circle around her, like a protective shell. He heard Melissa and Kate whispering about her, as he'd suspected they had before, but now they sounded sympathetic. Even Aidan seemed gentler towards her. But most respectful were the locals. Isaiah saw the way Rangi heaped extra food on her plate, the way Mary patted her when she passed by. And Isaiah had only said to her he was sorry, briefly.

Things had felt odd between them since she had refused to be drawn. A part of Isaiah thought she had orchestrated the scene on purpose; that she had never meant for him to draw her. Hannah had told him that Alexia was also going through a break-up.

It all made sense of her inappropriate laughter, her sullenness, her strange ability to absent herself when she was right in front of him. It made sense, but he wasn't sure how much of it was the grief and how much of it was just her.

'Come on, Isaiah. You're dreaming. We have to prepare the room.' It was Sam. He went with her to pull out chairs and move tables close to the walls. His day of triumph, the day of the calf, was yesterday. He'd woken with a strange feeling of elation. Today it was warm and they were having a meeting, their best attended yet. There were more protestors now than had been present at the start, maybe fifty in all. They laughed and joked and jostled for space. The mood was almost festive. Polly had been persuaded not to smoke in the presence of so many kids, though she had been resentful. She began the meeting with a choppily sung waiata, and started to speak.

The locals were unsure about the idea of a protest, Polly said. She held her tokotoko, and had on her brightest lipstick. In the absence of her cigarette she waved the holder, a little white thing that seemed to confer the same amount of power. What had happened when they'd protested before? At best, nothing. At the worst, arrests and imprisonments, and in the old days, death. In Polly's living memory there had been three land seizures. During the last one, in the seventies, the council had taken pā land and turned it into a reserve. The iwi had protested, but the seizure had gone through. Three of Polly's relatives had been arrested. Her brother was gaoled, and though it had been a short stay, he had not since returned home. Fifteen years later the council had sold the land to farmers, citing financial difficulties. The bush had been levelled.

The thefts of the thirties had been more straightforward. Polly had been a child, she said, when it started. But she remembered the raru that followed each new state-imposed boundary, how the meetings would drag on long into the night as the people argued about what to do. It was a grief to her then, she said, all that talk and wasted energy, and it was a grief to her now. But only through kōrero would they come to agreement about how best to fight. Then of course there were the bad early years, the years of Polly's grandfather. In those years there had been no time for kōrero at all.

'I say we take weapons.' Sam was fired up. The meeting room was crowded. Even the children hung about the edges, drawn in by the importance of it all. Isaiah had agreed with Melissa and Sam when they had wanted to lock the meeting down. But someone had the idea to have a protest, a large one, and now everyone vaguely interested was here to talk about it: the core activists, the locals, a few relatives and neighbours from close by. Taylor wasn't here. There were perhaps forty people in the room.

'I think that would be wise,' Kate said.

'What kind of weapons?' Rangi's face was strained with joy.

'They can't obviously look like weapons,' Sam said. 'That would give them an excuse to arrest us on sight.'

Polly lifted a hand. The room fell silent. She leaned forwards over the rug on her knee.

'We at this pā have never benefited from violence. Action, but not violence.' Her voice was quiet but her nostrils flared. 'If you are violent in response to the pākehā, they will have an excuse to crush you.'

'But where has peaceful action got you?' Kate asked. There were many nods in the room amongst the younger Māori.

'We lie down,' Matiu said. 'We always lie down. I offer no disrespect to those who have gone before. But what happened here in the 1800s? And in the thirties? And the seventies? We did what we have always done. We greeted the pākehā. Then they took our land.' The murmurings in the room increased.

'When they put up fences, we protested,' Rangi said. 'When they came later with bulldozers, we protested. And both times we went out there, with our hands up, and we said, Come, take it from us. We will not fight.' He looked around the room. 'When do we get to fight?'

'Open fighting is not the way,' Alexia said. 'They'd take us down fast.'

Isaiah was preoccupied with a new sensation, that of not being able to speak. It was as if he was clamped and held. People kept jumping in just ahead of him. He opened his mouth. Sam spoke.

'There are things you can do,' she said. 'In South Korea they have a long history of armed protest. I went on a march in Australia that a Korean group attended.' She laughed and suddenly he felt the full force of his feelings for her. 'It was a peaceful student march, but then the riot police showed up.

They were in full riot gear: shields, batons, masks. They came towards the front line, where the Koreans were. The white students just scattered. A few sat down but most just backed away. They were coming at us in a rush. One minute the Koreans were walking quietly together. Then they mobilised. They were all carrying banners with sharp wooden poles attached. They turned the poles around, points outwards towards the police line. Then, as if they'd practised, they formed a wedge shape, and charged the police. It was insane. All these young cops, they didn't know what had hit them. The Koreans drove right through them and out the other side and came back again on the attack. I've never seen anything like it. The cops were so stunned – no one was arrested – they just broke formation and moved away.'

'Far out,' Tama said, from the back of the room.

'We could do that,' Kate said.

'The charges for doing something like would be far more extreme than just for protesting,' Alexia said.

'No violence,' Polly said. 'Not now. What will you get if you bite their hand? Nothing but a smack in the head.' She banged her staff on the floor.

Isaiah became aware that people were waiting for him to speak.

'It's true, we have always backed away,' he said. 'We haven't fought since the old days. This hasn't exactly produced the best results.' The word 'we' felt strange in his mouth, but he forced himself to use it. 'But if we had been more violent, would it have been any different? Isn't there some kind of middle way?'

'What are you now, cousin, some kind of Buddhist?' Rangi asked. 'Thought you were all famous down south, for all those crazy actions you did round the nuclear confer –' Sam shook her head violently. 'You of all people,' he went on, chastened. 'Don't you want to show the pākehā what we're made of?'

'The time for peaceful resistance is over,' said Kate. Alexia rolled her eyes.

'At least we'd be sending them a clear message,' Sam said.

'What message?' Alexia asked. 'Who's going to care about your message?'

'If we undertake an action like this, people will have to notice!' Sam was furious. 'We'll make them notice! And if we lead, we pākehā, then they can't blame the violence on the iwi. They can't write us off as "violent Māori protestors". We'll make sure all the press photos have got white faces in them. They won't be able to sideline it as a Māori issue: they'll have to see it's environmental, universal, that more people care than Māori.'

'Then, when the papers come to talk to us, we'll show them all of it.' Matiu turned to Isaiah. 'You been taking pictures, eh? The dead birds, the fracking wasteland, they got to put that in the news.'

Isaiah nodded.

'Why would the pākehā care about a bunch of dead birds?' Rangi asked. 'You think they're going to put that on the front page of the paper: Poor Sad Māori Upset About Dead Pet Birds?'

'They will care,' Matiu said. 'They'll have to, but I don't want to be led by pākehā on our home ground.' Behind him, someone said 'Āe.' Te Kahurangi made a sound of assent.

'Why should we be scared of what they think of us?' she said.

'It's not about being scared,' Alexia said. 'It's about doing what's most effective.' Isaiah saw how she would be in a court-room pleading a case: meticulous, measured, infallibly reasonable.

'All your talk.' It was Lizzie – Ana, Matiu and Tama's mother. 'Why bother being reasonable when they think we're unreasonable anyway? Peaceful or violent, we can't win. They'll put the same picture in anyway, if it goes in at all.' She eyed Alexia. 'Why is it more effective to play it safe?'

'They see you as a minority group, with minority concerns,' Alexia said. 'If you take the peaceful approach, then at least they can't write your message off straight away.'

'But if we whiteys lead, they'll have to see that our concerns represent those of the wider community,' Sam said.

'You're not the wider community,' she said. 'You may think you are by virtue of being white, but you're not. Most people in this country wouldn't consider going to a protest armed. Most people don't care that you want to save this piece of land. Most people are just working, trying to feed their families, trying to get by.'

'Better keep your girlfriends under control, bro,' Rangi whispered to Isaiah. Was Isaiah that obvious?

Sam opened her mouth but was interrupted.

'She's right, dear,' Polly said. Her voice was soft. For a moment, Isaiah saw what Polly would see: the frayed corduroys bagging out at the knees, the old striped top, the nose piercing. 'Most pākehā don't care what you think. Most pākehā think you're a bunch of no good riff-raff, with no jobs.' She rearranged her shawl. Sam closed her mouth abruptly.

'You've tried speaking their language,' Bryce said. 'We've written to the council, we've objected in writing maybe a dozen times now. Taylor refuses to help us.' There were murmurs of assent from the group. 'You've tried peaceful protest for, oh, at least the last hundred years? And you live here on this small piece of land, when once you could walk from the mountain to the sea through your own bush, but now your water's going bad and your animals are sick. No,' he said, 'the time for peaceful protest is over.'

'All hail the new messiah,' Alexia whispered to Isaiah, who wanted to smile. But he had to speak now.

'I agree,' he said. There was a small silence. He was speaking to his people, who weren't yet his people, and his other city people, who were his but had never really been. The threads of obligation leading everywhere quietened his voice. But what was the big deal, if he advised them wrongly? Who else was going to advise them? 'I agree with you, Bryce,' he said. 'As long as we can keep our people safe. We have to do this in a careful way so that nothing can be pinned on us: no gaol terms, no charges.' This was a risky venue for conversations like these. There were too many people he didn't trust. But it couldn't be helped. 'We'll do this so that no one gets really hurt.'

'You mean none of ours, right?' said Matiu. He grinned.

'Well, okay then,' Sam said. The look she gave him said she might be open to a visit later. She stepped into organising mode. 'We'll need two metre-long staffs for the banners.' She was already taking notes. 'How many? And we need whiteys to agree to do the visible stuff.' Several of the white protestors raised their hands. 'We'll form the front guard, so we'll have to practise. We'll need to seem like we're not organised.'

'Shouldn't be too hard,' said Matiu.

'We need someone to go to town for materials, paint and the staffs. It should be someone who looks ...' Sam's eyes were on Alexia. 'You don't agree with this?' Sam asked her, almost gently.

'No, I don't,' Alexia said. 'I think this will give them an excuse to come down harder on you. But if this is what you all want to do, then I'll go and get the supplies.' Her thick brows drew together with the effort of saying it. Isaiah liked her face. There it was again: the thing about her that was difficult and earnest.

'We'll need some lengths of pipe,' he said.

'For locking on? We're planning an occupation, then?' Rangi asked.

'Not an occupation, an attack,' Isaiah said. There, he had said it. They had collected all the cellphones beforehand and placed them outside of the room, and Kate and Melissa had checked diligently for bugs. There were no unusual cars parked nearby. Still, he knew he shouldn't speak like this, but he'd never before spoken to a room of so many people poised to act. These were not city kids, constrained by their trust funds and university requirements. 'An attack on their house of power: the courthouse. They attack us, with their chemicals and trucks, ripping out trees, destroying the earth. So we attack them. Who could blame us? We'll slip the pipes up our sleeves, like batons. Does anyone have a welder?'

Matiu nodded.

'We'll need some kind of armour,' Melissa said.

'You'd know about that, wouldn't you?' Isaiah asked Rangi.

'What do you think, I slept through the Springbok tour?' Rangi said. His excitement was brimming over. 'We'll use the metal we've got here for body padding, but we'll need more.'

'Can you go to a climbing store, if there is one?' Isaiah asked Alexia. 'I'm going to need carabiners and some more harnesses.'

She nodded.

'Smoke bombs,' one of the protestors said.

'Grappling hooks,' said Matiu, breathlessly

'Flares!' Lizzie said.

Alexia rose to leave.

'Guess fighting just isn't in your nature, then,' Sam said to her as she was almost out the door. The women regarded each other.

'Give me a list,' Alexia said. 'I'll go to town today, and get whatever the hell you like.'

'What's got her so riled up?' Matiu whispered to Isaiah, who shrugged. People dealt with grief in different ways, perhaps that was it. He wondered about Alexia's partner, the ex Hannah had mentioned. What was he like? He imagined a clean-cut guy in a shirt and tie, short back and sides, and shiny shoes. He imagined him beside Alexia at a party, his hand in the small of her back. He stopped imagining.

There was a pause after Alexia left, then the talk went on.

20

'Alexia! Look at me!' There was a clomping sound, a thunk, maniacal laughter. It was Ana. She and Maitai and Tama were playing with a shiny pink thing on the deck of Lizzie's house. It was swelteringly hot. Alexia was passing with her guitar.

Ana had found a pair of high heels. They were bright pink, made of patent leather. Maitai and Tama were lying about the deck, and Tama's cat glowered in a corner. Alexia sat on the step, the guitar in her lap, and played chord progessions. Ana put the shoes on again and picked herself up from where she had fallen. Alexia started to practise scales, up and down, up and down, the notes flicking upwards in a staircase pattern, then falling. Te Kahurangi came out of the house, where she had presumably been visiting Lizzie.

'Watch me!' Ana walked a few steps in the adult-sized heels, and fell again with an exaggerated shriek.

'Thinks she's a real lady,' Maitai said, shaking his head.

'Thinks she's beauuuutiful!' Tama said.

'Try them on, Alexia!' Ana yelled. Alexia declined, but Ana persisted, until Alexia finally gave up the guitar to Te Kahurangi and allowed herself to be pulled by the hand. She was unsurprised when Te Kahurangi started playing Bob Marley, quite skilfully, the flat green notes making discs in the air. Ana shrieked and pushed and pulled until Alexia was stumbling around the porch in the heels.

'Oooh, ooh, Alexia,' Ana said. 'I'm gonna do your nails.'

Her own nails were a bright pink that matched the shoes. She ran inside and came out with a bottle of polish. The shoes were precarious. Alexia paraded for a few steps, for the amusement of Tama and Maitai. Then she tripped and nearly fell.

Sam was standing next to the porch with the compost bucket, which was in need of being emptied. Alexia felt the smile fall off her face. She stepped out of the shoes, wishing she was holding the guitar, though she was not sure why. Te Kahurangi stopped her playing.

'You should watch what you're teaching them,' Sam said. Her tone was reasonable, as if she was noting a room that needed tidying. 'We need to be careful with our young women's self-esteem. And besides, there are lots of things to do to prepare for the protest.' She stomped off in her gumboots. Sam was right: there was a long list of things to do. It was pinned to the wall of the hall. Alexia would go there soon. But she didn't envy Sam in her gumboots, and the thought of a hot-pink manicure made her feel quite happy.

Te Kahurangi broke into laughter.

'Stupid white girl,' she said. 'She's just an old second-wave feminist.' Her wide-set eyes were as innocent as ever. 'She doesn't understand femme power. She doesn't understand you can rip shit up and wear heels at the same time.' She shook her head. 'No real analyisis going on there.' Then she winked, causing Alexia to laugh so hard she had to sit down.

21

Alexia felt them coming. It started in her feet, a low, rhythmic rumble. The heat rose up through her shoes from the burning stones. The sun was high above them. The music rose up through her in the same way. The people were singing. As they drew near she saw their song. It was black and deep, deep green, and it hung about the entrance of the court, the notes burning into her retina like falling coins. The frontguard wore black. Behind them came the iwi, who were dressed casually and who brought children and kaumātua with them. Polly and Te Kahurangi and Lizzie were there. Polly walked near the front, stepping with care. The walk would have been a lot for her, though she always moved so energetically at home. She was leading the singing. With a small shock Alexia saw her for what she was, an elder leading her young people. Polly's pettiness, her belligerant pride, had blinded her to this. Polly's song drew her people after her. The lights circled her and fell, a halo of sparks.

After all the talk, it had taken them only a week to prepare for the protest. Alexia had arrived in town early. This would have put a distance between herself and the others, but she didn't care. She'd treated herself to a flat white and picked up some things she needed: moisturiser, soap, a nail file and polish. She didn't care if Sam would think her manicure frivolous. Now she stood near the courthouse and watched them come towards her. The old building stood grandly, its columns gesturing to the sky as though it held aloft some secular church. She had interned at a place much like it, walking the lofty halls, doing a senior lawyer's paperwork. She heard a low whistle and saw it as a faint blue trail in the air. Rangi was perched absurdly in a tree, close to her. She hoped he didn't think he was camouflaged in his combat boots amidst the sparse foliage. He ushered her closer.

'Sis!' he said in a stage whisper. 'You're blowing my cover.'

'You're not particularly well hidden.'

Rangi tapped the side of his nose.

'Ahh, but I'm the decoy, see?' She followed a flick of his eyes to a man sitting on a park bench reading a paper. 'There's the cop who's following me.' Now Rangi turned his eyes towards the top of the building that bordered the square. There was an almost undetectable movement, the tip of some silver object reflecting – a camera, she supposed, or binoculars.

'That's one of ours?'

Rangi nodded.

'Your boyfriend,' he said. 'He went up last night, with some of the others.'

'But it's three storeys high,' she said. The face of the building was smooth and apparently without purchase except for a few concrete ledges spaced far apart.

'Got a bit of experience, those ones from the south,' Rangi said, grudgingly. 'That boy's got a record. Breaking and entering, trespass, obstruction, wilful damage … they'll be after him for sure, if they can identify him. Run along now, girlie.' He ducked his head. The man at the park bench sat unmoving. Rangi was deluded if he thought that was an undercover cop.

Alexia hurried to the protestors and slipped in behind. She thought she saw Polly nod at her. Sam and Aidan and Hannah were disguised in their padded clothes. Te Kahurangi was holding the end of a banner. Wordlessly, she handed it to Alexia. It was not one of those with sharpened ends like the front guard were carrying. She watched the young woman's long hair as she moved away from her through the crowd.

There were several young people hurrying to the front: Matiu, others she'd seen around the pā, all moving swiftly. Perhaps they had decided to go against orders at the last minute. There were many people she had not seen before. The activists had done a good job of publicising the action.

The elaborate façade of the courthouse reared up before them. Alexia had a brief flash of the processes that might be occurring inside: the judge meting out judgement on a traffic fine, or concluding a custody case, or banging his hand on the desk to punctuate a comment. It was almost always a 'he'. She could hear the hum of the air conditioning and see the muted tones of the court upholstery. The song rose up and went on above her head. Then there was the sound of regimented feet behind them. People began to yell.

Polly's song changed. It went atonal and harsh, and the lights went green, black, black. Then the lights disappeared. Alexia was jostled from behind and crushed against a large man in front of her. Someone stepped on her foot. There was a great push forwards. To her left the children's mother, Lizzie, tripped and then righted herself. The woman had both Tama and Maitai by their hands, and her knuckles were white with the effort of keeping hold of them. Alexia dived for Maitai but missed and almost fell. The police line was not coming as anticipated from the front but from the back, where the protestors had gathered their children and those not interested in the attack.

The police had shields that covered their bodies from chin to knee, blue-black and glassy, and broad helmets. They came on in an unbroken line, hemming the group into a small space. Now from the pākehā front guard came a yell. Sam's voice rose through a gap in the noise.

'The people, united, will never be defeated!' Someone else, Melissa maybe, took up her chant. There came a push from the front and Te Kahurangi came flying towards her. She fell down, and Alexia lost her in the crowd. 'The people, united ...'

But the people weren't united, were they? They were walking separately towards their fates, the actions of those in front endangering those behind.

Children cried out and women called from the back to stand strong. The people in front chanted louder and louder. The singing rose again, fell, and then came completely apart. The police were advancing on either side now, closing in till the people fitted into a roughly square shape within the wider square. The tramp of their feet was loud but there didn't seem to be many of them, not compared to the protestors. The front guard screamed insults and taunts at the police. Polly's voice rang clear over the hubbub.

'Ake!' she called. Then more and more people around her yelled the word, and Alexia was calling it too.

There was an answering call from the rooftops around the square. Smoke bombs came down on the police, spitting coloured smoke. Lit flares were thrown from buildings. A figure belayed himself down the front of the courthouse. Smoke enveloped everything. The banner was pulled from her hand. Tama stumbled and his mother picked him up in one swift scoop. Cries came from the front. The front guard had turned their pikes outwards, and finally charged. Lizzie turned to run back, but tripped. Alexia caught her as she fell but Maitai had disappeared, and then they were all on the ground, under the thick layer of smoke and under people's boots. Someone kicked Alexia in the throat. Her face was close to Lizzie's. Lizzie pulled a scarf out of Tama's top, and wrapped it around the lower part of his face. She reached out to Alexia and pushed a bandanna against her mouth. She launched herself and the boy off the ground as Alexia was still stumbling to her feet.

She headed towards the front, not knowing why she was doing it, moving against the crush of bodies. Up there she heard a sound she'd never heard before: the crunch of metal hitting bone. The action seemed distant because of the smoke. The protestors swung the steel pipes they'd concealed in their sleeves. The police were hitting back. Someone struck her from behind and she fell to her knees. To her left Melissa fended off a strike with her forearm, then disappeared.

'Resistance! Resistance!' Sam was yelling.

Aidan was a couple of metres away. She splayed her hands on the ground, immobilised. She had been wrong to come.

Then there in front of her was Te Kahurangi. She saw grazes on the young woman's hands where she must have fallen and scraped herself. A policeman came at her from the front and she fell back. Struck in the face. Blood spilled from her forehead. Alexia pressed her fingers to her head. Te Kahurangi pulled away. The policeman came on with a baton.

Te Kahurangi's hands were moving behind her back, right in front of Alexia's face. She was slipping a shiv out of her sleeve, a razor stuck in a length of wood and bound with string. The cop swung his baton and it connected with the girl's shoulder. How old was Te Kahurangi? If she was eighteen and able to be tried as an adult … she started to bring her hand towards the cop. The years in gaol! Alexia plucked the weapon from her fingers and threw it, spinning, along the ground. She turned to run backwards, but the crowd was fighting behind her as well. The police must have got reinforcements from somewhere. She was trapped.

Polly was on her knees in front of the courthouse, in between the columns, in the midst of the fighting. She was singing. A figure in helmet and shield turned towards the sound. Smoke passed in front of Alexia's eyes, then cleared. He was advancing on Polly from behind; perhaps he could not tell how old she was. His arm went up and then came down. In the next gap in the smoke she saw he had pulled Polly upright. Her legs turned her around before she was aware of it. She pushed past Te Kahurangi. She passed Melissa, who was yelling incoherently. She passed someone she thought might be Matiu, but whose face was covered in blood.

The policeman was dragging Polly aside. Polly was completely composed. Her lips, as usual, had on their bright bow of lipstick, and she was singing again. Her legs were bandy and knocked along in their good black stockings. She had lost her tokotoko. The man dragging her had left his shield and mask on the court steps and was moving Polly quickly. Of course, she was so light, like a child. And she was offering no resistance. Alexia saw pinpricks of light rising as the faint notes came to her over the noise. She was sweating in the heat, and the other activists were too. She could smell them and the officers around her, a thick, animalistic smell. Polly's song made dashes in the air, like falling rain.

There was Polly's tokotoko on the ground. Carved and polished, with its eel head, the snout inlaid with pāua. Alexia picked it up and cracked it across the cop's shoulders. She raised it again, and hit, and hit. She would stop this. She would make him let go. The stick was light in her hands, a hot nothing. She moved faster than she knew she could. Then she herself was nothing – for one gorgeous instant, nothing but movement and air. There was a moment where she didn't know what happened, and then the policeman was on the ground, still facing away from her, clutching at his head. Blood was seeping through his fingers.

She heard the stick drop from her hands. There had been a blackness in front of her eyes, and now here she was, one foot still pressed against the man's side, while he curled into a foetal position, not moving. Alexia looked up and saw a figure hanging from the side of the courthouse, a balaclava-clad figure with a familiar profile. He swung away. Polly was prone on the ground. She raised her plucked eyebrows. Her mouth turned down at the corners and Alexia could almost hear her say, 'Well, who would have thought?'

This was why she never came to protests. Not because she was afraid of the police. But because she was afraid of herself.

22

Isaiah watched Alexia take Polly around the corner and disappear into an alleyway. He was hanging halfway down the wall of the courthouse, a balaclava over his face, smoke bombs attached to his belt, taking photographs of the scene with his digital compact. He was without a toehold, having rappelled down and locked himself in. He held it steady in one hand. He could not maintain this position for long. Aidan hit the ground and Matiu took a blow to the face. Melissa was trampled underfoot. Te Kahurangi was somewhere, but smoke got in his way. Sam was right at the front. When he dropped down she'd looked straight at him in the midst of her yelling. When she began to fight he'd braced himself: they'd agreed beforehand that it was too risky for him to get involved in the combat. He had let her down once before, at the fracking site. He wouldn't do that again.

From the middle of it all he'd seen Alexia emerge, eyes raised above the heads of the crowd, feet moving as if she was dreaming. Smoke passed between them, and then she was directly below him, raising Polly's tokotoko and striking something on the ground. The policeman took his hands away from his bleeding head and tried to find his assailant. He got to his feet. Perhaps Isaiah should swing out into the air and divert the cop's attention? But the man shook his head and turned back towards the courthouse. Isaiah sought the cop through the viewfinder, catching the dazed expression, the blood across his temple. The tokotoko lay on the ground.

The smoke was clearing. Sam still held her own with her banner-turned-spear, a fierceness on her face that she reserved for people in uniform. She fought cleanly, deflecting blows from the cop's baton as they fell. The intensity of the conflict was flagging as more of the protestors were brought to the ground. Some were pressed face down, cheeks to the concrete, handcuffed. Isaiah put his lens to his eye and clicked. Each time he pressed the button a feeling reverberated in his body like a stone falling into water. *There, there.* Hands being cuffed roughly behind an activist's back. A policeman striking Kate across the face. Aidan down and yelling, a boot swinging towards his head.

He flicked the camera into a pocket in his sleeve and hoisted himself up the wall. It was not his favourite camera – that would have been too heavy – but the photos would do the job. It would be helpful to have a record of events if anything legal were to come of this. He needed to get back on top of the building quickly. No one on their side would be left up here: Isaiah had dismissed them earlier on. It was up to him.

He swung out and back in and hit the building harder than he'd planned. Turning his foot side on in its rock-climbing shoe he smeared up the wall, adjusting the rope as he went. He slipped a couple of times, the rope breaking his fall. Amazingly most of the protest crowd had got away. There was only the core left, maybe twenty of them, but they were surrounded. Black figures came in waves from the exits to the square. He slipped again, found a toehold, and held, his body pressed close to the granite and his centre of gravity coming to where it needed to be. He crimped his fingers into a crack at the window's edge, locking them so they formed an anchor in the tight space. It hurt, and they would be bruised, but they held him long enough to allow him to reach for a hold on a window frame. He breathed in the smell of his own sweat. There was movement on top of the building. He leapt upwards for the next hold.

He caught and gripped, though his fingers were damp. He'd left the chalk bag in his pack in favour of climbing light – had enough gear slowing him down. He'd thrown most of the bombs he'd been carrying, but he now wished fervently for the chalk. It was summer and his hands were sweating horribly. Climbing like this was different from sports climbing: the gear for sheer building faces was weightier. You needed more rope length, more carabiners – Isaiah had seven left dangling from his belt – and the rope was twice as heavy as the one he usually climbed with. He heard a scream and, turning again, saw Te Kahurangi catch a blow across the face. He couldn't flip his camera out. He was using all his strength just to cling to the wall.

Isaiah dived upwards, muscles beginning to shake. Distribute your weight evenly on your legs. Don't lock too hard with your arms. Centre of force into the wall. His toes were slipping on the sheer face. He pushed and held. He wasn't breathing now: just working. He pushed. He knew he couldn't keep this up for long, but one, two more pushes, and he was there. He'd gained the lip of the building.

On the roof were five cops, no – six, standing casually against the sky. Isaiah lay on his stomach at their feet. He could flip himself off the building and swing free, maybe quick-release from his harness when he hit the ground, but his muscles had nothing left. One of the policemen tapped his foot …

… and Isaiah was on his knees, in another time, and in another place, surrounded by cops, and it was cold, and he was alone …

'Fancy seeing you here,' the cop on the roof said.

Isaiah's hands were wrenched behind his back. He told himself he knew his rights, he knew his rights. The tendons in his shoulders hurt. He was relieved of his remaining smoke bombs and flares. He was flipped onto his back. They took his carabiners, his concealed baton, and finally his camera. At least it wasn't the SLR. But fuck it was useful. And who was going to pay for another one?

'Shall we get the shoes?' one of the men said to another.

'What am I being arrested for?' Isaiah asked.

'Intention to damage public property. Trespassing. How's that for a start?'

One of the cops moved towards the doorway in the roof and opened it. Their prisoner was to be brought down the stairs and through the courthouse in a civilised fashion. A cop knelt at Isaiah's feet in a supplicating position. Isaiah had not decided to resist, but his foot moved away from the policeman's hand. He'd had his rock-climbing shoes only a few months: they were very expensive.

'I'll have you for obstruction,' the cop said. 'Your foot is obstructing my hand.' Even he seemed to think this was funny.

When they got down to the street, everything was too real. Te Kahurangi was bleeding from the head. Matiu was cuffed and thrashing, a cop kneeling on his back to hold him down. Sam had been subdued. She was talking loudly about the illegality of the arrests, which meant she was all right. Aidan was face down. Hannah was quiet but unhurt. They formed a line of bodies on the ground, maybe fifteen people. A policeman was being carted off in an ambulance and a paddy wagon had arrived. Lizzie was not in the line-up, nor Rangi. Isaiah was shoved down the front steps. Sam saw him and her face fell. He saw a movement to one side. It was Rangi, peeking from behind the corner of the courthouse. He was so blatant that Isaiah wanted to laugh. He raised his eyebrows at Isaiah comically, one by one. Te Kahurangi cradled her head in her arms.

'She needs medical attention,' he said to the cop holding him. The second time he said it, the cop spoke into a radio.

Everyone was being frisked. Melissa was weeping, unsurprisingly. He thought of Alexia and the staff, the blows going wide and striking, her seeming lack of control. At least everyone here was calm and co-operating. Isaiah was directed to lie on the ground. Someone who was presumably a sergeant circulated, giving orders. A small pile of weapons was accumulating. It was horrifying: smoke bombs, padding, knives, the short batons they'd concealed in their sleeves. There was enough there to put them all away, even the ones without a record. At least the fracking would be in the news, and it wouldn't all be for nothing.

'Search them again,' the sergeant said. He had a bag of their gear. He was putting cellphones and cameras into it: anything that could have taken images of the demo. Isaiah's body was wrung and sore, but he felt as if he could run and run. He knew this stage: this near hysteria after being caught, the weird false high. It would be replaced soon by exhaustion while they were all being photographed, fingerprinted and processed. With a group this large it would take a long time.

'Okay,' the sergeant said. 'Righto then.' He seemed overly cheerful. 'You've been warned,' he said to the group. He turned to his officers. 'Now let them go.'

Isaiah felt the shock go through the policeman holding him. There was a silence in which Melissa stopped crying.

'Let this be a lesson to you though,' the sergeant said, like someone's stern, good-humoured father. He placed the bag of cellphones on the ground and stamped on it with his boot. This was an entirely illegal destruction of property, but the man did not seem to care. The sergeant picked up the bag. His inferiors stood about, quietly, not moving.

'Did you hear me?' the sergeant said, to his officers this time. 'Let them go.' He turned away, taking the bag with him.

Te Kahurangi was placed on a stretcher. Aidan got up and brushed himself off. Melissa started crying again, and Sam leapt up from the ground. Matiu got up slowly. The cops began to uncuff their hands.

'What the hell's all this then?' Aidan said.

Sam began to scream.

'Arrest me,' she yelled to the cops. 'Arrest me, you bastards.

They're sabotaging us so they don't have to put it on the news!' she yelled. She neared the cop on Isaiah's left. She laid into him, striking at his face. 'Arrest me!' she screamed. None of the other activists moved. 'You bastards! Chicken shit bastards!' She hit out again and was deflected.

A cop came at her from behind and she bent under his weight, then threw him off. The sergeant took no notice. A young cop faced her.

'Why won't you arrest me? You dirty fascist pigs!' She spat into his face.

Isaiah saw shock register there, and disgust. Sam went on screaming. But the police withdrew.

23

Rangi was ranting about pressing charges, but no one was paying him any attention. A small group of them would be going to Te Kahurangi's bedside that evening. She was being held at the hospital to make sure she didn't have concussion. Matiu had needed stitches. He leered at Alexia from the passenger seat as she drove them home, inexplicably pleased with the bloody version of himself he could see in the rear-view mirror. Alexia felt drained and vaguely nauseous.

She was fairly sure she shouldn't be driving, but there it was. She had waited with Polly until it was safe to emerge and then rejoined the group in front of the courthouse. Sam's rage had been impressive. Aidan was draped along the back seat of the car as well, nursing his wounds. Hannah was riding with someone else. In the post-protest shock they had all piled haphazardly into different cars.

Alexia ground the gears of the ute. She had never been good with manuals. She drove carefully, wary of what her passengers might say as she slipped briefly into the wrong gear on a corner and quickly righted her mistake. She needn't have worried. In the rear-view mirror Matiu looked out of the window at the passing landscape, and Aidan had his hand over his eyes, one of which was swollen and bruised. Would Isaiah ever feel uncertain of himself the way she often did? One of the most attractive things about him was his ease, his apparent unconcern with how he was perceived. She recalled his fluid movement on the concrete surface of the building, graceful and assured,

144

making his technical feats with the rope and carabiners look like part of the body's natural repertoire. She recalled her own jerky movements below him, her sudden violence: how that must have appeared from above! She wasn't unaware of herself. She was, on the contrary, over-aware of everything, past and present. That had always been the problem.

'They were prepared for us,' Rangi said from the passenger seat.

She glanced at him from the corner of her eye. The beautiful moko spanned his cheek, the skin underneath it glowing. She was fascinated by Rangi, by his gruffness and tenderness. The face design was like a living sculpture. She knew what her father would have thought of Rangi; that he was a dole bludger, an ex-convict, a miscreant. She took a turn too fast and fiddled again with the gears. Then again, Rangi would probably like to consider himself a miscreant.

'Why do you think so?' she asked him.

Aidan jumped in. 'Obvious, weren't it? They'd called in the troops. They were kitted out proper in riot gear, helmets and everything. But those police were young. Their bosses weren't really threatened by us. If they were, they would've sent more experienced police. Those were fresh recruits, being given some experience. That was a training exercise.'

Alexia felt a thrill of anger go through her. The beatings she had seen, the treatment of Polly, the marks on Aidan's own face, the result of a training exercise.

'He's right,' Matiu said. 'Makes a lot of sense, from the cops' perspective, to train new recruits away from the main centres. Then if anyone messes up, there won't be any fallout. There'll be no media coverage of the protest, they saw to that. They were always going to confiscate the phones and the recording equipment. There's someone doing surveillance on us, or there's someone in the group informing.'

Alexia was aware of the silence filling the cab.

'S'all right, Alexia,' Aidan said. 'He doesn't mean it's you.'

Matiu quirked an eyebrow at her in the rear-view mirror, and she was grateful. Rangi patted her knee, which was inappropriate, of course, but she could let it slide. She pulled into the gate of the marae with a sense of relief. Why did it matter to her so much that these three men did not believe she was a police spy? A few weeks ago the proposition that anyone would suspect her of this would have been absurd. She could not have imagined herself being in this situation, nor caring so much about the opinions of people such as Aidan, Rangi and Matiu.

Her friends in the capital were ambitious lawyers-in-training, journalists and media people. They tended to be polished and articulate. They tended to be highly strung and well presented. They tended to be busy. Since she and Stephen had broken up there had been a notable absence of texts and calls. Aside from a few close girl friends, no one had been messaging her. But she had effectively gone off the map, away from the bars, the fashionable restaurants. She had withdrawn. But so many of these people she'd considered friends had turned out to be only acquaintances. So many of them must have decided, in that fraught period that followed her break-up with Stephen, that they fell on his side of the fence, not hers.

Rangi patted her knee again, reassuringly.

'Nearly there, bub,' he said. And though she had not been anyone's bub, ever, Alexia could have cried.

It was breakfast time. Polly was in the kitchen. Alexia touched her shoulder and pointed to the bandage around her knee.

'They said to change that evey second day,' she said. 'Do you want me to help you do it?'

Polly stiffened. Then she handed Alexia a mug of tea, and moved her mouth, ever so slightly, just at the edges. Alexia realised that this was Polly's version of a smile, reserved for people who were not relatives, who were pākehā, perhaps, but who had gained entry to Polly's sphere of affection.

'I'll be just fine,' Polly said. Alexia took her tea, tried to hide her own smile, and ducked away.

Tonight they were to hold their first meeting since the protest. Te Kahurangi was back from the hospital. She had been given the all-clear in regards to concussion and seemed proud of the cut that ran across her face and would probably be a scar. The bruises on Te Kahurangi's face were beginning to fade, and Matiu had had his stitches out.

After the demo no one had felt like planning or like taking action. They had been in some kind of collective shock. It had seemed enough to keep on cooking and feeding themselves. The disappointment was that, even with so many people injured, nothing had been in the media about the fracking, and very little about the protest. It seemed that the police had effectively silenced them. There had been a bulletin on the radio, but all it reported was that a small group of protestors had gone to the courthouse to protest fracking in the region. The reporter had referred to them as 'a Māori interest group'. There were no reports of the violence that had occurred. A local blog reported the action in full, but it had a very small readership.

The cameras and phones that had not been destroyed had proven difficult to reclaim from the police. Alexia, who was in charge of the effort, had come up against a series of bureaucratic glitches involving application specifications. No one had been arrested, and no charges laid, so there was no crime or record associated with the phones. Communications at the marae were stilted by the sudden lack of technology.

The feeling in the group grew into outrage, but the outrage had no proper object. Everyone was tired, and tempers were short. Alexia had begun to monitor what she disclosed and to whom. Rangi was restrained. Isaiah seemed rattled and unsure. The feeling was that there must be some step forward, some further act, but no one knew what it should be.

Then the more casual supporters began to leave. Numbers fell. Of the people who had been there at the gate at the beginning only about half remained. Alexia was interested to see who was at tonight's meeting. In contrast to the packed room of people who had decided on direct action, the gathering was a small one, a handful of people only, held in a back room. Polly handed out the digestives, but there weren't enough.

Isaiah hongied Te Kahurangi to welcome her back and spoke a few quiet words. Sam gave her a clap on the back and offered her some sunflower seeds, which Te Kahurangi politely refused, and Melissa and Kate sidled up to her, as if her heroism might rub off on them. Alexia thought she saw a new hardness in Te Kahurangi, almost a triumphant pride. The last thing Te Kahurangi should be basing her self-esteem on was how badly she had been beaten by the police. But then, what did Alexia base her own self-esteem on? Academic success? Both these things were problematic.

Matiu was speaking. 'The patupaiarehe have been at it again.' That surprised her. She always thought of him as a rational voice. Aidan and Hannah looked at him as though he were mad. 'They've been shifting things around at my place,' he went on. Melissa nodded. 'This protest got the fairies all stirred up, I reckon.'

'Patupairehe?' Alexia said. The bush fairies?

'All I know is stuff's been moving around that shouldn't be moving on its own, in the night,' Matiu said. 'I've been testing them. I started to leave stuff out on purpose, things they'd be interested in, flutes, shiny things, what have you. They've been moving them all over the place.'

Sam sighed audibly, and ate some seeds. Seeing Sam gnaw away, Alexia realised then that it was a nervous habit, like Kate's hand-wringing and Melissa's tears.

Matiu seemed thinner than he had a few weeks ago, and he had a frantic air. But then all of them, in the wake of the protest, had been oscillating between mania and apathy. Perhaps he was more worn down than she had thought.

On the other hand, a few nights ago she had heard, again,

the music in the forest, flutelike and faint, and seen its lights rise and burst above the trees. When she'd asked Hannah if she could hear this Hannah had shaken her head. Perhaps they were all succumbing to some kind of group psychosis?

'Those patupaiarehe giving you any tips on strategy?' Rangi asked. 'We're losing supporters like a leaky bucket. We're low on funds. Anyone got any ideas, patupaiarehe or not, I'd like to hear them.'

'We could sell Isaiah's pictures. We could have an art exhibition. We could all contribute. Even the kids. We could auction stuff off.' Te Kahurangi was inspired. The beating had galvanised her. Maybe good had come out of the protest after all. But even Kate and Melissa, usually so agreeable, seemed loath to commit to another event.

'I think for now we need to come up with some kind of holding strategy,' Isaiah said, softly. He surveyed the group. Polly, Te Kahurangi, Alexia, Rangi, Matiu, Sam, Melissa, Kate, Aidan and Hannah. 'How many of us are there left? Most of the Auckland group left last night, and the Hamilton group are leaving in the morning. Has anyone seen Bryce's wife? Or her partner? Maybe they've decamped.' Alexia felt the impulse to touch him, to hold his arm. She quickly censored the thought. 'We need to stop people leaving. We're haemorrhaging supporters.'

'He's right,' Sam said brusquely. 'We need to motivate everyone to stay involved.'

But by the end of the meeting they hadn't come up with anything. Alexia watched, bemused. Perhaps this was how wars ended. Maybe everyone just got tired, and gave up, and wanted to go home.

But for Matiu and Rangi and Polly and Te Kahurangi, this was their home. Isaiah was biting at his thumbnail, a nervous gesture she had never seen him do before. Then she realised: this was his home too. Isaiah was from here, he was iwi, she knew all that. The returning prodigal son. But his foothold here had been theoretical. She had assumed when this was over that he would return to the city. But now she realised that somewhere in the midst of the protest, maybe, this had become his place. If they all gave up on it and left, would they also leave him here, with the dead river and all the dying birds?

Polly ordered them all to have a good sleep. Something would happen to change things, she said. Something always happened. It was the only consistent truth of the world.

'Can I talk to you, Alexia?' It was Sam. Alexia supposed it would be rude to say no.

Sam led her to a tree outside, away from the others.

'I haven't told you, but I'm sorry about your grandfather,' Sam said. She put a hand on her arm, and to her surpise Alexia felt a softening in herself. She didn't want to cry in front of her. 'I really am sorry. The thing is, I keep noticing you tuning out, in meetings, or in the middle of conversations, whatever. I know you've been under stress.' Ah, this was what this was all about. Sam rushed on. 'My question is, are you going to be up for campaigning? Everyone thinks that protest was the worst thing that could happen. But I think things are just heating up at the pā now. You might not like what happens next.'

'What happens next,' Alexia said, to give herself time to think. She had been right not to cry in front of Sam. Nothing Sam did was accidental.

'You want to watch what you're committing yourself to,' Sam said. 'You want to be careful. I wouldn't waste my time up here, if I were you.'

A couple of weeks ago Alexia wouldn't have been sure where she stood. But now her feeling was that this work was much more important than anything else she had been doing for a long time.

Sixty years ago Papou had arrived in this country and decided to stay. After Greece the countryside was unbelievably green, he'd said, the farms unimaginably large. It was like a promised land. This had been the place they had run to from ruined Europe. The civil war had done things to people in Greece, Papou had told her, terrible things. Hunger twisted the villagers, and people who had once been friends sold each other out for food. Papou had described their first train journey here so many times that it hung in her mind like a series of photographs. She could see it: the train passing through the great green plains that spanned the distance to the mountains' feet, Yiayia and Papou looking out the window of the train, Baba – a baby – resting in Yiayia's arms.

Now this was the only place Alexia had. And it was being exploded, from underneath her. There was the police officer dragging Polly, her legs knocking on the ground. There was Papou in his coffin. Sam was waiting patiently.

'I think I might be ready,' Alexia said, 'for what happens next.'

'I guess we better get on with it then,' Sam said. They began to walk back. But then Sam spoke again, the words jolting out of her. 'He's not what you think,' she said. 'Isaiah. He cares more about this stuff than you realise.' Alexia nodded slowly. 'He cares more about the land, and the water, the pollution, than he cares about anything,' Sam said. 'He only cares about that.'

Before she slept that night Alexia listened to the whistles in the forest. They weren't birds, or anything mechanical, she knew it. The lights danced and fell before her eyes.

24

In his memory he was standing, in the front row of a protest, not the recent one, but one long ago. The cop opposite him was young. They could have gone to school together. Isaiah was yelling into a megaphone when the man pushed him.

The protest had been about rising fees at the university. It was a small group, and it was surprising to them that the cops had come down so hard. But they were young, and everything was surprising. Isaiah was shoved and a hot rush went straight through his body and floored him. *This is the way the world is.*

Then he was on his knees and the noise of the crowd rose and surged around him. They were angry he had been hit. He was puzzled, perplexed almost, at having his space violated like this. Later he would think how naive he had been. At the time he was concerned for himself, and for the young cop, who had broken the rules. One minute they were standing, chanting, and the atmosphere was almost jovial. The push had rent the fabric, and now everyone was in an uncharted place. He got to his feet and faced the man. His face was narrow and very lightly fuzzed with blond stubble.

'It's illegal for you to strike me without provocation,' Isaiah said.

The man nearly smiled.

Isaiah hit him. It was not graceful or nice or clean, like in a video game. It was sweaty and ineffective and imprecise. The blow hit the side of the man's chin and glanced off and Isaiah fell to one side, the cop crumpling under him. Then the other police were there.

Then he was on the floor, at the station. They'd taken his watch and he didn't know the time. They made him strip. They made him crouch down. They promised that someone would be along soon to do the body search. They told him that when the time came he should relax, not resist. That if he was tense it would make it more uncomfortable. He waited a long time for someone to come in, many hours.

Isaiah had made it through his rough high school on the coast without ever being beaten up. He had not been bullied. He had had exactly one physical fight with a boy, a conflict that had happened organically, after a miss-kick on a football field. He had never been one of those boys who had been taken to the locker room and had his head flushed in the toilet. You heard about things happening. You heard about such things, and you were always grateful it wasn't you.

Finally a cop came in wearing glove. He was an older man, accompanied by three other police. Isaiah assumed they were there to hold him down. They said for him to get onto his knees. His fingers seemed white in the harsh light of the cell, his feet narrow and hairless. He told himself he'd learn his rights, he'd learn his rights, that he'd be smarter in the future. He'd never let this happen again.

But they didn't search him. The gloved man's eyes were nearly compassionate.

'You can get up, son,' he said. The police with him seemed surprised. He turned to them. 'Sorry bastard's got nothing hidden. You can see that.'

Isaiah had managed not to cry.

Now Isaiah was the one in charge, sent to this other police station to retrieve their cellphones. He'd made the trip alone. Alexia was playing on his mind. As soon as he saw the concrete frontage of the building, he realised he should have brought Sam, who always had a bolstering effect. She would have approached the stern façade of the station with no more apprehension than if she was entering a schoolyard. He feared being enclosed.

Only Sam knew of this part of his history. He steeled himself and walked through the double doors. Immediately the smell was upon him. Surely all police stations shouldn't smell the same, and yet they did. There was that metallic, officious odour, the trace of the lock-up concealed somewhere. The front desk was before him. He composed himself. It turned out he didn't have to go anywhere else in the building. It was a simple matter: a form to be signed, nothing more.

When he got back to the marae he handed around the phones that had survived the protest. Sam took hers and put one strong hand over his, briefly, and then let him go.

25

There was absence and there was presence. And then there were things that were never really there. When Alexia had come here she was preoccupied with Papou, though she should have been feeling the absence of Stephen. Since the protest, she was preoccupied with the absence, not of Papou, but of them, all of them, everyone she had lost. The scenes played in her mind each night, but without the same edge of vividness, as if the action and the violence she had just seen had located her. Now there were delineations in the absence, as if it was itself a temporal thing. They were gone, and they were behind her. She couldn't quite see what was ahead. Papou, however, Papou was beside her, accompanying her every step.

Alexia was on her way back to her campsite when she saw Rangi coming. He drew near and, without speaking, nodded his head towards the trees, indicating that she should follow. Slowly she moved after him into the tight clasp of bush, the path narrowing quickly to a faint track. He took a thing out of his pocket. A small screen lit up, and she understood.

'Gonna save this for when we really need it,' Rangi said. Together they watched the figures on the small screen. It was the phone she'd seen him holding at the protest. Rangi had been their lookout and, like Isaiah, had been relegated to the sidelines on account of his police record. His phone must have been the only one that hadn't been confiscated. 'Didn't want to show it at a meeting,' he said. 'Don't know how I feel about the rest of them.'

'Thanks, Rangi,' she said.

On the screen she saw many heads from behind. The picture tilted and righted itself as the camera moved to a higher vantage point. The people were marching peacefully, banners upheld, the chanting coming to her eyes crackled and warped, and around the screen in front of her there were faint rising lights. The pattern was the same as the lights she'd seen in that moment on the march, and they started up a small fizz of panic in her. The courthouse was directly ahead. Alexia judged the police were already closing in behind. The camera weaved and dipped, then was hoisted higher.

Now she could see clearly what she hadn't been able to on the ground: the armed front facing the police. The police line moved. It was clear that they moved first, without visible provocation, though she knew the front guard had been mocking them. She saw Sam pushed backwards, recognisable even in the gear she was wearing. The phone jerked. When it came back to centre it focused on three cops, four, raising their batons. The protestors were falling back without fighting. The sound came intermittently, outraged cries and the singing still going on. Then came the cry, *Ake, ake, ake*. The phone cut out. Rangi pressed a button.

Another shot of the police line, from above. When had he scaled a building? Or was he again hiding in his tree? The police moved forwards and back, forwards and back. The crowd behind the militant front was thinning. Alexia saw half a dozen strikes fall. She knew the protestors were armed but from this vantage point it seemed one-sided, the armed and uniformed police set against a straggling crowd, with a child visible here and there. The protestors had succeeded in one thing: they did not look organised. The footage cut out. Rangi pressed the button again.

There were the protestors at ground level, recognisable and distinct: Aidan fighting, Hannah crouching down, Melissa lying on the ground, already cuffed. Alexia placed herself slightly to the right and, thankfully, off screen. The camera turned slightly, and found Te Kahurangi. Her face was bloodied from when Alexia had seen her hit. She was being set upon by three police. Her head snapped right, left, and then she fell. The camera lingered there. The screen shook, then held still. They kicked her, three large men in protective gear and boots. Te Kahurangi was splayed on the ground. She raised her arms to her head. Still the officers kicked. It went on. It went on. Just when Alexia was going to ask him to please turn it off, the screen went blank.

'Oh,' Alexia said. 'Oh, Rangi.'

'What do you think we can do with it?' he asked.

'What can't we do with it?' she said.

26

Isaiah began to go on long walks with his camera equipment, and while it was true that he was gathering evidence, it was also true that he needed the time alone. He worked his way far up inside the fracking land, beyond where they had explored before. A well was visible, its top bursting with flame. Around the base of the tower the land was scraped smooth, stripped of grass. A pond lay around it, extending off into the farmland. It was filled with frack fluid, the water grey-black in the daylight. The pond was less a hollowed-out bowl than a level layer of filth and detritus. He could see how rain would push the sheet of liquid further into the land, how the chemicals would spread. His back was to the mountain, where a bush reserve clad the lower foothills.

The sun was high and blue, and the mountain's snow had burned off except for a neat cap at the top. The landscape should have been beautiful. He took photos at the edge of the pool, its rim marked by bulldozer imprints. He hated what he saw, but he loved the feel of the camera in his hand, its coolness, its clean efficient design. The workers had laid plastic sheeting between the fluid and the earth. He found its black edge emerging from the orange clay like some exotic mushroom, and tested its strength and thickness with his hand. It was not much thicker than a rubbish bag, and the oily water was seeping around it already.

Close to the pool's edge he saw two kererū roosting, and a tūī drinking nectar from a kōwhai tree. He found a snail he knew was native; its curved shell a tight brown koru of a curl, more like a sea shell. The punters would love that. People were so fickle. A tūī had more pathos than a sparrow, a kererū more clout than a pigeon, and a shot of a rare kiwi coated in oil would be most valuable of all. He had no reservations about manipulating the public. The native fantails were too quick for his lens. He snapped several pictures in quick succession to splice together later with his editing software: tūī, tree, frack waste leaking onto the earth. He snapped another series: kererū, river snaking past frack pool, oil running towards it. And one more: kauri snail on leaf, wasteland with gas rig, smoky emanations.

Now he was in the shadow of the gas tower. The banks of the river descended almost to the level of the plain. His feet were hot in his walking shoes. The smell didn't make him lightheaded, as it had on his mission with Sam. He guessed the flame at the top of the well, erupting every few seconds, was burning off excess gas into the atmosphere. There had been that brief urge he'd had to have sex with her, just the moment before they'd seen the pit. His attraction to Sam had always surprised him. She almost had an air of asexuality. There was a sort of scrubbed quality to her hair and skin that made him think of girls' dorms in boarding schools, horses and private lessons. They'd slept together on and off for years, with interesting regularity, but since their reccie he hadn't had the urge, not once.

The banks of the river were slimed with run-off. Each new oily rivulet he framed seemed more meaningful; each frame more affecting than the last. Underlying his careful selection was a kind of drive, not a thought but more a bodily sensation like the need to eat or make love. It was a feeling of constriction that only let up as he photographed. The sun moved and details were thrown into relief. His body was shaking slightly.

He caught himself crouched, hot and ruffled, photographing a bird's nest against a backdrop of black river water, holding his hands still with a great willed force. The bird had used twigs covered in a slick film of fluid to build the lining of its home. He could not tell what kind of bird it was, but one of its chicks had struggled out and was lying on its side, quite still. It was a small thing, a pathetic thing.

This force in him, if it was translated into words, would say, *there. There.* How could they ignore this? The feeling Isaiah tried very hard to feel every time he visited the marae, the feeling he could see that Polly felt, and Lizzie, and even Rangi, when they passed the tukutuku patterns and settled under the high roof, was never quite present for him. But it was present for him here. His drawings, his photographs were just markers, odes to the unbelievable individuation of things: leaves, creatures, the land itself. The bird moved gently in its bed of waste.

He had a non-disruption policy when it came to animals. Of course he couldn't save it. You couldn't save everything. It might survive, adapting to its new environment. He jolted away. Each photograph he took was some kind of point in a grand argument he was having with an imagined public who in all probability didn't care.

Now he came to a valley, where the banks dropped lower still. Eels were swimming in the river's depths. There was lurid orange algae at the edges of the water. He found a sparrow, dead, took a photograph, moved on. He knew it wasn't the best image, not like the tūī and the kererū higher up, but still he clicked. He found two more sparrows further on, then a fantail. He found another bird, dead, a starling, its red legs sticking straight up into the air. He walked and stopped, walked and stopped, aware of his hunger and of his thirst, but there were always more shots.

This river fed straight into the pā. The water was their drinking water. He found a sheep – its carcass bloated and full. It couldn't have been long in the river. He'd have to ask Matiu about removing it, maybe come back and haul it out. But with so much other waste running into the river, how serious was one dead sheep? He photographed and photographed.

When he and Sam were on their way here there was some unspoken plan between them, some make-or-break idea he knew they both had. This place had always been his back-up plan, the place he would go when he wanted to settle down. It would mean a lot of work, of course, if he moved here. He would have to finally learn te reo, to study the customs. He didn't want to do it in the city. If he came here he could learn, but he wouldn't be doing it on display. It wouldn't be the cause for anyone else's celebration.

But the bank was littered with birds. He picked one up in his hand, letting the camera rest. Since he'd got here he'd become unsure of everything, even how he felt about Sam. Especially Sam. The dead bird was coated in a slick iridescence. He had wanted to have children here. He laid it down on the river stones.

27

Alexia had pulled the last clean clothes from the bottom of her pack: a short, black pencil skirt, a high-collared shirt. Her stocking-clad legs contrasted with her borrowed gumboots, a tragedy of stylistic confusion. Isaiah did not appear to notice. They walked without speaking through the bush, Isaiah carrying his SLR, Alexia with the microphone and tripod. He had an alertness about him when he was outside that he did not have at other times, as though he was reading signals not visible to Alexia. This, she understood.

Alexia enjoyed the bush as well. Since she had been living here (was she living here now?) she had noted a strange easing off inside her. It was probably to do with the quiet and the slowness of this place, all in opposition to her caffeine-fuelled, rushed, city commute. Maybe she could live here. But she didn't love the bush like Isaiah seemed to. And she wasn't quite enjoying herself yet. It was all Alexia could do get out of her tent in the mornings, after her dreams of knives and coffins and waves of earth.

Polly's house was tiny, set in the trees away from the marae. Alexia started to slip off her boots while Isaiah knocked. The door opened smartly. Alexia was caught bent over, one gumboot in her hand and the other one half off.

'Mōrena,' Polly said, and kissed Isaiah sweetly on the cheek. She led them down a dark hallway. Photographs were mounted on the walls, some decorated with harakeke woven into flowers, some with feathers. The glass in the frames gleamed, though the other things in the hall were dusty and untouched. Alexia understood that Polly must polish the glass often, moving from each picture to the next, touching the black and white faces behind the glass.

Her grandmother too moved through the house each day, carrying an incense burner and dowsing the icons with smoke, saying the morning prayers. When Alexia was a girl she'd helped, righting the frames, lighting candles, polishing the portraits of the saints. She stopped beside one of Polly's photos, and Polly turned and stared at her. Alexia didn't care: she was as affected by Polly's hall as she would be on entering a great cathedral. Isaiah had gone ahead into living room, his jeans disappearing through the door. Te Kahurangi was draped on the couch as though she lived here, which perhaps she did. Alexia left the hall reluctantly and entered Polly's small lounge. There was a coal range that the old woman apparently used, with a full coal scuttle next to it.

'You three sit here and I'll get you some tea,' Polly said. She went over to a stack of water bottles by the door. It was not all talk, then: Polly really was concerned about her water.

'No, Aunty, no tea,' Isaiah said. 'I've got to go to town for some supplies later. Shall we have a look at this water?'

'Cuz,' Te Kahurangi said urgently, but Isaiah was already in the kitchen. Instead she turned to Alexia. 'Doesn't he know anything?' she said. 'Way to go, offending an old lady, rejecting manaakitanga like that!' They could hear Polly in the kitchen putting the kettle on anyway, as though she hadn't heard him.

A loud bang came from the kitchen. Isaiah yelled.

Alexia and Te Kahurangi crowded into the doorway. Polly stood by the stovetop like a small, upright carving. Isaiah was flustered.

'Singed my eyebrows!' he said. There was a strong smell of burnt hair.

'The water actually caught fire?' Alexia asked. Then they were all speaking at once.

'I told you it had gone bad,' Polly said.

'Here I'll show you –' said Isaiah.

'Aunty wouldn't show me –' Te Kahurangi said.

'We have to film it,' Alexia said. 'This is insane.'

'What, you thought Polly was not telling the truth?' Polly asked. She turned on the tap. The small kitchen filled with a sulphurous smell. 'Stand back,' she said, grandly. Alexia saw that her moko lines were chiselled in. She must have had it done when she was very young, when they still did moko like that, with hammers and a thousand tiny blows. She had a vivid image of Polly being held down in some private space, desperately holding her face still. Polly let the water run for a moment, and then produced a match. It would have taken days for them to complete a moko like that. The elderly woman struck the match and held it to the flow. The three of them jumped, but nothing happened. Polly took the flame away and then touched it to the water again – a moment when it should have gone out.

A flame exploded out of the tap. The air was sucked towards it. She noticed Te Kahurangi was holding her hand.

'Kai hamuti!' she said.

The water ran and the flame danced around it. It was bright, a foot high, half a foot in width. It grew larger and brighter in the dim kitchen. It struck Alexia as biblical, as though she were watching brimstone fall from the sky, and the effect was very much like her private lights, and this made her feel guilty, as though she, Alexia, had personally put it there, as though it was a consequence of her presence. The flame grew larger still, reaching the edge of the sink and passing beyond it, nearly reaching a tea towel close by. Still, they watched. Te Kahurangi took her hand away from Alexia's and wiped it on her thigh.

Polly twisted the tap off. The flame leapt away down the plughole like an animated ghost.

'Shoo, shoo,' Polly said. She hustled them out into the lounge and rushed about, opening windows, while they all began to gasp.

'Bad,' she said. 'Bad water, bad air.' Alexia was feeling ill. Next to her, Isaiah bent over, clutching his stomach. 'What do they think I'm supposed to drink?' Polly said. 'How do they think I'm supposed to cook my kai? All my life, I've drunk from our stream. What am I supposed to do now?' She spoke to Alexia. 'Complain to the council with more of your big words? Fat lot of good that'll do.'

Alexia had thought she'd been useful with her words, her ability to speak the council's language. Now she saw it was one more thing that made her stand out. Te Kahurangi sat on Polly's couch as if it was her own. Alexia supposed it was her own, or would be one day, and the bush, and the land around it. There was a silence in which Alexia did not speak. She had been raised to respect her elders. Isaiah was quiet, taking deep breaths. Polly still waited for a response. Alexia felt herself blushing. She signalled Isaiah with her eyes, but he said nothing. But why was the woman choosing to pick a fight with her? She hadn't come and personally polluted Polly's water.

'Come on, Aunty, she's just trying to help,' Te Kahurangi said. Polly seemed to let it go.

Alexia hated Isaiah for a moment. He was so unaware sometimes. Had he even noticed her discomfort? But he still looked sick. He was bent over, huffing a little.

When Alexia had met Stephen's parents it was a cool affair: dinner at a nice restaurant, with formal table settings, the kind of place she didn't know how to behave in. Her family usually ate with their forks in one hand and a piece of bread in the other, picking at bones and fish. She hadn't learned Englesika table manners until she was quite old. Stephen's parents had inquired, politely, as to her origin. 'We used to have a cleaner who was Greek,' his mother had said. 'No,' Stephen's father corrected her, 'Rosa was Italian.' Stephen had raised his eyebrows at Alexia across the table. 'Don't worry about it, guys!' he'd said, loudly. 'Greek, Italian – it's just about the same thing, right?' His tone was so light that they'd all laughed, even Alexia.

Isaiah sat up with some effort. Alexia forgave him. How could you hate a person who had no idea what he was doing?

'I am too old now to fight,' Polly said. 'You must all do something, anything, before we have no air left to breathe.' A look passed between her and Isaiah. Alexia thought she might be imagining it, but then Isaiah nodded slightly, as though in agreement with a statement Alexia had not heard.

28

Polly had given him a sign, he was sure of it. She had stood in her kitchen, seeming to hold the flame with one hand, controlling it, with the lighter in the other. She had been weirdly impervious to the fumes. And then she had pretty much told him straight up that he had her permission to flout her rules. To act, whatever that act might be.

Isaiah began to jump the fence at a quiet place up the river and go onto the fracking site more often. The noise of the drilling went on late into the night now, causing a vibration in the ground. Orange scum filled the river. Polly's private veggie patch was drying up, and her water was still flammable. Everyone had started to view the produce from the gardens suspiciously. Between the marae and the mountain, many wells were now visible.

He would take a back-up memory card for the camera. He would take some fruit and some water, and tell himself he was being useful. When he got back he would hide the evidence, changing his muddied clothes before Polly could see. Even now felt he should maintain the impression that he was a good boy, like his father, and that he wouldn't endanger the pā by breaking the law.

He was washing yellow clay off his boots out the back of the kitchen when Rangi spoke.

'Bro,' Rangi said.

'How do you do that? Just appear?' Isaiah continued to rinse his boots. He'd heard a rumour about Rangi's guerrilla army training, about how they had taught him to move without sound. Rangi had also told Isaiah he'd been apprenticed to a kaumātua up north, tutored in the ways of the bush. Perhaps his stealth was a combination of both influences.

'Māori bush magic,' Rangi said. 'Some wicked mud you got there, eh. You make sure to get it all off before Polly sees.'

Isaiah assumed Rangi went out to the frack site himself at night, treading his own paths. He had seen more than one hole cut cleanly through one of Taylor's fences. He didn't think it was anything to do with the bush fairies.

'You missing your girl?' Rangi asked. 'What's going on there? You guys hit a little bumpy patch? Come on, tell your uncle.'

Isaiah was genuinely perplexed, and thought it best not to answer. Did Rangi mean Sam, who had – perhaps obviously – cooled off over the past few weeks? Or did he mean Alexia?

'I'll bet you five dollars you're too chicken to call her.'

Isaiah let out a huff of air and sat back on his heels. He considered how long Rangi would take to go away if he didn't answer. But his curiosity kicked in.

'Call who?'

'The Queen of England, who do you bloody think? Ms Acropolis, your long-lost love.'

Isaiah pursed his lips, and took a swipe at his boot.

'Rangi, we're not in primary school.'

'I bet you ten dollars.'

'It's not like that, anyway.'

'There's not much happening around here. Why don't you call her up, ask her if she wants you to come visit her in her tent?'

'What are you, the pā relationship counsellor?' Isaiah stopped scrubbing. He was thrown. He wasn't sure how he felt about her anyway. And he hadn't thought Rangi a particularly perceptive type.

'Oh, come off it, cuz. Everyone's been waiting to see what yous are gonna do.' Rangi smiled. 'Anyway, she's recently bereaved. All you need to do is just be sympathetic. She'll love you forever. Classic. In with a grin.'

'You're disgusting, Rangi,' Isaiah said.

Rangi waggled his eyebrows up and down. 'I bet you a twenty you won't make a move, bro,' he said. 'Don't push me to twenty-five. I can't afford it.'

'There's Sam to think about.' Isaiah had said it half to himself.

'Thought yous were "non-monogamous",' Rangi said, putting the quotation marks round the words with his hands. 'And I thought she had given you her blessing.'

Where was Rangi getting his intel? He'd never bought the slow country cousin act. Rangi rolled his eyes.

'For someone who's so popular with the ladies you haven't got a clue. Go on, put Sam out of her misery. I think you'll find she won't be surprised.' Isaiah did not answer. 'Do it in the name of honour, then,' Rangi said, 'if you won't do it for carnal reasons. You've been letting it drag on with Sam long enough. And remember what I said, eh? In with a grin.' He slouched off, leaving Isaiah to frown at his departing back.

29

Alexia was dreaming about a man tied to a track in front of an oncoming train. There were rescue teams trying to save him, but they were too far away. She saw the man with hideous clarity as the train approached. She half knew she was dreaming but could not pull herself into consciousness. She was running but her feet would not touch the ground, spinning instead in a circle just above the scraped earth, tracing wide, pointless revolutions. The plain was naked, all burnt reds and oranges. The only green spread in a pool around the man, as though he'd gathered the grass to himself. She could see the police and, further off, a fire truck, but even the authorities seemed helpless. She was closer to him than they were, and the train was bearing down on him.

It hit him, and she opened her eyes.

She crawled out of the warm fug of the tent, her eyes struggling to adjust to the brightness outside. There was the mountain, remarkable in its symmetry and unclouded today, super-real. Under its flank lay the bare fracking land, but from here all that was visible from where she stood was bush, and green farmland beyond that. She could understand why tourists came here. She tried not to think of the image left over from her dream, from the moment after the train had passed and all the rescue attempts had failed.

Aidan and Hannah were up already, cooking. Bryce came into the clearing.

'Something's happened. You have to help,' he said.

Was it to do with Polly's flammable water? Bryce turned and walked away without explanation. Aidan was not pleased. But they all followed him quickly down the path to the pā. Bryce moved fast on his long legs. The back of his denim shirt appeared and disappeared through the foliage. Where the path opened out into field Aidan took Hannah's hand and they began to run.

Now Alexia too heard the waiata. She couldn't understand the words, but the notes had one clear meaning. White falling sparks. There had been a death.

The voice called with such urgency that she began to run as well, blocking out the lights that interfered with her sight. As she arrived in front of the marae she looked for the crowd that would be at the entrance to the pā, but no one was there. The call was coming from down by the river. She started toward the bridge. Everyone was running that way, the children and the older people too. Matiu caught her up. There were tears streaming down his face. Rangi was there, running beside her. She could not see Isaiah. At the bridge the people were leaning out over the water. Some were weeping. Polly stood at the creek's bank, singing her sad song. Alexia was brought up short by the parapet of the bridge.

There was no body, no dead person. Instead, there were the bodies of the eels, varying in size and age, varying too in how much life they had left in them. Some were clearly dead but others writhed violently, moving away from the water with strange blunt movements. Some had burrowed their heads into the slimed banks. The largest were metres long and thicker than one of her thighs. Once she noticed the first one she saw them everywhere, some hunched dead along the bank she'd run past, others wrapped around the base of the bridge, so many, a litter of huge bodies.

Isaiah arrived, sweating, his shirt unbuttoned. His hands went to his camera. He seemed to have several. This one was heavy-looking. Then he was clicking, clicking, moving among the bodies. She stayed, affixed to the bridge by Polly's waiata. She tried to block it out but could not.

A child's voice rose above the song. Under the bridge were Tama, Maitai and Ana.

'Mako,' Ana said. Alexia saw that she had her eel by the head and was pulling at him, as though if she got him out of the water he would live. His mouth was opening in what appeared to be pain. Ana offered him a sock filled with bait, but he didn't move. She took the food from the sock and threw it in front of him on the ground, but he did not shift towards it. Tama tried to pull her away. The girl wouldn't go. She sat down, cradled the eel's large head in her arms and began to cry. Then she hit him. Still, he did not move. She hit him again, a small, furious blow. Now Tama did manage to pull her away.

'He's my eel!' she said. She looked frantically up at the adults. 'Why don't you do something?' she screamed. 'I hate you!' She fixed her eyes on Alexia, as though she was responsible. 'He's my eel, and now he's dead!'

They started to bury the bodies. Alexia had never touched an eel before. She worked with Rangi first, then Matiu, then, finally, Isaiah. The eel skin was wet and soft, but rough if you stroked it in the other direction. Some of them seemed dead but when she touched them twitched to life. She couldn't tell from their milky blue eyes which ones had gone yet. One she and Rangi carried was still all the way to the burial pit and then suddenly squirmed. He took a stone and beat its head. She was sure she heard him sob as he was doing it. Some of the eels who had been dead for longer were beginning to smell. Alexia's arms were covered in the thin orange slim that coated them. Her hands began to sting and itch. The eels were surprisingly heavy, and the work made her sweat. The people grew thirsty and tired, but it occurred to no one to stop.

Ana sat at the river's edge and wept. She cried for a while like a child, and then she began to weep formally, a repeating, wailing cry. Alexia worked around her in the mud, seeing the child rock back and forth on her heels. She tried as hard as she could to block it out but Ana's song was too insistent: the white sparks of grief rose and fell until Alexia was nearly overwhelmed. Eventually Ana's mother, Lizzie, took her away.

When it came time to take Old Mako, Alexia was working with Isaiah. Alexia and Isaiah hauled together at the eel, who was larger than the rest. Mako was bleeding from the mouth and his blood dripped onto her hand. Isaiah took the tail end. They had not spoken. The labour caused her face to flush red, and they were both covered in earth from the pit. She had a stupid moment of vanity. Here she was, worrying about her face, her hair, when Ana was grief-stricken, when all the adults were crying. Alexia worked her muscles harder, and put on a burst of speed, but then she tripped and fell, dropping Old Mako's body. The eel fell with a slick thud.

On her knees on the earth she saw as if from a distance that she had cut them on the stones. Now she was bleeding. She felt lightheaded. There was a touch on her back. Mako's head beside her suddenly writhed, the jaw opening and shutting, and then he was still again. Alexia gagged, once, twice, but nothing came out.

'Take a deep breath,' Isaiah said, quietly. The other workers passed around them as if they weren't there.

'A breath,' Isaiah said. Alexia listened to him, and took one. She was so nauseous that at first she didn't notice his arm around her waist until he had pulled her up. But when he took his arm away, she wanted him to put it back.

That night they all agreed something must be done. Sam said they should go ahead with that concert, to raise funds. This time, Alexia agreed to play.

30

Polly was eating in a disgruntled way, and muttering about her water, as she had begun to do regularly. It was the night before the fundraising concert. Isaiah took the seat next to Alexia.

'The kai moana's good,' Rangi said to her. 'You should have some more. You could do with some more fat on your bones.'

'It's not up to you to decide whether I need to be fatter or not,' Alexia said.

'Frosty,' Rangi said, but in a pleased way. Alexia glanced at Isaiah. She wasn't blushing, not quite, but he still felt implicated, as though it was he who had made the inappropriate comment. They were eating raw fish, except for the cooked mussels, which Isaiah liked. Hannah picked at her meal. Aidan was staring at the seafood heaped on his plate with an uncharacteristic torpor. But still they all ate, as though eating was some proof of their political commitment. Matiu and Bryce had collected the kai themselves at the coast just down the road.

'I like the food, anyway,' Alexia said. 'My family worked in fish shops when I was growing up. You don't have to convince me.' Then she ducked her head. She often did that, he'd noticed: volunteered some personal information and then fell silent.

'More than I could say for some of them,' Rangi said. Melissa, Sam and Kate – the vegans – were eating in the lounge. 'The way some people been eating salad round here the gardens won't hold up much longer. It's just not sustainable.'

'And whose fault is that?' Matiu said. 'Production's down on last year.'

174

Everyone over at Bryce's table laughed. He was entertaining them. He had come in wet, quite the hero, carrying the crate of seafood, his shirt half-stripped off.

'It's the fracking waste,' Rangi said.

'Are the gardens really dying?' Isaiah asked.

'It's only a matter of time. The land's being poisoned from underneath. I went up there this morning. Here, smell my clothes.' He held his sleeve out to Isaiah and Alexia, who both sniffed at it. It was there, the smell he had encountered at the frack site, then in Polly's kitchen, a sulphuric scent of rotting things. Alexia met his eyes.

'Better do good at the fundraiser tomorrow, hey?' Matiu said. 'Or we'll have to cart you and all you white fellas back to the city.' He didn't smile.

31

The next day Alexia woke with nausea and a pounding head. She'd gone to sleep late, unable to settle, considering the songs she would play on stage. She didn't have the beautiful amp Stephen had bought her the year before. She didn't have her acoustic guitar with the electric pickup. She had only the old acoustic that she'd found in the communal hall. Her head emitted waves of pain, and her stomach was clenched tight. She stumbled out of the tent. Hannah was sitting by the fire. She was curled into herself. From the bush behind them came a heaving sound. Alexia's stomach pitched and fell, a craft in a violent storm.

'You too, then,' Hannah said.

Alexia crawled into the bush, in the opposite direction from Aidan's groans.

Her heaving went on and on. At last it was over. There were the karaka leaves and there was the rich soil. But everything seemed off. Her lights were everywhere, but there was no accompanying music. They flashed in incomprehensible patterns. There was a buzz in her ears like static and the tips of her fingers were numb. The foliage was water. The lights came on, all colours, sickeningly random. Her bare feet did not shift or change, but the dirt underneath them had an unmistakable sentience. The lights themselves had aura, circles encompassing circles in fractaline iterations. She tried to block it out, but it didn't work.

When she got to the wharenui she found that Rangi was

sick, and that Matiu was still in bed, and Te Kahurangi had not yet emerged from Polly's house. Polly was at the kitchen table peeling potatoes, seemingly fine, though she admitted to having had a little trouble with her stomach. She studied Alexia, as if measuring the extent of her weakness. Alexia straightened up. Aidan and Hannah dragged themselves in to see what could be done. There was an air of muted panic. Everyone tried to communicate as if through a fog. The guests would begin arriving soon. The only activists who were well were Sam and Melissa and Kate, and Bryce's wife and her partner. All the bloody vegans. Melissa was counting tickets into numbered batches. Sam brushed past her with an air of righteousness. Bryce came in with a lockbox and put it on the table.

'Aunty,' he said to Polly in greeting. Polly patted Bryce on the cheek. Isaiah burst through the door with a certain drama. He seemed very unwell. His eyes seemed to cross as he stood there. He was paler than she'd ever seen him, his olive skin sallow.

'Alexia,' he asked. 'How do you feel?'

Alexia did not wish to be the centre of attention. Aidan stood up, then sat down again, then stood up and hovered near the other door.

'I feel ... like you do, I think,' she said. Isaiah grabbed at the door frame. In his other hand he held a piece of paper.

'No, I mean, how do you all feel, specifically?' he asked.

'Sick, man,' Aidan said. 'Sick as a dog's bollocks, if a dog's bollocks could get sick.'

'Wait, do you have ... numbness and tingling around the mouth ... dizziness, double vision ...' Isaiah was reading from the page in his hand. Alexia drew close to him. The sheet was titled 'Toxic Shellfish Poisoning: Coastal Safety Warning'. Isaiah went on. 'Potential respiratory issues, vomiting, diarrhoea ... Does this sound familiar to any of you?' His eyes were jerking strangely.

'I have numbness –' Alexia said, '– in my fingers.' Their

voices came to her as if through water. She always knew she should be vegan. It would be easy. She would feel morally upright all the time. She wouldn't have to worry about food poisoning.

Rangi came in. 'The kai moana,' he said. 'I don't think it was just off, either.'

Isaiah brandished the paper at him. 'It's the shellfish,' he said. 'It's toxic.'

'I've been bloody seeing aura, mate,' Aidan said. He laughed, a little hysterically. 'Thought it was some kind of flashback.'

'It must be PSP,' Bryce said. 'Paralytic shellfish poisoning. We should have known.'

'You've heard of this?' Isaiah asked.

'Don't worry, it will pass,' Bryce said airily. 'It usually lessens within hours. It's happened at other sites, overseas. Of course, it has to be the fracking. There were the eels, and the gardens. It stands to reason the kai moana isn't safe either. I don't know what we were thinking.' To Alexia he seemed surrounded by an ethereal ring of lights, one slender hand reaching out to console Polly. 'Your kai moana is not safe for the people,' he said. 'The levels of toxicity in the river are too high.'

'How long will this last?' Polly asked. 'When will we be able to eat from the coast again?'

No one answered her.

'This is the only time,' Aidan said, and doubled over suddenly. He raised a finger and his upper body with a great expenditure of will. 'The only time, bar Bangkok, I'll grant you, that when I made it to the shitter I didn't know which end to point at it first. But at least in Bangkok I'd had some fun beforehand. This is just the total fucking shites.'

32

Isaiah's legs were wobbly and his head ached. He kept seeing things flash and shift at the edges of his eyes, turning, and finding nothing there. It was like the time he took mushrooms. The weird charged colours were there, and the tension in his body, and the feeling he had been poisoned.

They had decided to go ahead with the fundraiser, though the main act would not play. Aidan and Hannah had crept back to their tent, defeated. Even Polly had made a small concession to illness and was resting with her feet up on a couch. It was like seeing a piece of wood relax. She was so small, lying there and sipping at her water, that Isaiah had felt an inadvertent surge of affection. The only people left standing, the vegans and vegetarians, were all useful organisers, but none of them could play. The only one who could perform and who was still able to walk was Alexia.

Isaiah went into the little room behind the stage.

'How many of them are there out there?' she asked. Maitai was at her side, stroking her arm. Isaiah had a moment of extreme covetousness. There was her arm, with its silver bangle on the tan wrist: Maitai's hand on it. It was just an arm, he told himself. And attraction was just that, attraction. It didn't have to mean anything.

He had thrown up many times, and he was supposed to be the MC.

'I'd say about a hundred,' he said. He was being conservative: the hall could hold two hundred, and was now almost full.

They had made big prints of his photos, and Melissa had written accompanying blurbs. Now the punters were circulating, unable to avoid his pictures. At the very least he was showing the locals what was going on.

'I can't do it. I don't know Hannah and Aidan's set. I can't play it by myself. There's a huge amount of time to fill in. I don't know what you expect me to do. I'm too sick,' she said. Though she was wearing a pretty dress, a frothy thing in blue and green, she smelt ill. Why did she even have such a thing with her? But then, she usually appeared more formal than the others. He probably smelt the same.

Maitai glared at him. 'You don't have to get up there,' he told Isaiah.

'Actually, I do,' Isaiah said. Fine-boned arms and pretty dress or not, Alexia was being a princess. Did she think she was the only one having a hard time? But she was only meant to be the back-up, after all, and now she was their main act. People had paid for this. He relented. 'You'll be fine, Alexia. I'll take up as much time as I can. Rangi said he'll play something as well, and Matiu. But you're the headliner.'

'I think I have to throw up.'

'Me too. But I'm still going to get up onstage.' He left her with Maitai.

In the bathroom, as he splashed water on his face, he realised he wasn't sure where his confidence in her was coming from. Sam thought he was a fool when it came to Alexia. He gathered as much from her glances. She could imply a particular judgement with what he thought of as one of her 'non-looks'. Sam thought Alexia was conservative, limited, deeply traditional, selfish and possibly an informant. Isaiah still doubted this last suspicion. Surely an undercover cop would know better than to turn up to an activist hui in office clothes and fancy shoes? A cop would have formulated a better disguise.

Sam was sorting money at the door. Even though Isaiah felt wretched he still had a trace of excitement. There were farmers and townies and local iwi, kids and older people too. Everyone had called in favours and used their connections. Sam was folding bills in a pleased way. She and Melissa and Kate bustled around, competently, fixing up piles of pamphlets. Sam had on a headscarf and long, dangling earrings. She was in her element.

'You look terrible!' she said.

'Sam, will you do the kōrero? I don't know if I can.'

Sam laid a cool hand on his forehead. He experienced a slight jolt of excitement. It was just Sam, of course, but he was all pent up and all stressed out. The sickness had done odd things to his body.

'No,' she said. 'I think you should do it. You're the one that knows how the powerpoint runs.' She smiled her no-nonsense smile. 'You'll get through it! I have complete faith in you. You know who I'm not so sure about though? Her over there.' She nodded towards Alexia, who had hovered near the stage, seen the crowd and was retreating again to the back room. 'The only time I've heard her sing was at the pōwhiri. Sure, she has a nice voice, but she was lacking in soul, wouldn't you say?' Sam shrugged. 'It's just, we've promised these people entertainment. I guess it's just a matter of taste.' If Sam ever sniffed, she would have sniffed now.

'The last thing I expected of you, sweetheart,' he said, 'was for you to turn into an aesthetic snob.' Sam only smiled.

There was a last-minute glitch with a microphone, but Matiu fixed it. Then it was time. People rustled and giggled and fell silent as the lights were turned down. Isaiah stood behind the lectern with his mouth dry and his hands clasped together. He told himself he was giving a speech at school. He started the display. A shot of the mountain. Here was the difference: it was not school, not another meeting, not a practice run. This was his own mountain, under threat.

He started his mihi, which he had finally perfected. The

shots kaleidoscoped through the damage he'd found at the frack site. His voice cracked but he was used to public speaking and spoke through it, knowing that soon he would be lost in the thread, able to tell the story.

He described the effects of the fracking. He described the risks. He touched briefly on the recent reports, on the science. But he knew what they were interested in were the sensational aspects: the dead birds, the poisoned soil, the flaming water. He showed a brief clip of it. The audience moved and murmured.

When it was over Isaiah felt a brief satisfaction and then, coming down from the stage, crushing exhaustion. But no one came on after him. He went up a couple of steps and signalled wildly to Sam. Rangi and Matiu got up uncertainly from where they sat at the front of the hall. Then Maitai emerged from a side door, dragging Alexia by the hand. Her cheeks were red, and her hair was a huge dark mess, moving and alive. Isaiah realised he was standing half on the stage, half off, staring at her. He must be sicker than he thought. He got down. Maitai took the microphone. He placed Alexia in a chair put there for the purpose and she picked up the old guitar.

Maitai launched into a speech. He smiled out over the crowd and showed the gap in his teeth. At the back, Mary and some other aunties beamed. His mother Lizzie waved. Polly sat as she always sat, bolt upright, unsmiling.

'And thank you all for coming to see our show,' Maitai said, finally. 'And thank you for helping to save the pā from the frackers. And this is Alexia. She will play some of her songs.' He climbed down, very proud of himself.

Alexia did not speak. The audience rustled. The hall was stuffy and thick with used air, but there were no fans, and it was the middle of summer. Still, she did not open her mouth. Her long brown fingers lay lax on the guitar strings. Isaiah began to panic. More rustling. Someone called out something rude from near the back.

'I'm going to,' Alexia said, looking as if she might pass out.

'Microphone!' someone called out. Sam turned the volume up.

'I'm going to play,' Alexia said. Everyone waited to hear her say what she would play, or to tell a pleasing anecdote. But she just started to strum. The song was bland and formulaic: a call to arms, a call to save the environment and end the fracking. Even in his strange, almost euphoric state of illness he could hear that her voice fell flat. It was Aidan's song, and without his accent and Hannah's vocals there was nothing to it. Alexia finished and did not play on. The audience did not applaud. She was focused on the microphone. She was not such a good musician after all, he thought, but still, so very photogenic. He had the urge to leap up and explain to everyone that she was sick, that she had not had time to practise, that none of this was her fault. He wanted to take photos. The silence lengthened.

Suddenly she broke into an unfamiliar rhythm. The sound was traditional, Middle Eastern, maybe? It took him a few moments before he decided that of course it must be Greek. But it wasn't the cheerful canned Greek music of kebab shops. It was inexplicably modern, the base tempo taking on extra, off-kilter beats, the guitar hit by the flat of her hand setting up a low hum that underlay the beat. Rangi raised his eyebrows. It was dancing music, for all its experimental undertones. Sick as Isaiah was, he felt like dancing.

She started to sing. It was strange music to hear at a fund-raising concert in the middle of rural New Zealand. As she went on singing, odd things happened to her face. She stretched her mouth into awkward shapes to accommodate the words, which switched from Greek to English and back again. At times it seemed to sound classical. It was a song about a lion and a rabbit, some revised nursery rhyme. She increased the tempo. She scrunched and twisted her face. The music was poppy and weird and off key. It was not quite regular enough to be satisfying. Her face was entirely mobile; relaxed one second, contorted the next. She was no longer embarrassed. She increased the tempo again, adding more layers under the notes, with here and there an oddly ringing slide: things he knew were not a part of the old music but her own elaborations upon it. She increased the speed again, playing double-time. He remembered some footage he'd seen somewhere of Greek dancers, their hands linked with handkerchiefs, moving around the room in a circle. The music's tempo would start slow, then double, treble, till the dancers were running and leaping and it became a contest to see who could keep dancing.

'Opa! Opa!' Alexia yelled into the gaps between the notes. Raised hands, white shirts, black pants, kicking legs, broken plates. She played faster. She sang, face wrapped around the words – a marvel of effort. Her cheeks were glowing. She watched the ceiling. She played so fast now that Matiu and Rangi, who'd been stamping on the floor, stood up. Maitai and the kids were dancing. Isaiah stood up. Alexia was wailing now. The notes rose and rose and, suddenly, stopped. Her face was blank and calm.

'Got any more like that one, sis?' Rangi called up onto the stage.

She smiled, and played another. Isaiah stood for the whole performance.

Afterwards, when Rangi and Matiu were safely installed on the stage, playing more reassuring reggae tunes, Isaiah passed Kate and Melissa whispering near the door.

Kate shrugged. 'If you're into that sort of thing,' she said. 'Don't know if the locals liked it.'

Isaiah felt the grin slip off his face. He was foolish, foolish. He must not be thinking straight. He turned to Melissa.

'It was all right,' Melissa said. 'I guess.' He walked away, chastened. Of course, he'd been in the front row, watching only Maitai, Matiu and Rangi's response. Now that he thought of it, no one else had stood up. He had no reliable impression of how she had been received.

*

Isaiah brought a bottle of water into the side room. Alexia was slouching on the couch with the guitar. He offered her the bottle and sat down. Her eyes were unhealthily bright.

'You were …' he said, but she leaned close to him suddenly, and tucked her head under his chin, so she was almost under his arm.

'Shut up,' she said. 'Just shut up about it.'

'You …' he said.

'I was perfect,' she said, into his armpit. 'Apart from the start, of course.' Her hair tickled his nose. She pushed her head into him roughly. 'Entirely unsuitable, I know, for an environmental fundraiser. But what else could I do? It's all I really know how to play.'

'I seriously doubt that,' Isaiah said. She seemed on the edge of sleep one moment and wired the next.

'You don't need to flatter me.'

'Are you still seeing aura?' he asked. 'On stage it was like you had sparks coming off you.'

'Those little flashing lights? They were real,' she said. She laughed as if at a private joke, and put her hand on his leg. 'I had a dream about you. We were riding in a car very fast. It had no steering wheel and we were in the back seat: it was like it was driving itself.' If he responded to her advances now, was he taking advantage? She moved her hand up his leg. Was he sicker than her? If he was, did that mean she was taking advantage of him?

'I didn't know you played classical guitar,' he said.

'One of my closely guarded secrets.'

His judgement might be impaired, but he didn't want her to move her hand. 'I didn't know a new interpretation of Greek folk music could bring a small-town audience to its feet.'

'Only the front row,' she said. This might be regrettable later, he thought, and put the thought out of his mind. 'The car in my dream crashed,' she said. 'Can I put my arms around you?'

'I don't see why not,' he said, trying for lightness. She met his eye, and then anything he was trying to do or not do fell away. They sat on the scratchy couch, with the sound of Rangi's voice rising to the *chinka chinka chink* in the hall outside. She placed one arm, very slowly, around his shoulders and brought her cheek in close to his. He brought his opposite hand round and placed it on her wrist. He wanted in a deep part of himself to run out of the room. They sat like that for a minute or so.

'Oh well,' she said. 'It was a good thought, anyway.' She got up and went towards the door.

But this was too much. He got up too and grabbed at her. His lips met hers, but only briefly, like on the first day they met. His glasses crashed into her nose. She righted them.

'I didn't want to rush,' he said.

'I'm a straight-up kind of a person.'

'It's just that I don't know what.'

'I'm an all or nothing type. I'm just saying it now. I'm just saying.'

Alexia led him away down the corridor and into the night. He made sure they went out the back way, away from Sam and the departing guests.

Isaiah kept reaching out as he followed her into the bush to touch her back, her shoulders, her hair. She did not speak. Someone smashed a bottle in the car park, and someone else closed a door. Isaiah jumped, a jump all out of proportion to the noise. He worried again that he was not at all well. The moon was shadowed and it was very dark. It struck him that if he was to do anything, any nefarious anti-fracking activity, that tonight would be a good night. All the people at the fundraiser would be his alibi. No one would suspect Alexia of anything, because everyone thought she was so uptight.

They worked their way under some larger trees. The ground was damp, and he couldn't see the sky.

They were far from any comfortable place. But this person was Alexia.

'I can't believe you told me about that dream.'

'I can't believe you let me get up there, when I'm so sick. I should be in bed.'

'We should be in bed.' Isaiah felt himself smile. 'Are we too old for these sorts of encounters? Please don't judge me for this.'

'Promise that you'll love me in the morning,' Alexia said jokingly, but her eyes might have been full of tears. He wondered if he should stop, but she bent her head to his.

There were some moments of urgency. If it wasn't so warm they wouldn't have been able to do this. Still the ground was cool, even in the summer. Eventually Isaiah found his wallet and, inside it, the bright packet. Soon he was with her. Then she was over him, he underneath. There was a twig in her hair and it was dim so he had to imagine her face. He held her down on his hips. She was rough. He thought that he was meant to like it, the roughness, but he didn't. He stroked her face. There was a moment of calm where he held her to him preciously, his desire curiously stalled.

There were contours to be discovered and memorised. She leaned down and he held her still, she slightly unwilling, as he kissed her. But as soon as he moved again she started to butt against him; he couldn't match her rhythm. He tried to cup her in his hands but they were still too clothed. It was dark and impersonal. She moved and moved and made sounds. He put his hands where she wanted. He lay on his back, the stones driving into his shoulder blades. He found it all too hard to make real and, when she made the many noises and climbed up into them and out the other side, brushing her fingers down his still clothed chest, he found it even harder to believe.

She lay next to him.

'I'm sorry,' she said. 'Do you want me to …?'

'No,' he said. 'Don't worry.'

He lay on his back, happy to be rid of her, and sad that he was happy. He felt a sense of guilt, not because of Sam, but because he had built Alexia up in his mind, and when it happened he had not fully been here. He had remained closed.

He'd have to explain that it couldn't happen again.

'That was terrible, wasn't it?' she said.

'Did you really …?'

'I don't know what's wrong with me. It's purely physical. A lot of women would hate me for it, of course.' She laughed.

'Alexia,' he said. He was surprised to feel her hand on him. The packet lay discarded off to one side.

'Well,' she said. 'It's not as if you …'

'No,' he said. 'It would be highly unlikely.' He wanted to kiss her again, but then he thought of her jolting movements. It quelled his urge.

They rearranged their clothes, awkwardly, and started back towards the hall. Behind them the great swathe of bush lay between them and the fracking site. A place of towers, exploding earth.

'Sorry,' she said, suddenly. 'I'm all over the place at the moment.'

'Me too. I still feel sick.'

'No, it's my grandfather. I don't know how to talk about it. I keep going back there, in my mind. I'll be sitting in a meeting and then I'll be back in my grandfather's house. It's the nature of absence, I guess. But I almost feel like it's an addiction. I see him: I see all of them. I can't give it up.'

He waited for a moment, wondering if he should hug her. He didn't.

'I understand, I think,' he said, cautiously. 'Some people leave absences we don't know how to fill. It's a part of life, I guess. It's natural, right?'

'You don't understand at all.' In the dark her eyes were tearful or furious; he couldn't tell.

'I've never had the chance to understand. But I have an absence in my life, one that I can't fill.' This was reasonable, he thought, considering.

'Oh, of course.' She seemed suddenly appalled at herself. 'I'm sorry. I didn't mean to be mad. You just seem so rational all the time, so cool. Even about all of this …' She waved her hand towards the fracking site. 'Injustice. You seem so calm.'

'Believe me, I'm not.' How could he tell her that he recognised the thing in her that was defensive and cruel? In Alexia, it was close to the surface and fun to poke at. But it was also dangerous.

'Really?' There was something mocking in her voice underneath the humour. 'Really, Isaiah?' He wanted to take her back into the bush, to take her further in than she had ever been, and show her. He put his hand on her arm.

Afterwards, as they walked back together, she said something he didn't quite catch.

'What's that?'

'*Music*, I said. Music.'

'What about it?'

'I can see it.'

She explained. He wasn't sure what it was that she was offering; some tale about a different way of seeing. She gave it to him like a gift, one he wasn't sure how to take. For a while she explained about the light show that accompanied her musical notes. It had happened when she was a teenager, she said.

Isaiah felt like he needed to reciprocate. He told her about his mother, her endless stories about his father and how he had grown up out of touch with the marae. But it seemed as though she'd expended the last of her energy out there in the bush.

At the hall they parted like casual acquaintances. How tired she looked! How rough she'd been, rude and abrupt. How surprised he was by that. She waved at him as she went away quietly, hunching over, into the crowded hall.

33

When she played the fundraiser, Alexia had thought only of Papou, his gnarled fishmonger's hands, his eyebrows moving expressively on his face. She'd noticed Isaiah noticing her, of course. She'd seen his foolish expression. His was the only face that distinguished itself amidst the blur of the other faces in the audience.

After what happened in the bush her knees felt raw and bruised. She trailed away from him and found herself, still half wanting to throw up, in the bathroom, in front of the mirror. She tried to flatten her hair with her palms. There was a twig in it, which she hastily pulled out.

It had been ridiculous and teenage. It had been absurd, what they had done together – much like Alexia herself. There was make-up smudged around her eyes. She closed her eyes and hummed. When she opened them, there they were: the small, darting lights against the dull concrete of the bathroom wall. She hummed gently, the notes gradually ascending, and the lights circled her face and lent her a halo of sparks. It was a trick she'd learned to make herself feel better.

She hummed hard. The small lights danced. But her face, with its long Greek nose, its straight eyebrows, was still there behind them.

34

Some people left the pā after the concert. There was a general feeling of malaise. They had made money, though, just enough for those remaining to stay.

Now Polly had dispatched Alexia and Isaiah to get the lockbox from Bryce's camp. Since the night of the fundraiser they had not spoken of anything significant. That night hung between them, unexplored. Perhaps for the better. Perhaps that was it, and it was finished, and he would have to do nothing further. Why would he want to be with someone who made him feel so uneasy? Perhaps it had just been sexual tension, combined with Isaiah's frustration about the campaign. Perhaps all they had needed was this single dramatic act, this violent act, and now it would all go away.

Sam had to be told, of course. She had taken the news with her characteristic stoicism. She complained, though, that she hadn't been informed prior to the act. She had been calm and professional, and left Isaiah with a feeling of relief. The thing that surprised him the most was her lack of surprise.

They didn't speak on the way to where Bryce was camped. When they arrived Bryce's wife and her girlfriend were sunbathing topless in the clearing, though it wasn't warm. Steph and the girlfriend came over. She was a deep, even orange. A scarf was draped around her neck, concealing one nipple. It only emphasised her nakedness.

'We're here for the lockbox,' Alexia said.

'Gidday to you too,' the girlfriend said. 'Oh come on. Seems like everyone's so tense these days.' There were prayer flags hung from the trees with tino rangatiratanga patches on them. In a way this typified Bryce's approach. Two bikes lay in disrepair by their campfire. Bryce's wife had been tinkering with them. Naked bike repair. Isaiah was impressed.

'You two didn't get sick?' he asked.

'I'm vegetarian,' the wife said.

'I'm vegan,' said her girlfriend.

'Where would the lockbox be?' Isaiah asked. The woman led them to Bryce's van: a blue, older-style camper with a white awning. Inside it was dark. The walls were lined with reclaimed wood and someone had installed a structure around the bed, a carved thing made out of driftwood pieces. The bed was unmade and the pillows were thrown about. He wondered if they all slept together here. The lockbox was on the bedside table. Underneath it were Bryce's books: *The Art of War*, *The Complete Karma Sutra*, *Political Persuasion*. If Bryce was an informant, his disguise was thorough. Alexia sat on the bed, bouncing slightly. On the roof was a cloth mandala, and light came from the stained-glass window behind the bed.

'This is my family's worst nightmare,' she said.

'Would you live in something like this?' Isaiah asked.

'Depends on who it was with,' she said.

There was a shelf on the wall. It held a pressed leaf, a note-book and a package of papers.

'I don't know,' Alexia said. 'The other night. I don't know what …' She put her head into her hands.

'But you were great!' he said. 'I mean, you played great.' He realised too late she might not have been discussing her musical performance.

'I'm meant to be a lawyer,' she said.

'Are they mutually exclusive things, being a musician and being a lawyer?' He was still investigating the shelf.

'It seems like that sometimes. I'm meant to be studying for my qualifying exam. At this rate, I'm not going to pass.'

He grabbed at the package of papers and opened it before she could say anything. Then he sat beside her on the bed.

'"If you do not cease and desist our group will be forced to take violent action,"'Alexia read aloud. '"Following your lack of response to our applications we will take matters into our own hands."'

'These letters are addressed to the council,' Isaiah said. He leafed through the pile. 'And the newspapers. Look at this. He's used capitals for the whole letter here. It's like a threat. It's insane!'

'Surely he wouldn't have sent these?' Alexia said. 'How could he have thought this was remotely acceptable without asking everyone?'

'I'm pretty sure he doesn't care about what the group thinks,' Isaiah said.

'You're going to take them?' Alexia asked. He was shoving the papers into his jacket. She reached her hand after them and then took it away again. 'Leave them. Or he'll know that we know.'

Isaiah shook his head. 'Come on,' he said, and grabbed the lockbox.

'Find what you were looking for?' Bryce's wife asked.

'Got everything we needed,' he yelled brightly. 'Cheers!'

On the way back, Alexia did not speak. She seemed distracted. He wondered if it was her synaesthesia. He had googled it, of course – what a world she must live in – but he was reluctant to ask her about it.

35

Hannah had gone to help with breakfast. From where Alexia and Aidan sat in their camp, they could see a fracking tower. Until now they'd been shielded from the reality of it by the bush. The fracking went on far into the night, distant rumbles shaking the ground. Alexia wasn't sleeping well. She was finding meetings tiresome again. There had once been a strategy; but now it seemed the only strategy was a kind of flailing outwards, a contacting of uninterested parties in the hope that they might be heard.

Alexia's new problem was the sparks and lights. They had begun to come when there was no music present. She saw them all the time: in meetings, over people's heads when they were talking. Playing over the edge of the bush, at dusk. She spoke of it to no one. Each time, she strained her ears, but there were no sounds accompanying the lights, or maybe a few tiny notes, seemingly coming from far away.

When they'd arrived here in spring the grass was still lush and green, but now all the colours were steely, as if the cool air had drained them of warmth. The nights had grown longer. Summer had been hot and full of frustration, the long, dry days burning into evenings full of guitar notes. It was hard to feel sensual in autumn. She just wanted to stay warm.

Alexia looked at the thing piercing the sky. There were two types of well. Some were smooth flues of white concrete and others were constructed, like this one, of interlaced steel. They would drill an experimental well, and if gas was released when they pumped frack fluid into the earth, they would reinforce the structure. As the fluid spread out horizontally, discovering fissures in the rock, there were attempts to channel whatever came out of the earth up into the well. She didn't see how they could expect to control everything that was released.

'That thing,' Aidan said. 'It's like the machines have come to conquer us. The Tripods and the Daleks. Except that one's on fire.' At the tower's top was a plume of flame, which burned and ceased irregularly. The tower was built on one of the many small maunga between the pā and the mountain. The maunga were associated with various spirits, Te Kahurangi had told her.

The fire against the sky made Alexia wish for one of Isaiah's cameras. She felt a flicker of what he must feel: a drive to have it all recorded, to have it visually understood.

'Exterminate,' Alexia said. 'Exterminate.' Her impersonation of Daleks was fairly rusty. 'What are we on now, our fourteenth appeal? Or is it the fifteenth? What will they have left at the pā, if we lose?'

'There isn't any recourse to justice left for them,' Aidan said. 'What will they have when we all bugger off home? Poisoned water, a big file of rejection letters from the council, and a gorgeous new view.'

'Bugger off home?' Alexia said. But of course, there had been the fundraiser and all their hopeful articles, and nothing had come of them all. They'd written to the papers and the radio and the TV news in vain. Now it was down to tedious correspondence between the council and the pā: *Your application could not be considered at the council meeting because it did not have the required number of signatories. As you are writing on behalf of a trust, all signatories must be present for your appeal to be considered. Your application was tabled this week due to other issues which took priority. Please accept our sincerest apologies. Your application has been declined.*

It was left up to Alexia to field the letters. It was a lesson to her. Schooled as she was in the processes of the law, she expected things to take a long time and to be frustrating, but she had not expected the governing bodies and the media to be quite so elusive, or to answer applications with such outright dismissals. She had never acted on behalf of a rural community before. What would she do herself, if all of this didn't work out?

'Are you buggering off, Aidan?'

'You mean, have I given up?' Aidan took a sip of coffee and glared at the well. 'I haven't given up.'

'So what are you meant to do in a campaign like this, if it all fails?'

'Come with me,' he said.

The stash was hidden not far from where they were camped. There were a lot of flares stored in a plastic container, under the cover of leaves, in a deep hole. Aidan brushed his boot over the ground to the left and right of the container, and she saw more lids. He opened one.

'Skyrockets!' she said. 'I haven't seen those since I was a kid.'

'Would you shut up!' Aidan said. 'Jesus, Mary and Joseph. If you are an undercover agent you're not a very convincing one. And not a very clever activist, neither.'

'Did you think I was an undercover agent?'

'Well,' Aidan said. 'Of course not. But Sam now, she was certain.' He lowered his voice. 'You didn't bring your phone?' She still found his caution hard to take seriously, but she handed her phone to him and he slid the battery off the back.

'Why rockets?' she asked.

'It's a one-step process to turn them into explosives,' Aidan said. 'Nothing major, just something that would cause damage to their equipment.' Hannah must know about the stash. Did Isaiah? Did Polly? Te Kahurangi, surely, would have jumped on the militant nature of all this with delight.

'I hope you're not going to hurt anyone,' she said.

'Little Miss Goody Two Shoes, are we now? Didn't seem like you were so peaceful when you were beating that cop with Polly's staff.'

'I was provoked,' she said. She still wasn't sure how she felt about it. She was embarrassed she'd acted that way, sorry she had caused harm. But she had felt, also, the beginnings of another feeling. She knew it had been stupid, but she was a little impressed with herself.

'Well,' said Aidan, spreading his arms wide. 'So was I.' He scraped his heel over more patches of dirt, and more lids emerged. Ammonium nitrate, gelignite, cans of petrol.

'What's that for?' She pointed to the fertiliser.

'That's more complicated than the rockets. It's a two-step process to turn it into something useful. And this,' he said, pointing to the gelignite. 'We're lucky enough to have a healthy mining industry just up the road. It's not hard to get hold of this if you know someone who works at a quarry.'

Alexia supposed this answer had always been here, waiting for her. He was right: all their attempts at peaceful negotiation had failed. All their lobbying and letters, all of her measured words. Aidan was in his element, riffling through the boxes, explaining items like a child with a train set. She found it hard to connect his excitement with the things that were happening in her head: screams, a siren, people running, maybe Syrian, maybe Palestinian, a camera wobbling as the cameraman staggered back, bodies half covered with sheets, women screaming in the midst of rubble and dust.

'You're not even listening!' Aidan said. 'We'll use these things responsibly, of course. It wouldn't be without a precedent, if that makes you feel any better. Did you not know about the anti-apartheid militants in the eighties? It wasn't so unfashionable to stand up and fight back then. You remember the tour?'

She was sitting on the ground, her head close to her knees. 'Of course,' she said.

'The leaders of that movement were trained in guerrilla warfare. All those people, they're academics now, politicians. You were probably taught by some of them. Haven't you seen the footage?' She had. 'Those front lines were briefed and organised. They weren't sitting ducks like us.'

'But Aidan,' she said. 'No one's attacking us.'

Aidan's face changed. The suddenness of it scared her, as did the closeness of the copse, with all its open boxes like so many plastic coffins. 'I stand in solidarity with the indigenous people of this place,' he said, 'who have been robbed and oppressed, and who are now being poisoned. I thought you did too.' She felt as though the trees themselves were waiting for her response.

Alexia said nothing. At length he closed the boxes and pulled her from the clearing.

'No word of this to anyone, right?' he said. He did not smile.

'What does Hannah think of all this?'

'She doesn't know,' Aidan said. 'She's more the earth mother type than a warrior.' He gave her back the battery from her phone. He seemed so easygoing with his blond dreadlocks, his patched cut-off jeans, his wide grey eyes. She had instinctively liked Aidan when they met: his musical aptitude, his warmth. He didn't seem to subscribe to the same rule book as some of the others here, who were judgemental about such things as the consumption of meat. From the outside he and Hannah seemed to be a couple miraculously free from tension. But Hannah was his girlfriend, his bedmate, his musical partner, and he hadn't told her about this cache. Instead he was telling Alexia.

'I don't know where I stand on the kind of direct action you're talking about myself,' she said.

'These people, they've had their land took off them. Now the company's coming in and blowing up what they have left, poisoning it, till they can't drink their water, and their animals are dying and they can't even breathe. In this context, damaging a few bits of the coloniser's weaponry could be seen as self-defence, don't you think?'

She made a non-committal noise. They were passing the urupā. She knew it was important to listen, to figure out exactly where he stood. But the lights were there again, her lights, dancing faintly above the graves. She strained her ears but she couldn't hear anything.

'You see this marker here?' Aidan asked. There in the long grass was a large, rounded stone. 'That marks the place.' In answer to her silence he went on. 'You've heard about the aukati? The line the soldiers forced the people back to in the 1800s? That's away over there in the bush. The people won't set foot there. But this stone marks the place where they killed their chief. He was a well-loved leader, by all accounts. Their last. The chief was killed here after they surrendered. The soldiers shot him, in front of his people. It was only a couple of generations ago. Every local who walks past this place, this is what they're thinking: that's the place they murdered him. There's blood all over this land – their blood and the Crown's. They live it every day. History's not separate for them. And it's still going on – the injustice. It's more insidious now: it's chemicals and pollution, not guns. You can't tell me it doesn't make you want to fight.'

'I guess I'm just not a very violent person,' she said.

'Not violent!' Aidan said. He began to laugh and, slowly, she began to laugh as well, though she was not sure why. 'Not a violent person!' They laughed and laughed.

36

Someone had sabotaged the fracking site. Everyone was talking about it at breakfast. Matiu had been up early milking the cows in the upper paddock and had seen the police cars. He'd peeked over the fence and brought back the news. Sam, Melissa and Kate were whispering excitedly, and Aidan was aglow. Polly was not pleased. She presided over the breakfast table like some kind of silent goddess, her mouth turned down at the corners. Damage had been done to a truck; it wasn't clear what or how. Isaiah felt a small thrill pass through him at the thought. It was a thing he would like to do, if he wasn't constrained by his position. If he wasn't constrained by reason, as well, and by the law. How deeply he wished he was not constrained.

He decided to take photos of the damage, if he could. He wanted to survey the scene. He might be able to figure out what had been done, and how. How had they got onto the site without being detected? He waited till evening, till the action died down. Isaiah headed up the path, camera around his neck. The air was cooler than it had been for months. He would have to resurrect the fleece from the bottom of his pack. He'd not needed it since spring.

'Uncle Isaiah, wait!' Tama called. 'I have three important things to tell you.' He had followed without Isaiah knowing, which was impressive. The boy had a way of talking that commanded interest. Isaiah didn't particularly want a hanger-on, especially a child he needed to be worried about, but Tama had said 'uncle'. Was this the first time? The second? Isaiah was an uncle now.

He picked Tama up and slung him over his shoulders. 'You can come with me,' he said. 'But only because I'm staying close to the fence.'

'I'm looking for my cat.' Tama held him closely about the head, and Isaiah held the boy's bare feet.

'Tell me your three things,' Isaiah said.

'A taniwha came to me in my dream last night,' Tama said. 'And Mama's got a baby, but it's in her puku. And this is the last thing.' He reached down and passed Isaiah something. Isaiah opened his hand. In it was a key: large, machine cut, with sharp edges.

'A taniwha, a baby and a key?' Isaiah said. 'Who's your mama having a baby with?'

'Rangi,' Tama said, matter-of-factly. 'He's gonna be the dad. The taniwha got big,' he went on. 'It ate one of their masheens, it said.'

'Rangi!' Isaiah hadn't seen Rangi so much as interact with Lizzie in the meetings. Maybe he'd just agreed to stand in, in the father's absence. Or maybe he really was the father. Isaiah remembered his lone reccie up the river, the dying bird slick with oil in his hand. Lizzie stayed on the marae in a family house, but the way people lived here was changing already. The child would not have the childhood Tama had. Lizzie was hapū! In Isaiah's plans to come here, to stay here, was a child, or children, kids growing up freer than in a city, closer to nature. He began to almost jog along the path.

'Yeah, so what?' Tama said. He nearly fell off Isaiah's shoulders. 'The baby's gonna be a boy,' he said.

'Did that come to you in a dream too?' Isaiah asked. 'Or did Lizzie have a test?'

'Nah. Just, I asked God for a boy, cos girls are so annoying,' Tama said.

'Which god?' Isaiah asked.

'That Jesus one,' Tama said. 'All the other ones are busy. '

'Don't you think Jesus is busy too?'

'Nah. All the others are looking after the trees, or whatever. But he just hangs out up there on his cross in that church in town. I don't know what he's doing up there, just hanging around.'

'What was your taniwha like then?' he asked.

'Eyes like massive jools,' Tama said. 'Head like a hammer. All these patterns on its bum, like a waka carving. And it got stronger, it said, cos it ate a orange truck. It's our taniwha. It lives in the river. You didn't know?' Isaiah shook his head.

The path wound through the thick bush. Isaiah set Tama down and took his hand in his own. A little further up the bush cover dropped away. Isaiah made Tama get down low and, crouched like this, they advanced along the fence line. He got his camera ready. There was a commotion behind him as the damaged truck came into view. Tama was leaping on the spot.

'A orange truck! Just like she told me! Just like she said!'

There were no police now, just footprints and traffic cones. The truck was orange, which could be a young boy's informed guess, perhaps. He would question Tama later. If he knew about the truck already, he or some of the other kids must be coming up here alone. Isaiah knelt and clicked. There was wide hole in the truck's side. He took a close-up of it, the sharp edges of steel bent open like tinfoil. Stretched around the cab of the vehicle was a strip of police tape. A line was traced in white around the site.

It was marked as a crime site. They would outline a damaged truck in white; they would photograph this piece of private property because a company owned it. But no one wanted to publish his photographs of dead birds, the damaged land lying open and oozing fluid, toxic chemicals leaching into the earth.

Tama yelled. He was a little way off in the bush. Isaiah began to run towards him, but the boy was already coming back with something in his arms.

'My cat!' he said.

The creature was dusted around the ears with twigs and greatly displeased to have been found. The adrenalin brought on by Tama's scream made Isaiah's hands and face hot. He hadn't been careful enough. He hadn't been watching. Taylor had said there were pits and soft places in the ground. Tama could have easily been lost. The small boy was flushed with happiness.

Isaiah collected both Tama and the cat and carried them back towards the pā. He felt a sharp thing knocking against his leg: the key.

'Where did you find the key, Tama?' His voice came out sterner than he'd meant it to.

'They told me not to tell.'

'Who told you?' He stopped walking. He had suspected for a while one of the others was a plant. What if they were trying to plant evidence?

'Geez, don't freak out. The fairies, uncle.'

'The fairies?' Tama's eyes were candid and completely honest.

'They said go onto the bush path, down lower than here. They said to look in the yellow mud. They sung it at me. You wouldn't know their language. It's older than te reo. But then, you don't know that language, either.' How was it possible for a six-year-old to be so imperious? He didn't believe Tama was guided by the fairies, rather that he and the other kids had been involved in some sort of dare. It would all come out in time.

By the time he got to Lizzie's place it was dark and Tama was asleep in his arms. She opened the door in a slip and then stood back, hiding herself behind the door frame. Perhaps she was expecting Rangi? He passed her her sleeping son. The cat had run away as soon as they got to the pā land. He could not tell if Lizzie's stomach was bigger yet.

'Naughty boy,' she said. 'He told me he was with Rangi.'

'Went up the river,' Isaiah said. 'Found his cat.'

'Thank you,' she said. 'He's been crying for her every night.'

'He was pretty happy. I was up there looking at that truck. There was police tape and everything. They'll try and pin it on one of us, for sure. Wilful damage.'

'What truck?' she said. 'We been over at the coast at Tama's aunty's memorial. We just got back tonight.'

'A truck was vandalised.' Isaiah said.

'Tama had a dream about some truck being smashed up,' Lizzie said. She laughed quietly over the sleeping boy. 'Said it was the taniwha done it.'

It was only after she closed the door that he remembered the key in his pocket. Was the key from elsewhere? What did it open, anyway?

It was hard for Lizzie to feel comfortable around him – he could tell. He was a city kid and she was a country one, but it was more than that. Isaiah had to work hard not to feel like an imposter around Lizzie, around all of them. His mother wasn't from here, after all.

Isaiah's mother had met his father at the ministry, where she was working as a social worker, fresh out of school, back when you could get that sort of job without qualifications. He liked to imagine her as she would have been then, not yet in her twenties, dressed in a seventies mini dress with some obnoxious print, and getting away with it because of her blonde hair and blue eyes.

He had not inherited anything of her appearance. Isaiah looked like his father. Strangers would approach them on buses to inquire about his origins. Most assumed his mother was his babysitter or his nanny. Even now, when they went together to cafés, they got the odd curious glance. He could imagine the possibilities scrolling through people's minds: maybe she was an older woman having an affair, or a woman mentoring a disadvantaged youth. He had grown used to his mother fielding their questions.

'No, this is my son,' she would say. 'Yes, by birth.' His

204

mother would stare at them with her large eyes. 'His father is Māori,' she would say, loudly. As he grew older, the shame and embarrassment crept in, until as a teenager he would duck his head.

They'd had a fight about it once. He'd asked why it was people's business to know what his background was. He could be Pakistani or Lebanese or anything for all they cared. It wasn't like he would go up to a white person and demand to hear about their 'backgrounds'. So why did she even bother answering them?

She had got upset in her usual, embarrassing way, and ended up crying: large, excessive tears that conveyed bafflement more than grief.

'But aren't you proud that you're Māori?' she'd asked him.

'It's not that ...' he'd said, and hadn't known what more he could say.

37

They were in the kitchen, peeling spuds. Alexia was not romantic about communal living. Rangi, Matiu and Polly were all bent over their various tasks, working efficiently. So they all got along. So what? Sam, Melissa and Kate viewed the locals and their lifestyle with a vampirish admiration. Alexia had heard Sam say how much she liked Māori culture, with its emphasis on the collective, with the manaakitanga, the wider family structures ... she could wax on about it for a long while.

Since the blow-up after the funeral she'd texted Katherine a few times. She'd heard from no one else, but Katherine was friendly. They were probably all preoccupied with their grief, she told herself. It affected people in different ways.

Alexia dropped a spud in the bucket, started on another. She'd noticed the kind of people who talked like Sam did about family were generally those who had just a little familial responsibility, who probably saw their grandparents once a year at Christmas, whose grandparents, in fact, would probably be cared for by others. Who was caring for Yiayia? She dug the end of the peeler deep into the potato's black eye.

'You don't have to murder it, sis,' Matiu said.

'Cup o' tea.' Rangi came into the room gasping. 'Cup. Tea.' He sat down with a thump, expecting to be served. In a moment, Matiu was at his side. It was always Matiu who got up when someone came in, who attended to Polly, who anticipated everyone's needs. Rangi was more dishevelled than usual. He seemed to be shivering. It was autumn, but it wasn't yet that cold.

'Who do you think we are, your slaves?' Alexia said.

'It's your people that turned mine into slaves,' Rangi said. 'Not the other way around.' But he was distracted. Matiu put a teabag in a cup and filled it from the Zip. He brought it to Rangi.

'Sup, cuz?' he said.

'Nothing,' Rangi said. 'Got to talk to Polly, that's all. It's not right, Matiu.'

'What's going on?' Alexia said. But it was coming out anyway.

'Got to call a tohunga, maybe,' Rangi said. 'The lights round the urupā, they're not looking normal.'

Matiu put a hand on his shoulder. 'You been seeing things?' he asked.

Rangi slammed down the cup of tea. 'What I been seeing ain't nothing on what some others have been seeing,' he said. 'Just fairy lights. Just a whole lotta nothing.'

'It's just the stress, cuz.'

'Stress doesn't make you see things that aren't there.'

'Tama's been having all those dreams,' Matiu said. 'About the spirits. You know his nanny comes to him. Was it round her grave?' He sat down at the table.

'Whatever the hell it is it's not meant to be there,' Rangi said. 'I'm down with the ancestors, bro, but this puts the shits up me. Dancing lights ... Bet you think we're all crazy,' he said to Alexia.

'Not at all,' she said. 'Not even a bit.'

'Well, then, how's this?' Rangi said. 'That Tama's granny never liked me when she was alive, and she don't like me any more now she's gone. Said we're doing nothing about the fracking. Said we're all just gonna give up.' Alexia saw tears in his eyes. Without meaning to she sat and embraced him awkwardly from the side.

'It's okay, Rangi,' she said. 'I see lights too, you know.'

He stared at her. 'What kind of lights?'

'I see them when I hear music,' she said. 'Sparks, flashes, dancing flares. There's a medical term for it. Synaesthesia.'

'Oh, we got a term for that in the reo,' Rangi said. 'We call that just being mental. Ha ha. Jokes.' But she could feel him shaking. 'Don't yous tell anyone,' he said to them. 'Got to go talk to Polly. Those old people, they got to stay in the ground.'

38

'First they dirty my air. Then they set my water on fire. Now they take my key. Who would take my key?' Polly asked.

Isaiah looked around at them all. As the year waned, it seemed their paranoia had grown. Even Polly wasn't immune to it. She was staring them down, each of them. The sky outside the meeting room was a slate grey. Polly wore a scarf of purple and gold, and pink lipstick.

Alexia was wearing red, a colour that brought out her complexion. Her black hair fell against her shirt and she wore gold hoops in her ears. Next to Sam and Melissa and Kate, who dressed boyishly, her decoration seemed showy. Sam had the nose piercing and the plug in one ear, but none of them wore typically feminine things. Alexia wouldn't be out of place playing a guitar on a street in Spain. She moved her hands restlessly on the table. He wished to hold one in his, to still it. He was so confused by the feelings she evoked in him, after their misadventure on the night of the fundraiser. He told himself that he just felt protective of her, because she was grieving. In the past, he'd slept with people sometimes just the once, and found that the tension was resolved. He'd been hoping this would happen with Alexia. He watched her lips moving on her cup. He told himself a lot of things.

She was fragile of course. Prone to bouts of anger, and politically conservative. And she saw music. What did she see? Did she see sparks as everyone was speaking? Did she hear colours, too? He would have to ask her about it. He would, after the meeting. He made up his mind. He would just go up to her, and ask her about herself, as though there weren't other concerns, as though the land was not being destroyed underneath them, as if their campaign wasn't failing.

'Patupaiarehe. That's who took your key.' Rangi ducked his head as if he expected a smack. The key Tama had found lay on the table.

'It was you who took it,' Polly said. She blew a plume of smoke up and into the air. No one was bothering to argue with her any more about smoking in meetings, not even the vegans. Rangi shifted in his chair and raised his hands palm outwards.

'Aunty, no!'

'You're a good-for-nothing brute,' Polly said.

Rangi stood. 'It wasn't me,' he said. 'I might not care too much for the law, but I don't bloody lie.'

'Well, not often, anyway,' Matiu said. 'And then, only by omission.'

'Where did Tama find it?' Polly turned to Isaiah.

'Up the river,' Isaiah said. He didn't believe it was Rangi. It wasn't his style. His guess was Aidan, but Aidan was quiet, eating his biscuit. No one looked guilty.

'Well,' Polly said. 'Maybe it was the patupaiarehe. The bush fairies,' she clarified, for the pākehā.

'There haven't been any over this way for a long time, Aunty,' Matiu said hastily. He made as if to roll his eyes.

'They're real,' Polly said. 'And they're mischief-makers. Your great-grandfather saw one, over Tūhoe way, in te Urewera. That's where they used to live. Not round here. It was a long time ago.' Again she adressed the pākehā. 'They have orange hair, or white, and pale skin like you. But they're not human. They're atua. The Tūhoe say they're little people, but I've heard in other tales that they're as big as you and me.'

'What does the key open?' Sam asked.

'The key unlocks the gate to the upper paddock,' Polly said. 'The one near where they found that vandalised truck.'

Melissa let out a little puff of air. Sam picked up the key. Alexia shifted in her seat. Again Isaiah thought of what Sam said of her: that she was an undercover plant. A man had been working undercover in one group Isaiah knew of, keeping up a relationship with a woman for about a year. He had been outspoken in strategy meetings, often urging the activists to more militant activity. Isaiah tried to meet Alexia's eyes but she was fixated on the key. She projected guilt, but he suspected it hadn't been her. Then he remembered her wielding Polly's tokotoko, and doubted himself again.

'If there were any fingerprints, they'd be wiped off by now,' Sam said.

Polly told them that there was only one key and that it was kept in her secret box.

'The earth mother is angry,' Melissa said. Her eyes filled with tears. 'What are they called?' she whispered. 'The fairies? Patu–'

'Patupaiarehe,' Polly said.

Te Kahurangi came in and sat down beside Polly, all quick movements and long limbs. She noticed the key. She didn't offer apologies for being late, as Isaiah would have done. He supposed this was a consequence of her being young, with all the blithe confidence that entailed. But also she had grown up here; this kitchen was her kitchen. Te Kahurangi didn't need to apologise to anyone. It was there in her openness, in the way she held herself. Isaiah envied it.

'What's that?' she asked. Her wide-set eyes were virtuous.

'It's a key for somewhere you're not meant to go. And someone took it, that's all I know, patupaiarehe or not.' Polly left the room. Isaiah supposed that meant the meeting was over. Still Melissa's tears dropped onto the table.

'What was that all about?' Te Kahurangi asked.

Melissa sniffed. 'The earth,' she said. 'The earth is …'

'Oh for God's sake,' Sam said. 'No offence, Melissa.' She turned to Rangi and Matiu. 'I'm not discounting your lore or anything but …'

'Everyone knows our stories are true,' Matiu said. 'But some think they're true true, while others think they're true only in the metaphorical sense.'

'Like your Bible,' Rangi said.

'Nah,' said Te Kahurangi. 'Their Bible's full of shit!' She doubled over in laughter.

'But your great-great koro saw one once. A patupaiarehe.' Rangi was daring Matiu to disagree. Te Kahurangi picked the key up.

Alexia was quiet. Since the night of the fundraiser there had been a new thing in her that worried Isaiah. Perhaps she should be packed up and escorted away, for her own good. He had a brief fantasy in which he was the one escorting her, and she was grateful for it. But where would she go? Sam would tell him he was removing Alexia's agency with such a fantasy. And she would be right.

'So the key went missing?' Te Kahurangi asked. 'And Aunty Polly thinks it was the fairies? For real?' Matiu tried to shush her but she started to laugh. 'Little fairy people with green eyes and red hair!' she said. 'Creeping round at night and magicking keys away, when they coulda just jumped the fence!'

'How did you know what the key opens?' Isaiah asked her. She turned her guileless gaze on him.

'I've seen it before.' She shrugged. 'I've stayed with Aunty a lot.'

'This is the earth's only defence,' Melissa said. 'After what happened to the eels.' She was crying full force now.

'Well, they do say the patupaiarehe protect the tuna,' Rangi said. 'They woulda been pissed about the eels.'

'We need to talk about some things on the agenda,' Sam said. Isaiah knew he should help her steer the meeting in the right direction, but he was watching Alexia. Her eyes were focused on the wall beside Sam, moving in small jerks. She was seeing the music now, then. He listened, straining his ears. But he couldn't hear anything beyond their voices and cars in the distance.

'The patupaiarehe protect the tuna?' Alexia asked Rangi.

Isaiah felt a ridiculous jealousy.

'They take little girls like you deep into the bush and …' He gestured with his hands.

'Shut up,' Matiu said. 'Well, they have been said to abduct people. Women and children. But they bring them back, afterwards.'

'After what?' Alexia asked.

Melissa pulled a tissue from her pocket. Everyone was ignoring her, but she sobbed anyway. She addressed the table top.

'It's all happening, just like I knew it would. The taniwha. The spirits. All the old things are coming back to fight.'

'What kinda whack shit has she been smoking?' Te Kahurangi said. 'I got to get me some a that.'

'Do the patupaiarehe play music?' Alexia said.

'Flutes,' Rangi said. 'They play their flutes at night, in the bush.'

Sam banged the table with some force. She hit a pen, which shot across the table into her other hand. She flipped it with great dexterity so it balanced on its end on the wood. Then she caught it and laid it down, next to the key, with precision. Everyone in the room watched her. It was a move Isaiah had seen her perform before, at times when meetings were well and truly lacking direction. They had discussed leadership and charisma, authoritarianism and collective decision-making, the dynamics between those empowered to speak and the silenced. Earlier in their relationship, they'd talked until they were blue in the face. But despite all her principles, Sam was not above seizing power when things were out of control.

'We need to get this campaign back on track,' she said. 'What are the key issues we need to discuss?'

'Guess the main issue is who is it that's running round in the night stealing keys and blowing shit up?' Te Kahurangi said. She laughed uproariously. Rangi joined in, then Matiu, then, uncertainly, Alexia, who was jolted out of her quiet. Isaiah permitted himself a smile. But Sam would not allow distraction for long. There was a long list of banal actions to agree upon before they were released.

As they left the meeting house Alexia turned towards her campsite. He had not got the chance to talk to her. The meeting had gone on way into the evening and Alexia had grown increasingly withdrawn. Now she was walking quietly into the dark away from him. He had wanted to ask her what it was she'd been watching in there, but Sam was standing close behind him and so he didn't. It was Rangi who moved after her.

'You stay out of the bush at night,' Isaiah heard him say. 'All this funny stuff going on with the voices in the bush, the lights. Whether it's people or patupaiarehe doing the damage, it's not good for a girl to go out there alone.'

Isaiah heard her start to protest.

'Yeah, but, if you been hearing flutes,' Rangi said, 'I'm just saying, stay away from there.'

Isaiah watched them fade into the dark.

39

'Matiu!' His long, looped figure was bent over the fence. He didn't move. Alexia touched his back.

'Jesus!' he said. 'Some way to sneak up on a bro.' She'd always felt a personal sympathy for Matiu. What would it be like to play the country cousin to Isaiah's prodigal son, and to defer to all of Rangi's demands? To be the one always baking scones for whoever came to the marae, doing what needed to be done? She pointed to the buds in his ear.

'What are you listening to?'

'*The Very Best of Mozart,*' he said. 'I find it soothing.'

'Matiu!' she said. 'I thought you'd be a Vivaldi man.' He grinned. Now she could see he was watching two men at the edge of the fracking site. 'What's going on?'

'You don't have your phone on you? They can listen in through that, you know.'

'Back at the campsite. Don't you think you're being a little paranoid?'

'Just because you're paranoid ...'

'Doesn't mean they're not out to get you.' Matiu moved his head towards the men.

'I've been watching for an hour,' he said. 'Those two up there are plain clothes. I'm sure of it.'

'Police?'

'They've been going up and down the guard towers asking questions.'

'How do you know?'

'Look at their car. Generic Honda Civic, beige, town plates. There's a huge aerial, see? That means they've got a radio. I think there's concealed lights under the grille of their bumper. And check out the way they're dressed.' He snorted and offered her an ear bud. Piano sonata number eleven, *Rondo alla Turka*. She mourned her record collection, and then felt guilty for missing it more than Stephen. 'See how fake-casual they are?' Matiu asked. 'No jeans, right, but those light-colour pants that white dudes wear. What is that colour anyway?'

'Beige?' Alexia asked. 'Khaki? Cream?' The music was building to a crescendo and she was lost in it. It was mostly very subtle, Mozart: pastel-hued notes bursting delicately to the upper left of her vision.

'The sort of pants you make someone iron before you wear them. And shirts. And sunglasses, for Christ's sake. What else could they be but police?'

'Oil magnates visiting their site?'

'Those people stay away from the dirty business,' Matiu said.

'What are they looking for?'

'You didn't hear?' He took the ear bud out of her ear. 'Some more stuff on the frack site's been sabotaged. Thought everyone knew.' He put the buds into his ears, both of them. She tugged at him. 'Okay, okay,' he said. 'Some tyres were slashed on a guard's car. We know that because our good friend Sammie was doing a patrol.' He frowned. 'So, if it was her, you wouldn't think she'd …'

'What else?'

'More wires were cut round the fence line. That could have been anyone. Then last Friday, shots were fired at a tower. You really didn't know this?'

'I knew about the fence lines being cut. If there were shots fired, why didn't we hear anything?'

Matiu shrugged.

'Maybe we did. Shots are fired round here all the time. People hunt. Rabbits, deer – up the mountain – boar. Taylor over there probably has a gun. Most people do. But these shots hit the base of the tower closest to us: there, you can see it. Could have been any one of us. The last thing was I heard some … bites got taken out of a tower base, higher up.'

'What do you mean?'

'Someone used explosives. Left marks like huge teeth would make. Didn't make a shitarse bit of difference, though. The tower's still standing. You can't blow up concrete, except with something big.'

'So it's not you, then?' His face went still. She felt suddenly remorseful. Eventually he sighed deeply, like the kaumātua he no doubt aspired to be one day.

'If you were me, and this was your land, what would you do? What would be the most useful thing, the most helpful thing, for the land itself?'

'What do you think happened to the tower?' Alexia asked, after a moment.

'I don't know how it was done,' Matiu said.

'Tama keeps dreaming of a taniwha.' It was out before Alexia could stop herself. Tama had told her the night before, brimming with a child's conviction. 'He's sure it's real.'

Matiu shook his head in a pitying way.

'That Tama has heard too many stories,' he said. 'There hasn't been a taniwha in these parts since 1869.'

40

The fences had been cut again. Isaiah and Alexia were going up the river on a fact-finding expedition. Kate and Sam and Melissa were in town, and Rangi and Matiu had farm work to do. Polly had assigned the mission to them, peering shrewdly at Isaiah over her cigarette holder. And they were taking Ana – she'd begged to come.

'What's this important business you've got up the river, then?' Alexia asked Ana.

'My brother,' Ana said. She let go Alexia's hand and skipped ahead. 'Tama told me something. I just wanted to find out what it was about.'

'What did he say?' Alexia said.

'"Knock three times, knock on wood." Just an old rhyme my nanny used to say.'

'Your nanny who died? Are you having funny dreams too?' Alexia said.

'Nah, not me.' Ana turned to face them. Framed in the bush in her white T-shirt and cut-off jeans and dark hair she seemed unworldly, a sprite of some kind. 'But Tama's a weirdo. You could say that, you could say he's a matakite, like he can see stuff other people can't. Maybe.' She laughed – seemingly this stretched even her own view of things. 'But Nanny tells him when stuff's going to happen.'

'What does she say will happen now?' Isaiah asked.

'He doesn't know this time what she means. He said she's all like, "Knock three times, knock on wood, knock three times and make it good." She used to say that when she was alive.'

'What does it mean?' Alexia asked. The hair on her arms was standing upright, and Isaiah felt voyeuristic for noticing. They were climbing high up now, Taylor's bald land curving away from them, the wells rearing up ahead. It shocked him every time: the garishness of the yellow clay, the crane-like towers.

'She used to say it when we came out of the urupā. Takes the tapu off.'

'I see,' Isaiah said. Ana seemed so invested in the children's romantic version of events. He suspected she believed in all of it, the fairies, the ghosts, everything.

Ana walked ahead, humming to herself.

'You believe in ghosts?' he asked Alexia. Too late he remembered about her grandfather, about his recent death.

'Who doesn't believe in ghosts?' she answered, lightly. 'Some of the best people I know are ghosts.' She continued ahead of him. Her shoulders were tense.

The wells spoiled the bush line and the clear view of the mountain, but in a way Isaiah welcomed it. At least the threat to the land was a concrete thing that everyone could see. The act of fracking was so direct, so unapologetic, the towers like architectural odes to industry, and their explicit purpose: to exploit the earth's resources, to get right down into the rock and literally explode it.

Isaiah fitted the lens on his camera and took some shots in quick succession. The burn-off of the gas had not yet started. Construction was still in the interim stage. They would pump the chemicals down soon, but it could still be stopped. The fracturing would not yet have begun. He counted three, four more new wells off in the distance, like absurdly magnified telephone poles. There were about forty on the site now, and the count was growing.

'Here it is.' Alexia was pointing to the fence. Ana and Isaiah came abreast of where she stood. Ana was humming to herself, nearly skipping along. There was the damaged fence line, its wires ripped and stretched like old elastic bands. It had separated completely only in two places. The rest was warped, as if something had leaned up against the fence, exuding a great force. He had the camera focused, his eye pressed to the lens, before he was aware of movement.

'Step away from there,' a voice called out. 'Move away.'

It was the Māori guard who'd apprehended him and Sam the night of their reccie. He was approaching, carrying tools. He spoke so urgently that Isaiah stepped back and put his hand on Ana's shoulder.

'You should be ashamed of yourself!' Alexia called suddenly. 'Turning your back on your own people!' Isaiah turned to her, confused. Confrontation hadn't been in the plan. Ana went still under his hand. Alexia's face was twisted and there was a wildness in her voice. The security guard stood up, seemingly confused as well. 'Traitor!' Alexia yelled. Her voice rose to a scream. The guard met Isaiah's eyes and backed away a few steps. He spoke into a radio: there would be reinforcements arriving soon. Alexia yelled and yelled, producing a stream of abuse. The guard didn't answer.

She picked up a large rock. Isaiah let go of Ana and stepped forward to stop her, but it seemed Alexia couldn't hear him. She threw it. The guard put out a hand and fended the rock away. Alexia picked up another rock, and another. The man was a bigot, conservative, closed-minded, an oppressor, and she would stop him. A rock glanced off the man's head. He began to run towards the fence, towards Alexia. Isaiah tried to grab Alexia but Ana was there ahead of him, placing herself between Alexia and the fence and the man, and Alexia tripped and fell to her knees, shoving Ana forwards.

Ana jolted and lay on the ground.

Isaiah realised at the same time as the guard. Together they ran a few steps, a long few steps, on either side of the fence. But the guard was there first, pushing at Ana through the fence with his rubber boot. She lay on top of a wire. She jolted again, a little jolt. Alexia was still on her knees.

Isaiah swerved to the side and picked up a long branch. He knelt and pushed Ana off the wire with it, rolling her onto her side. Spit ran out of her mouth onto the ground.

'She all right?' the guard asked.

Alexia cupped the girl's face in her hands. Isaiah pushed her off. But Ana opened her eyes and, in one swift movement, stood up. Isaiah was so relieved he laughed. Ana's eyes were too wide.

'Enough voltage to stun cattle,' the security guard said, apparently shaken. He eyed Alexia. Isaiah patted Ana as though she was not quite solid.

'Knock on wood,' she said, faintly. There was the branch in Isaiah's hands. Ana shook her head and laughed, but there were tears at the corners of her eyes.

'You hurt?' Isaiah asked, but she shook her head no.

'Been shocked before,' she said.

'Keep the kids away from here,' the guard said, roughly. 'Keep them out of all this. There's weird things happening on this site.' He handled a wire in his gloved hand. 'No wire cutter did this!' He didn't seem to be accusing Isaiah but rather asking a question. Isaiah threw the stick away. Ana began to leave.

'Them's taniwha tracks!' she yelled. 'Those wires were bitten by taniwha teeth! And the patupaiarehe are coming again in the night, did you hear?' Isaiah hurried after her. She might need to be checked out by a doctor.

'She'll be all right,' the security guard said. 'She's a country kid, like me. When you grow up around here you have at least one run-in with a fence.' Alexia started down the path after Ana. 'Hey,' the guard said, quietly. 'That's some crazy woman you got there. I'd watch out for that one, if I were you.' He shook his head. Isaiah did not feel inclined to disagree.

On the way back he piggybacked Ana, who was now limp and quiet. Alexia followed meekly, her breath coming in little gasps, as though it was she who had been shocked. What the hell had happened to her? Her anger had come out of nowhere. Isaiah found himself too angry to speak.

Ana's mother Lizzie was unfazed by the news. It had happened to the locals often enough walking around the pā in the dark. Ana went off sulkily after a brief moment of drama. Finally Isaiah got Alexia on her own.

'It was inexcusable,' he said. 'I can't believe you'd speak that way in front of the girl, or act that way. What were you –' But then he stopped. Her shoulders were slumped, she wouldn't meet his eyes. The mountain behind her was veiled in cloud, as it was most of the time now. He missed the clear days of spring.

'I don't know what happened,' she said. 'I didn't mean –' Her hair fell over one eye and she brushed it back. 'I just lose control sometimes,' she said. Her voice was very low. 'It was like I woke up and there was a rock in my hand.'

'I don't buy it,' Isaiah said. 'That was you, there, yelling those things. Some part of that was Alexia.'

'You didn't grow up like I did,' she said, almost viciously. 'I can tell from the way you talk. You want them all to like you, the local iwi. But you're not like them. Everything's rational, with you. Everything has to be considered, and scientific, and evidence-based. You think any other way of being is inferior. You don't understand real emotions. You don't allow yourself to. Of course it was me; of course I picked up the rock. I'm different from you. Sometimes when you feel things strongly, these things happen.'

He shook his head. She was tricky. Did she know what she was saying? And there was this allusion to the things that she had experienced. He wouldn't ask her. If she wanted to talk, she could. But Isaiah didn't play that kind of game.

'You threw the rock, though,' Isaiah said. 'It's always your choice, whether to throw it or not.' He watched her go back to her camp, the heavy curve of her hair moving slightly, her awkward loping walk.

41

They were having a small, informal meeting. Alexia much preferred larger gatherings, where the tone remained political, and where the statements and discussion were regulated, somewhat like a law court. In these smaller gatherings she had to sit close by Sam and Melissa and Kate, losing the buffer of her anonymity. It was harder to remain quiet, which was Alexia's agenda. She feared if she spoke her mind honestly she would just piss everyone off. Te Kahurangi was there as well, and Matiu, and Polly with her bright lipstick, and Bryce.

Matiu was making the tea as usual. As he opened a fresh packet of biscuits, Alexia noted the ease with which he remembered everyone's preferences – the way he had of sliding your cup in front of you without you noticing he was there.

'Did you hear?' Te Kahurangi said. 'That shellfish. It wasn't the fracking after all.'

'Eh?' Rangi said. 'Our kai moana wasn't bad before.'

'I got a call from my aunty up the coast,' Te Kahurangi said. 'She said they had the same thing a few weeks ago. So they called a guy in to take some samples, and sent them to a lab. It's just the next beach over from where we go. It's not the fracking. Their streams are all mucked up from other stuff. I told her what happened to us, the hallucinations, the sickness, everything. It's not the wells. It's just your standard run-off from the farms.'

'Well,' Polly said. 'It makes no difference. Still can't eat from our own coast anymore.'

Aidan seemed annoyed. He appreciated a straightforward case.

Isaiah entered the room. He was wearing green trousers and a black T-shirt, despite the freezing cold outside. He carried a sheaf of papers in his hands.

'Did your aunty say there was anything we could do about the kai moana, cuz?' Rangi asked.

'Nothing,' Te Kahurangi said. 'Apparently the Ministry of Fisheries said it was unfortunate. Said to wait till next season. Said there was nothing to be done.'

Isaiah smiled. Alexia saw many things in the smile, including satisfaction and a calculated pleasure. He laid Bryce's letters down on the table.

'"We will take further violent actions immediately,"' Sam read aloud, '"if you continue fracking activities on these lands."' She rifled through the papers, spreading them across the table. Bryce had kept copies of everything. 'Where did you get these?' she asked. Melissa and Kate and Matiu crowded around to see. 'Who even writes paper letters anymore?'

Rangi stayed where he was, his eyes moving from Isaiah to Bryce and back again. Te Kahurangi lounged casually by the door. '"We are issuing a warning,"' Sam went on. '"If the fracking does not cease we will ..."' She laid the letter back on the table. 'Where did you get these?' she asked again. Her voice was almost soft.

'Where did I get them, Bryce?' Isaiah asked. His eyes flicked to Alexia and then back to Bryce. Here was a part of Isaiah that Alexia did not trust, the part that obviously enjoyed such moments. Isaiah was too nuanced, too self-aware. Throughout all of this Bryce's face had stayed placid, unmoving. Now he moved casually and grasped a letter between a finger and thumb.

'Did you go through my things?' he asked Isaiah.

'We went to get the lockbox,' Alexia said. 'He's been writing letters ever since he got here,' she said to the others. 'Letters to the council, to the police, to newspapers. They start out as requests.' She pulled out a letter spelled out in capitals from the bottom of the pile. 'But they end up as threats.' Now Sam was looking sharply from Isaiah to Alexia and back. Alexia couldn't help it, she felt a little thrill of satisfaction, and then guilt.

Bryce regarded Alexia in an interested way, much as he would regard someone suggesting a good idea. He nodded enthusiastically.

'Right,' he said. 'All right then. Yes.' He seemed to change the way he was sitting, to become some larger version of himself. 'These are mine,' he said. 'Yes, they're mine. And yes, I spoke for all of you.' He nodded his head.

Polly banged her tokotoko on the ground. Sam's characteristic smile had left her face. Isaiah patted Sam's hand like you would subdue a loyal pet, Alexia thought. What could be worse for Sam than Isaiah having a sexual encounter with someone else? The thought that Isaiah had plotted some political intrigue, and that she hadn't been involved. He was cruel, and didn't even realise it.

'You went above the people of this land?' Polly asked. Her nostrils were wide. Her eyes glared. Alexia was afraid of her. 'Those letters are poison,' she said. 'You put those messages out into the world, on our behalf? You think we don't have troubles enough?'

Bryce stood up, and then fell to his knees. Alexia began to laugh involuntarily. No one else did.

'This is no joke,' Bryce said. 'Polly, I ask you and your people's forgiveness.'

'You can't be serious,' Isaiah said.

'Aunty,' Bryce said, 'I did it for us.'

'Don't listen to him,' Rangi said. 'He's full of –'

'Watch your mouth, Rangi,' Polly said.

'You did it for us?' Sam had fully recovered. 'You spoke for us and for the people of this pā for what reason exactly? Are you sabotaging us? I thought it might be you who was working against us. The undercover cop.'

'But surely informants wouldn't bother making such stuff up?' Matiu asked.

'Informants work in strange ways,' Sam said.

'I'm not working against you,' Bryce said. Alexia found herself strangely convinced of this, though she would prefer to believe he was guilty. 'I've been upset, like all of you, at the way our attempts here have been failing. We've acted optimistically, assuming we could change things. Assuming, perhaps, that there weren't higher powers involved.'

'What higher powers?' Rangi asked.

'The local council and probably the government,' Bryce said. 'They all have some investment in the fracking. Economic motivations.'

'What are you saying?' Isaiah said. 'That we shouldn't bother to resist?'

'No!' Bryce seemed genuinely appalled. 'Just that we shouldn't have bothered trying to resist honourably, with applications and protests. We aren't dealing with forces that existed in the past. This fracturing of the land,' he said. 'It has the potential for utter destruction, you all know that. It can ruin the air, the water. It can trigger earthquakes, tidal waves. This kind of insane piercing of the earth, it hasn't been seen before. We should meet force with force. What they're doing to your land, Aunty, should be illegal.' He was focused on Polly again. 'It's a violation of natural law. I say we should meet that illegality head on, with some illegal acts of our own.'

Alexia and Isaiah exchanged glances. Bryce came across like a mad zealot, but his opinions were not that far from Isaiah's. But Isaiah was shaking his head. This was not the point, of course. The point was that Bryce was a madman, and a culturally insensitive one at that.

Matiu leaned towards Bryce.

'She is not your aunty,' he said. 'Why did you speak for us?'

'Everything's falling apart,' Bryce said. 'I've seen it happen before with social movements. It all starts out well. But humans were meant to fight in short bursts: we're not built for the long fight. Before you know it the energy wanes, and it's all over.'

'So you did this for us,' Isaiah said slowly, 'to get the powers that be to act against us, in order to give us some more motivation? To make us angry enough to act?'

Bryce nodded. Melissa started to cry.

'You expect us to buy that?' Sam said. 'What kind of activist tries to get his comrades in trouble?'

'A desperate one,' Bryce said. 'I needed to make an impact.'

Polly rose from the table. She went to Bryce. She reached out her hand and stroked his chin. Then she slapped him very hard – one, two – across the face. For a moment Alexia saw Bryce's mask falter, his face slipping into shock.

'I always thought you were a little strange,' Polly said. 'From the minute I saw you I thought, That man's a man of the people, but he doesn't have any real friends. Now I know you're not just strange,' she said. 'You're totally off the wall pōrangi insane.'

'I move that disciplinary action be taken by the members of this group against Bryce,' Sam said. 'For implementing actions without a mandate.'

'Oh I think you'll find there are a few people around here acting without a mandate,' Bryce said. He was flinching a little from Polly's blow, his eyes filling with water.

'Rangi,' Polly said. 'Te Kahurangi.' Her voice was low. 'Get this man off our land.'

Te Kahurangi jumped up with joy on her face. Rangi stood, his large hands stretched out.

'You may not return,' Polly said.

They gave him till nightfall and, as Alexia understoood it, Rangi all but kicked him back to his camp, where his wife and wife's girlfriend were understandably upset. But the women decided to stay on – apparently they owned the camper – and Bryce was forced to leave with only his pack.

That night at dinner, Te Kahurangi described Bryce's frantic packing, his escalating threats. It was cold outside, so cold, and the wind was up. Alexia couldn't imagine where Bryce was camped now, out there in the wilderness.

'Called me a fascist,' she said. 'So I called him a cultural imperialist guilty of micro and macro aggressions. That shut him right up.'

'That's what shut him up?' Rangi said. 'Thought it was my boot up his arse.'

42

Isaiah put the thing on the table. It was a small, unprofessional mess of wires and electrical tape. 'I found it under the mudguard of my car.' They all looked at it, Alexia with shock, Kate eagerly. Polly touched it with her finger. He saw them go through the same stages he had: disbelief, bemusement, fear. He had called a closed meeting, so only a few of them were present. They were huddled in the wharekai.

'It's a bug?' Polly asked.

He nodded. 'I don't know what it is they suspect us of, but it's important.'

'We're going to have to take precautions,' Melissa said.

'Don't worry,' said Rangi. 'I always take precautions.' But under his humour there was disbelief.

'Cellphones, landlines –' Sam said – 'they definitely aren't safe anymore.'

Polly lit a cigarette, ignoring Te Kahurangi's glare.

'We live in a culture of surveillance now,' Kate said. 'We have to assume we're being listened to, every phone call, every conversation. That they can hear.'

'But isn't it illegal to bug us without a reason?' Matiu asked. 'I guess it was Bryce and all his lovely correspondence.'

'If they don't have a reason the evidence would be inadmissible in court,' Alexia said. 'But laws can always be changed retrospectively.'

'How do you know so much about it?' Isaiah asked.

'I did an assignment.' He wasn't sure, but she seemed to blush.

Polly tapped her cigarette holder on the edge of the ashtray with a clink.

'What could you have said anyway to get you in trouble?' Te Kahurangi asked.

'Let's not discuss any specifics,' Melissa said. She spoke in an exaggerated whisper. 'Any speculation about actions we may or may not initiate should be avoided from now on. We shouldn't use our real names.' Isaiah hoped she wouldn't cry. She was a strangely colourless woman. He knew about her ex-husband and her upbringing. He always tried to be patient with her.

'Now you are being ridiculous,' Matiu said.

'She's right, though,' Rangi said. 'We should be careful in meetings.' Polly loaded another cigarette into her holder. Had she already finished the first? He noted her movements were a little frenetic.

'How are they going to listen in on us?' Alexia said. Despite the bug sitting on the table she seemed unable to accept any of this.

'It's not a nice feeling to know your conversations have been listened to,' Isaiah said gently.

'But how do you think they're listening?' she said. 'Surely no one's bothered to sneak into my tent and install a bug in there. You think there's a cop behind that wall with a cup pressed to his ear?'

Polly exhaled pointedly in Alexia's direction. Alexia coughed.

'There was a group of animal activists up north that was infiltrated by an undercover cop,' Melissa said. 'Afterwards, we did some research about the police: what equipment they use, what their processes are. It's pretty sophisticated stuff.'

'The police, sophisticated,' Matiu said. He and Rangi began to laugh.

'She's right,' Kate said. 'They can easily listen in to conversations on your phone. They don't even have to do anything physical to it. They can track you and locate you using your phone too: that's GPS, that's pretty straightforward. And they can bug you.' She gestured to the thing on the table. 'They'll have people hacking our email lists, of course. We should assume those are not secure. Anything said over email should be regarded as public.' Kate was in her element. Her long hair was pulled away from her face and she was speaking fast. It had been Kate who had stayed up late with him researching this information, after it came out about the group up north. They had shared pizza, only taking breaks to write things down. How good it used to feel to work with someone so dedicated.

'And they'll have people tracking the websites we visit on the pā computers,' Kate went on. 'If you have anything private to do, then it's best done from a cafe in town.' Rangi and Matiu stopped laughing. 'They can also listen in if you're just sitting talking, like this, in a room.'

'You mean, if they haven't even been inside it?' Te Kahurangi said. 'How?'

'All they need to do is sit somewhere nearby. They have a thing that emits radio waves and bounces signals back from the window panes. They don't even need to be on the property. They can do it remotely. They could be listening right now.'

Everyone was quiet.

'Like, through the walls and everything?' Te Kahurangi asked.

'Through the walls,' Isaiah said.

'You seem almost pleased about this,' Alexia said to him. 'This isn't some kind of Bryce-like act in which you try to get us all motivated, is it?'

He didn't know how to respond, least of all because he hadn't thought of that.

'You people think someone's bothering to spend all this time listening to you talk about nothing?' Te Kahurangi asked. She was so sunny and unparanoid in her sneakers, with her taniwha tattoo. Te Kahurangi still believed the best of the world, despite what was going on. He wished he could preserve that for her.

'Well, what do you think that is on the table?' Kate said.

Te Kahurangi shook her head.

'It's just all so Orwellian,' Matiu said.

'We're living in the future,' Rangi said. 'Back when we got cellphones, I said it: the government will find some use for these things, and it won't be a good one.'

Kate lifted one hand. She wrote large letters on a piece of paper and held it up so they could all see.

If you need to talk about anything suspect, write it down, then burn it.

Te Kahurangi thought this was hilarious.

'You really expect us to do that? In twenty-four seconds, this message will self-destruct!'

'You are way too young to know that phrase,' Matiu said.

'I have an interest in classic TV,' Te Kahurangi said. 'I have hidden depths that you wouldn't know about.'

Polly drew her cellphone from her pocket and placed it on the table. She put it in the ashtray with her cigarette butts, took the piece of paper from Kate, and tried to set the phone on fire.

'No, Aunty!' Matiu said, hurriedly patting out the flame. 'It makes no difference! We all have them.'

Polly accepted her phone back with reluctance. 'So now we cannot speak freely on our own land,' she said. 'I suppose it was only a matter of time.'

43

In the days after they'd discovered the bug they all had more energy, as though the authorities' interest was a sign of affirmation. Alexia had found in herself a greater commitment to the work. It was only at night that she thought of Papou. The Family would be thinking of him too, speaking of him. His kindness became a story she told herself over and over; his winning mildness, his belief in her. The Family had still not contacted her, aside from Katherine. That day, after the funeral, Katherine had pulled Alexia along the path away from the house. She'd insisted on taking her home, and on making her a cup of tea. She'd sat on Alexia's couch, feet curled under her, and flicked her hair.

'They'll get over it,' she told Alexia. Alexia did not think so.

As she lay in her tent alone with the rumble of the fracking moving through her body, a great, formless anger would well up in her, a targetless thing that was perhaps useful.

Alexia heard the knock before anyone else, but she let Te Kahurangi answer the door to the wharenui so she could continue her conversation with Sam.

'Yes,' she said to Sam. 'I understand that.' Sam's skin reminded Alexia of oatmeal. 'But it's no good. The wording has to be more moderate if we expect anyone to read it.'

'But this *is* the fallout of colonisation,' Melissa said. She and Kate were supporting Sam, who shook her head. Melissa wrung her hands and picked up the scarf she was knitting.

'It's just that no councillor is going to respond well to reading that,' Alexia said. Sam made an impatient noise. They were all so unrealistic, so distanced from the way real people thought. But who were real people? Were her family real people? 'I'm going to take out the bit about the proletariat, too,' Alexia went on. 'I hope you don't mind.' Throughout this all Isaiah remained silent, supposedly focused on the papers before him. But then he looked straight at Alexia. He didn't smile or wink, but it was as if he had.

A dog ran into the hall.

'No dogs in here!' Polly yelled.

With the dog came a tall, thin man who Alexia knew at once must be Taylor. While his dog was frisky, rushing around the room, the man seemed to slink, as if his body wished to excuse itself. Isaiah had had a bruise on his hand for days after his visit to the farmer's house. He had seen the dog and was backing away.

'Take your dog,' he said, 'and get out.'

'God help me,' Polly said. 'I will raise a stick to that mutt.'

'She's not a mutt,' Taylor said. 'She's a pure-bred border collie. Besides, I'll only stay a minute.' He draped himself over a chair.

'Did anyone say you could sit down?' Polly banged her tokotoko on the floor. 'Matiu!

'Rangi! Kick this fella out!'

Te Kahurangi realised who Taylor was.

'I'd watch it if I were you,' she said.

'That's not very neighbourly,' Taylor said. He was on the edge of tears.

'You have no business here,' Matiu said. The dog made a pass at Isaiah. Alexia was aware that Sam was smirking. Sam and Isaiah's relationship was a mystery to her.

'Call Francesca off!' Isaiah said.

'That's not Francesca,' Taylor said. 'That's Petunia. The rest of them: Daphne, Francesca, Petal, Rose ... they're all sick.' He shook his head. 'They've gone bush. Think they might have kicked the bucket. I keep searching up on the fracking site but I can't find them. It's crazy what they've done up there. It's like the end of days.' He spoke blearily into his cupped hands. 'We're all done for,' he went on, in his Dutch accent. 'We're all up the boohai shooting poukakakas, up shit creek without a paddle.'

'Good God, man,' Rangi said. 'No one talks like that anymore.'

'I know,' Taylor said. He sobbed.

'This is ridiculous,' Sam said to Polly. 'You can't just let this farmer walk in here and say he's had a change of heart. What are you going to do, Taylor? Pull the towers down? Blow the wells up?' Her voice dropped nastily. 'Ride on in here on a white horse and save us all?'

But Taylor could not be further humiliated.

'I just want to help,' he said. 'I'll do anything.'

Sam turned to Polly. 'Surely you're sick of crazy well-meaning pākehā turning up hoping to solve your problems?'

'Oh, you'd be surprised how tolerant we are,' Polly said. Alexia suppressed a smile. 'But no, Taylor, it's too late. You held the title of our lands. You could have fought it. And now you come here hoping for forgiveness from us all?'

'Shall I get my chainsaw?' Rangi asked. He was joking, but Alexia was aware of real anger in the room, real fury. Taylor did not seem to feel the group's antagonism. He seemed barely lucid, almost on another plane. Te Kahurangi's face was twisted. Kate and Melissa took a step towards him.

'Go home, Taylor,' Polly said.

He got up to leave. 'You think I'm not ethical,' he said. 'But I didn't have the resources I'd need to fight it. I'm telling you, I will help.'

Rangi held the door open with his beefy arm.

Alexia turned her back on the farmer, along with all the others.

44

Isaiah waited till he and Sam had finished up the dishes. Then he took her hand, which was still slightly squeaky with suds, and led her outside. She did not resist. Her face was closed. If she'd thought he wanted romance he couldn't have dealt with it right now.

'I need to talk to you about something,' he began, once they were seated on the steps. Sam's expression changed, and he saw how she might appear in a few years: harder, more resolute. The sun glowered low on the bush line. A fracking tower tapped out its disconsolate rhythm in the distance, punctuating the gusts of wind.

Then Sam laughed.

'Oh!' she said. 'Finally. Bloody hell, Isaiah. How long have we known each other?' She continued to laugh, but quietly now, and with less humour. 'I'm not blind.'

Isaiah said nothing. Sam was not blind, and apparently Rangi wasn't either. But it appeared that he was.

'It's fine,' she said. 'How long has it been now that we haven't really been together?'

He didn't answer this either. He knew he wasn't doing well. Guilt rushed over him. Sam began laughing anew, then put her hand on his. Did she really care so little? As always, he found it hard to decipher what was Sam, and what was Sam acting how Sam thought she should act in alignment with her principles. Wasn't she moved on some level? But she beamed back at him, with the tanned skin from summer still glowing on her cheeks, and her smile, as always, broad. He would never know where she got her optimism. Maybe it was a genetic chemical disposition he had missed out on.

'I love you, you know,' she said, lightly. 'You're my best friend.' Her smile got wider and she squeezed his hand roughly. She was holding back tears. This was the key to Sam, he realised, and couldn't believe he was conscious of it for the first time. The more affable and the more friendly she appeared, the harder she was trying to be all right.

'You're my best friend too,' he said. 'I'm so sorry.'

And now he was almost crying, and Sam was holding him gently, as if he was an injured animal. He bit down on his own hand so as not to be audible to anyone inside, and they rocked back and forth and watched the light of the sun retreat, until the spotlights from the towers took over, and filled the sky with artificial light.

He waited a few days, in which he took his book and drew a lot of plants. Since his conversation with Alexia he'd not wanted to draw people anymore. He drew rocks and trees, and tried not to draw too many dead birds.

Every time he tried to talk to Alexia she shut down and shied away. Once she made an excuse that she had to see Polly, once she let Ana drag her away by the hand to have her nails painted. Isaiah had tried hinting that they should have a discussion. He had tried joking about it. At breakfast he had kept his voice low and attempted to make a direct request: 'Alexia, I would like to see you on ...' He had been about to say 'on my own', but halfway through his sentence she turned elaborately away from him at the breakfast table and began to talk to Rangi about going to town for groceries.

Late one night, in desperation, he texted her. He resisted the urge to add in any pretence that the text was practical in nature. He wrote that he would like to 'talk things over', that he thought there were 'things they needed to sort out'. The words were clumsy, but he didn't know how else to go about it. He asked her to call. He would not tell Rangi, even if Rangi owed him twenty dollars.

Alexia did not respond for three days. During this time she was conspicuously absent from meetings. Aidan told him she hadn't been feeling well. Hannah told him she was getting through some paperwork. He even heard a rumour she was finally studying for her bar exam, that she was considering leaving to go and sit the test. He grew slightly panicky. She wasn't at meals, aside from breakfast, where she avoided his eyes.

On the fourth day his phone rang in the middle of a meeting. He took the call outside.

'It's Alexia.'

'You're calling,' Isaiah said. He couldn't keep the joy out of his voice. He began to walk towards the hillock that had the best cellphone reception. She must be down by her camp; there was a good spot there, close to the road.

'I'm calling. What have you told Sam?'

'I talked to her. Everything's out in the open.' Isaiah was aware that he was rushing the words.

'What exactly is out in the open?'

'She knows that I might be interested in pursuing ... something with you. Sam said she's all right with it.'

'But I'm not all right with it. I'm just not that kind of person. I can't pretend to be. And for all your "open relationship" talk, I don't believe that Sam is, either.'

'I wouldn't speak for Sam.' He crested the hill, but the reception was fluctuating wildly.

'Last time I checked, open relationship wasn't a euphemism for "letting tired old relationships drag on while you sleep with other women".'

'You're assuming a lot, Alexia,' Isaiah said. 'It's not like that. Not anymore.'

'It's just that I don't think I can do it.'

'Do you mind if I come and talk?' he asked. 'I can explain better in person.' They had broken up, he and Sam. It was final. It was real. Since their conversation he hadn't missed her in an active way – she was there as much as she had ever been – but just because they had officially broken up didn't mean he wanted to rush anything with Alexia. It also didn't mean he wanted that possibility to go away.

'There's the issue of us being very different people,' Alexia said. He remembered her hovering over him, the disjointedness of it.

'Everyone's different,' he said.

'I think … you want to destroy things,' she said. 'To strike out at things that are wrong. I'm not like that.' He said nothing. 'Really, I just want to make music,' she said.

'I don't think we're so different after all,' he said. He left a space. 'And I'm not all about destroying things. I'm eager to rebuild this community. But how do you repair something so broken?'

'The best you can hope for is to contribute a few fresh notes. That's what I think.'

'I think it's defeatist to think that way.'

'I don't feel defeatist. I think I probably feel more hopeful than you.'

How had they even begin talking like this?

'I am hopeful. I am hopeful the system may break down. Or that we may overthrow it.'

'You sound like Bryce.'

'Someone has to sound like that. Maybe I'm more hopeful than you.'

'My hopes are more realistic.'

'Well, I'm hoping something will come out of that night in the bush, in the end.' She didn't answer. 'Can I come and see you?' Again, she didn't speak. 'I'm aware you've lost someone close to you. I just want to talk. I'm not in a rush.'

'Not tonight,' she said at length. 'But soon, Isaiah.'

He came down off the hill happier than he had been for weeks.

45

The day dawned clear and bright. The mountain's flanks were covered in snow now, and as she was leaving her tent she dived back in immediately, seeking her warmest winter fleece. She had been given this by Mary with a pitying expression; she said it had been her eldest grandchild's. Alexia's coat was muddy from being kept on the floor of her tent and her breath steamed. The sky was steely and the air felt like snow. She wondered if it fell this distance from the mountain.

That morning at breakfast Matiu prevailed upon them to give up their camp and come inside. There was room now, he said, now that the many other protestors they'd make space for were gone. Aidan and Hannah had always had their van, of course, but they admitted that even that was growing freezing in the mornings. Alexia had a four-season sleeping bag, but the nights were almost intolerable.

Matiu put his hand on her arm.

'We wanted to encourage others to stay,' she said. She still felt she took up too much space here.

'I don't think any more are coming,' he said to her gently. 'It's more a time of endings than arrivals, don't you think?'

'Our Zen philosopher!' Rangi said to Matiu. But he grew serious. 'Nah, you guys got to come in from the cold. You can always sleep in the marae.'

In Alexia's mind the marae was for ceremonial meetings, but she supposed this was exactly what it was used for: to house manuhiri when it was cold.

'There's that whole place next to Lizzie's house that Alexia can have, with Aidan and Hannah too.'

'That's if they want to give up their free-loving combi dream.'

At the other end of the table, Hannah was nodding furiously.

'About bloody time we came closer,' Aidan said. 'I'm freezing me nuts off out there.'

That night they packed up their camp, and came inside. Alexia couldn't help feeling hopeful, like it was the beginning of a new chapter.

46

Isaiah was sitting on the porch of one of the small houses in the evening. Sam offered him her sunflower seeds. Despite everything, the break-up, the people leaving, the general air of disillusionment about the pā, his friendship with Sam seemed better than it had been in months. Now she was full of smiles. They'd come out of an arduous meeting, in which Rangi and Matiu had diverted the talk to the gardens: the kūmara were drying up and the silver beet too, and what was to be done about it? It had appeared at first to be Matiu's fault: he had not properly supervised the irrigation of the plots. Then it appeared to be Rangi's: he had suggested that the kūmara be planted too early to have a good yield. Now it was evident that the gardens were suffering from the same toxic run-off as Polly's veggies. The root crops refused to grow and the lettuces had turned black. The pā was lower on winter stores than it had been for years, and the money from the fundraiser would only go so far to bridge the gap. Then the depressing business of their latest application to the council had come up, and after a lot of legal language from Alexia, they had learned that there were no large or straightforward things to be done, only small, frustrating things.

Now Sam leaned against him in a companionable way. Alexia was playing guitar at the end of the porch. She did not seem to notice. Melissa and Kate were sitting on the steps. Mary was knitting, and Polly sat in her wooden chair. Hannah was doing the dishes in the wharekai, and Rangi and Matiu were up to something behind the house. Te Kahurangi was absent, but she often was in the evenings. He supposed she was somewhere doing things on social media. He chewed the seed and spat out the outer layer. It lay on the ground like a small cockroach.

'I never liked them that much anyway,' he said.

'I know,' Sam said. She beamed. Perhaps now that the issue of sex was out of the picture, their friendship was magically healed?

Then the noise came, like nothing he'd ever heard: a tearing and a thunder.

There it was, against the winter sky, a large, misshapen sun. Then they were all on their feet watching the ball of light move upwards and out and down from the sky. The sound went on and on. Sam grabbed at him and Melissa bowled them both onto the deck. She was screaming but he couldn't hear. The rumbling went on and the ground shook under their feet and they were inside of the sound. Rangi came around the side of the house, yelling. Alexia sat transfixed with her guitar, her hair thrown back, face coloured red by the light. He tried to get up but could not.

When the great noise was over the shouting began. Matiu came running up from somewhere and Polly was yelling in te reo. The ground shook, then stopped, then shook again. He watched with a calm he knew was false as a crack opened up in the path to the marae. He watched it widen. The earth moved and stilled, moved and stilled. Sam pulled her cellphone out and began dialling. Kate hyperventilated in the corner of the porch. He saw that Melissa was, peculiarly, tearless.

One of the towers visible from the pā was on fire. As he watched, hand going to the pocket where his second-best camera was, the ball of flame moved downwards and dispersed. Now a huge piece of the building tumbled and fell.

'Police, ambulance, fire,' Sam was saying into her phone. 'I don't know. All of them. All three.'

The earth moved and shook.

'Gas masks,' Isaiah said, but no one seemed to hear.

What the thing could have released into the atmosphere, he didn't know. He went down the steps to Alexia and touched her back and they both stood very still. If something was very loud, but not music, did she see her lights? Was that why she was staring in this enraptured way at the sky? The earth kept moving.

'Come away from there!' Polly yelled. 'Come into the field. Get everyone out.' She sent Melissa off to find the children and their mother Lizzie. Mary ran onto the deck.

'Who has done this thing?' she yelled. Mary had always the been jovial, practical one. It was Polly who had led the speeches and the talk, while Mary ran the wharekai behind the scenes. Now she was ready to fight. 'Which of you has done this?'

No one answered. Polly put a hand on Mary's shoulder. Mary calmed herself, and then crouched to comfort Kate, who was muttering and shaking.

'Not safe there,' Polly yelled to Isaiah and Alexia, who had failed to move. They walked a few steps, quickly, out into the field. Isaiah was aware of things being organised swiftly around him. Mary came and went with blankets and a battery-powered radio. He marvelled at the way Polly walked strictly upright through the little shakes and the big ones, as if unafraid, when even Rangi crouched down.

'It must have released some gas underground,' Isaiah said to Alexia. She was mute. He took deep breaths but could detect nothing except the air: perhaps they were far enough away. He had always been proactive under pressure, but now he had frozen up. The ground moved and Alexia put her arm around his waist. Rangi and Matiu were talking in te reo. He listened hard, and found that he could understand. Had this happened organically? He didn't have time to wonder.

'I'm coming with you,' he said. They did not argue. He unwound Alexia's arm and held her hand for a moment. She made to come with him but he shook his head. 'You should stay here.' She seemed about to argue but Polly waved to her. Alexia went. Isaiah walked with Rangi the truck.

Rangi drove slowly, waiting for each new tremble to subside. At the entrance to the fracking land the way was barred. As Rangi parked the ute Isaiah saw an ambulance pull in: how it had got there so quickly he had no idea. The security guard refused them entry. Rangi argued. The guard spoke into his radio.

'Nope,' he said to them, and turned away. Rangi moved forwards, as though he would strike him. Isaiah stepped in.

'We're from the pā,' he said. 'We have relatives in there. We only want to know what's happened. Are our people safe?' It was the same thing that Rangi had said, but the man turned to him as if he was relieved. Isaiah kept his voice low. 'Anything you can tell us. Anything at all.'

'They're saying it was sabotage,' the guard said. 'Someone set explosives on the tower. Must have been near the gas outlet. Looks like it was deliberate.'

'Is anyone hurt?' Isaiah asked. 'Should we move our people?'

The guard didn't answer. Isaiah saw that there were no protocols in this situation. The guard probably understood the risks less than he did.

'If these guys don't even know how dangerous it is, we'll have to go back,' he said to Rangi and Matiu. 'We'll have to move them out to somewhere safer.' He made as if to walk away.

'Wait, I'll call management,' the guard said.

The site manager arrived.

'I'll ask you to stop harassing our people,' he said.

'We're not harassing them,' Isaiah said. 'I think you'll find your men would very much like to know what is going on as well.'

The other guards were collecting around the entranceway. 'There's been an accident,' the man said. 'Someone's been hurt.'

The ambulance drove past towards town, its lights flashing.

'Only one?' Rangi asked.

'Just the one seriously injured,' the man said. 'He was on patrol.'

Matiu tried a few names. Isaiah recognised some of them. At one, the man grimaced.

'Oh,' said Matiu. It was the security guard Alexia had abused, the one related to Ana. 'Have you notified anyone?'

'He's not dead,' the man said quickly.

'We will pass on the news,' Matiu said.

'I can't authorise you to contact the family.'

'We are the family,' Isaiah said. He was surprised to hear the pride in his own voice.

47

'Oh God, oh God,' Kate muttered.

Te Kahurangi widened her eyes at Alexia. 'I just *can't* with her,' she mouthed, and Alexia almost laughed.

Mary had got over her fury and was trying to persuade Kate to drink some tea. She could be so patient. The shaking had subsided but still came at intervals. Polly organised her people as if she had practised for it. Alexia was put to work serving biscuits. She was grateful for the job. The thinking was that the series of small quakes had been brought on by the explosion. Circulating amongst them was the term 'aftershock'. No one mentioned the other word, the more frightening one: 'pre-shock'.

A head count was started. Te Kahurangi stood at Polly's right hand, counting people off. Matiu and Isaiah and Rangi were accounted for, and Alexia and half a dozen other activists. There was Hannah, but where was Aidan? The head count halted for a few moments and people made nervous comments about 'The Irish'. But suddenly Aidan burst from a bush, accompanied by Bryce.

'Burn!' Aidan yelled. 'Them fuckers are burning!'

Bryce had lost weight. His cheekbones had taken on an austere quality. He must have been camping out near the boundaries of their land. The thought made Alexia uneasy. She waited to see if anyone would take issue with his presence, but everyone was otherwise occupied.

'Burn!' Aidan yelled. He danced a little dance and raised his hands towards the flames as if warming them. 'Celebrate the capitalist apocalypse!'

Polly appeared to notice Bryce but shook her head as if she had more important things to worry about. Mary was pulling at her right arm. Alexia caught the words 'told you', and 'pākehā'. Polly seemed to be trying to calm her down.

Hannah walked over to Aidan. There was a new tremor, but she didn't bend.

'Aidan McBurney,' she said. 'Sit down and shut the hell up.' Aidan did as he was told.

'He's right though,' Bryce said, with a trace of his former force. 'They deserve it.' He spoke too fast. But then they'd all been getting a little manic. There was Sam's recent strange elation, Matiu's quiet rage, Melissa's increasing self-righteousness. And Isaiah was always so quiet. You never knew what he was really thinking.

The earth shook, very slightly. How had she even come here? Papou came to mind, holding out a ripe tomato for her to eat.

Polly pulled her pearl cigarette holder from her pocket. She inserted a cigarette, pre-rolled, and lit it. She considered Bryce for a moment. Then, with a gesture that was almost queenly, she lifted one finger and pointed towards the ground.

He sat down with a small huff. Polly began to address them.

'We have people at the site,' she said. 'Relatives.' Te Kahurangi carried on with her head count. Alexia too was counting between the tremors, seconds not people. The tower was burning at a slower pace. What was there to burn? As far as she knew it was all iron and steel. It must be gas burning, still flowing up from the ground. The tremors were getting shorter, each not as strong as the last.

'Forty-eight,' Te Kahurangi said.

Maitai was calling out. 'My brother,' he said. Alexia put down the pot of tea and went to him. 'My sister.'

'Where's your mother?' Alexia asked. She put her hand on him: he was cold. She found a blanket.

'Away at my uncle's,' Maitai said. 'Me and Ana and Tama, we stayed here, with Mary.'

'Where are Ana and Tama?' Now the people around them were listening.

'Tama's cat,' Maitai said. 'They went to find it. Tama wouldn't go alone. Isaiah made him promise.' He jerked his head up the river, behind which the tower burned. 'They went up there,' he said. 'Past the place where the taniwha lives.'

Alexia drew her jacket around her.

'Polly!' she called. But Polly had already heard. A wave seemed to go through the old woman's body, a sort of long exaggerated jolt. Now Polly bent slightly at the waist, ever so slightly, and leaned on her tokotoko. Then she met Alexia's eyes, and pulled herself up.

Sam reached again for her phone. But whoever she called would have to come all the way from town. No one would be here for hours.

Polly let out a call, a call that rose as it went on and that contained things Alexia did not wish to see. It was only red. It turned halfway into a short, blunt song, a sharp thing with an economy of words and notes, then cut off.

'Who here will go and look for them?' she said.

Alexia gathered the few remaining children into a room off the wharenui. She put on a cartoon. They all watched it, including her, happy to forget what was going on. The earth had stopped moving. Maitai still gripped her by the hand and would not let go, though she sensed he was embarrassed by this.

Outside, Mary was handing out torches and Polly was splitting people up into search parties of two or three. Te Kahurangi was with her wherever she went, running, fetching, moving, entirely in her element. Of the pākehā left at the pā only Aidan, Hannah, Sam and Alexia would be sent out: they had just enough knowledge of the paths they must search. Alexia took Maitai to Te Kahurangi, who stared at her cousin blankly.

'You need to stay with him,' Alexia said.

Te Kahurangi pulled Maitai roughly alongside her. 'Don't you piss off anywhere without telling me,' she said.

'But this is mad,' Kate said. Melissa nodded through her tears, which had finally started. 'We have to wait for the emergency services. This violates the rules of a safe rescue. You all know it does. Any one of you could go missing on this search.'

Polly glared at Kate.

'Get the radios, Te Kahurangi,' she said. 'Get the maps.' A wooden table was covered with a large map, which Polly segmented with a red marker. Each pair was given a shortwave radio and flare, and allotted a segment of land to search. They were so swift, it was as if they were prepared. But of course. They had lost someone to the bush before.

'You are not to go off the paths,' Polly said. 'Keep within the old boundaries. Check within your area, then return. Stay in your groups. If you are not back within two hours, the searchers will be coming for you too.'

Alexia was matched with Sam.

'I still think we should wait for the authorities,' Kate said faintly.

'We will work with the authorities,' said Polly, 'when the authorities show up.'

They were almost ready to go when a woman rushed into the room. She had a dog with her.

'That's Taylor's farm hand,' Sam whispered.

'I need help,' the woman said. 'Please.' Alexia could see the whites of her eyes. 'It's just crazy, with the explosion and everything. It's just that Taylor…' She sat down suddenly, and began to cry. Alexia thought what it must have been like to hear the sound and see the explosion and feel the earthquakes in the farmhouse all alone. 'He went out looking for his dogs. He's been going further and further into the bush. They were sick, you know.'

'When did he leave?' Polly asked.

'Earlier today,' the woman said. 'Didn't have any gear with him. He traipses about all over that land.' She gestured towards where the tower burned behind the drawn curtains. 'I wouldn't want the mad bastard to come to any harm.'

Now Polly turned to the searchers.

'We have three people to search for,' she said.

'Aunty, no!' Te Kahurangi said.

But Polly said nothing, only held her palm out towards Te Kahurangi, as flexible as a stone.

Rangi, Isaiah and Matiu returned, and there was a quick exchange of information. Mary rushed off to call someone about the hurt guard – she needed a landline, as the pā was still short on cellphones. They decided not to evacuate. The three men insisted they join the search. Polly handed them the last of the torches and radios.

'Take care of yourselves,' she said. She was speaking to Isaiah, but Alexia didn't think he noticed. He didn't seem to notice Alexia either. She remembered the warmth of him beside her after the explosion. In the distance the tower fire burned low but still lit up the sky. His eyes were on the mountain. The searchers called out to each other as they crossed the field, cheery comments about having a cuppa and a kai after they found the kids.

Alexia and Sam walked close together. Isaiah was walking up ahead with Rangi and Matiu, the sound of his voice floating back to her. Soon Alexia and Sam came to the edge of the field and entered the bush. The searchers separated. Sam fiddled with their laminated map before pointing to the track they would take.

'Can you believe how organised they are?' Alexia asked.

'I can believe it,' Sam said.

One by one the voices of the others faded, swallowed by the wall of bush.

The sound under the trees had a special quality. It was muffled and magnified at the same time. Alexia immediately began to hear echoes that weren't real, cries that sounded weirdly joyful from further off under the trees. She knew it was just the other searchers talking, their voices distorted by the bush, but at each new sound she felt a kind of panic. Sam strode on in her combat boots, apparently unfazed. If anyone would find the children it would be Sam, defender of innocents, protector of small things. Alexia felt oddly reassured to be with her.

They began to yell the children's names in turns. The odd, disembodied noises went on. The bush was damp and cold though the night was not wet. Several times Sam inadvertently bumped a tree branch and it flicked at Alexia. She pointed the torch down at the ground a couple of steps ahead of her feet so Alexia could see the trail. The night closed around them. The noises continued: cries and strange cackles, birdlike and surreal. Could Sam not hear them? She said nothing. They came to the river. Here was the clearing and a convergence of paths. The burning tower was visible from where they stood, turning the slick water red.

'Second to the left, upstream,' Sam muttered. She peered at Alexia. 'You okay?'

'It's just,' Alexia said. She felt suddenly physically weak. 'Bit noisy in here, don't you think?'

'It's just the others calling,' Sam said. 'Here.' She thrust her hand towards her. Alexia opened her hand and found a pile of sunflower seeds. Not knowing what else to do, she put them into her mouth. Sam seemed satisfied. They began working their way upstream. Now they were closer to the fire a dull glare hung in the air and Alexia could smell it; not smoke, something more toxic.

'Tama!'

'Ana!'

Tama was stupid, stupid. Stupid boy! Stupid cat! She could not allow herself to think too hard about what it was they were doing, the potential scenarios ahead. It was easier to be angry. She walked hard into the gradient, throwing herself at the hill.

48

'I'm going back,' Isaiah said. 'I'm going to get some gear, then I'll head further up alone.' He changed direction suddenly. Matiu frowned under his headlamp.

'What's that going to achieve?' he said.

'The kids'll be okay,' Isaiah said. He was convinced that this was true. He trusted them. 'They're clever kids, local kids; they won't have gone off the path. And they wouldn't have got far in anyway. Someone will find them. You guys will find them.'

'And what the bloody hell are you going to do?' Rangi asked.

'I'm going up to look for Taylor,' Isaiah said. 'He's been lost all afternoon. When Search and Rescue come it might be too late. It's cold. The kids wouldn't even have been near the tower. They know by now not to go on the fracking site.'

'Don't let him go, Rangi,' Matiu said. 'He's gone insane.'

'I know where he would have gone,' Isaiah said. 'I'm going to find him.' He ran some steps back down the track.

'But we've got the radio,' Rangi said.

'Don't worry about me,' Isaiah said. 'I'll leave records of where I'm going. Promise.'

'Yeah, and aren't you the most trustworthy guy in the world,' Rangi said. Isaiah was already moving out of earshot. 'Don't worry,' he heard him say to Matiu. 'He won't get any further than the river.'

Orienteering. Abseiling. Rock climbing. Mountain climbing. Isaiah had done them all. He had always known there was something coming – the imminent global economic collapse. The fall, and then the mayhem, and then the critical adjustment period, while people looted and fought and established new ways of surviving in the absence of nation states. He would welcome it, if it came. Or perhaps it would come in the form of a natural disaster. He'd never taken anything for granted: the continuation of life as he knew it, the soundness of the economy, the stability of the natural world. When they'd decided to come here he'd spent a significant amount of his savings on shoes. Sam had hassled him about it. She got all her clothes from op shops, and would never indulge her feet in such a way.

'What are you running from after all, that you need such expensive shoes?' she'd asked.

'The apocalypse,' Isaiah had told her. 'The impending apocalypse.'

Now his apocalyptic shoes carried him well over the rough ground. He'd got the pounamu out of his pack, where it had sat since that unsuccessful meeting. Around his neck it was as cool and as heavy as ever. He would earn it tonight. Rangi was right, he was mad to go in alone. It was the exact opposite of everything he'd been taught about survival. But he was sure he knew where Taylor was. He would go in, travelling at speed with his head torch and compass. He could do the half-hour walk to the mountain's base through the open farmland in a quarter of an hour, if he went at a run. He would climb for an hour, two, at the most, which would put him beyond when Polly wanted them all back. The pack on his back with his flares and matches and survival blanket was light, streamlined to fit his body. He would make his way through the bush up the spur of the mountain that he would choose as if he was Taylor, as if knew the land well and was searching for some lost dogs.

When Taylor went up it would have been light. He must have scaled the spur and come down off it onto the mountainside, maybe following a noise in the bush, and got lost in the waning light. Isaiah would make his way up, following the ridgeline, till he came out in the sparser bush. He'd been up that way once before, photographing birds. There the bush thinned and opened, the trees dwindling into smaller versions of themselves, the dense foliage transitioning into alpine cover and the air cooling. There was only one place a person would go in this area if he wanted a view. Taylor was guilt-ridden and weak, and enamoured of his dogs, but Isaiah did not believe that he was stupid.

There would not be snow tonight, but the air was cool and clear, and it would get colder as the night wore on. It was about eight o'clock. Isaiah knew sometimes his actions could be questionable in other people's eyes. He knew sometimes he acted against the accepted codes, but it was always for a good reason. If Taylor had been out since early in the day and the rescue teams took too long to find him, there would be a good chance he'd develop exposure. Isaiah knew the terrifying largeness of the land.

On this side of the mountain there were no paths or trails. The closest hut was a day's walk away along the tops of the mountain's flanks where the bush gave out, and the closest road would be a day or more away, if you were headed in the wrong direction. Taylor would know the lie of the land, of course, and hopefully would do what you were meant to do if you were lost: either stay still or find a river or stream to follow downwards, or climb a ridge and follow that. But Isaiah suspected that Taylor had got turned about. It was easy enough to do.

Isaiah had studied maps of the area for many hours, trailing his fingers over the marked ridges and valleys, the topographical legends of the terrain. Every time he'd hesitate on a different ridge or hill, hating himself for it, wondering. He knew the clean green lines and blue threads of river on the page were deceitful. It seemed so straightforward, so easy. There were protocols to follow if you got lost. You would mark your place by taking note of your surroundings. You would stay put or, if that failed, climb a hill to get some idea of your position. You would build a shelter. You would think of the people at home.

But the symbols on the map were nothing like the things they stood for. A thin blue line was a minor stream, which in a storm could flood to head height. A thick blue line was a river, which if you were fording it alone could take you under. A track line was the fantasy of safety, one which in real life could slip and fall down a bank, give way or disappear. A bridge was a sometimes a vulnerable span of wood, sometimes only three steel wires, upon which you must balance with your pack. A yellow triangle was a hut, warmth, heat, light in an unknown place. This side of the mountain was all hills and valleys, blue lines and brown, indicating surges in height, rocky outcrops, ravines. There were no huts, no intersecting paths. Isaiah knew the maps better than anyone. He jogged on, the pounamu cold around his neck.

He came out into open farmland, found the stile and climbed the fence. The tower was a little way off, still burning in a satisfying way. Near the fracking site there were no bird calls, no sounds except the wind. The emergency services would be there soon: fire engines, ambulances. Some of them would be heading to the pā to help in the search. But finding Taylor was up to him. He began to run through the long grass. The bush line came into view quicker than he'd thought it would. He saw the place where he estimated Taylor would have gone in, where any logical person would have gone in, and headed towards it. The earth dropped away behind him so he could see it all laid out: the tower, the small trucks like sheep on the plain, the pā lands bushed and indistinct. He stopped and caught his breath.

He felt sick. But he'd trained himself for this sort of physical trial. It was only Sam who really knew the weaknesses in him, who knew how reckless he could be. It was wrong to like Alexia quite so much. She didn't know him. His thoughts were coming too fast, like his breaths. And it was irresponsible and impulsive to go into the forest alone. But he was the fittest person for this job. Traitor or not, Taylor was a human being. He still had a chance. Isaiah would not let him go.

He flicked his headlamp on, and went in, moving quickly. He began to call Taylor's name. In his mind he cast the map out like a blanket unfurling. He could see it in three dimensions, almost: the river coming down here, the lesser rivulets going into it at intervals, the angles, even, of the rising ground. He was climbing very quickly, scrambling hand over hand up the steep bank. It levelled as he knew it would. His legs had started to cramp and burn, but he ignored them. He had a bottle with electrolytes in it, if he needed it, not now. Further on, there was a cliff he must negotiate, and then, perhaps after half an hour, he would come out into sparser bush. He called out for Taylor.

He thought he heard an answer. It was off in the bush, a little to the right: from the wrong direction for someone climbing the spur. He moved that way. He yelled as loudly as he could, but there was no response. It had been maybe three-quarters of an hour and his throat was growing hoarse. Suddenly he felt at his collar bone. There, lying against it, was the pounamu, warm for the first time.

He turned and turned, calling in all directions, and heard the sound again, a weird, low calling that circled in on itself like a repeated note. A cooeee? His headlamp bounced light off the grey wall of leaves, showing the ripped gap where he'd come up and the bush ahead. He felt the great mass of fear and panic held at bay just beyond the torchlight, and the great, mounting cold. Why had his father left the pounamu if he'd meant to come back? He changed direction slightly towards the origin of the sound, feeling invulnerable. This bush was his, after all. It was all pā land, once, all of this mountain, and all the lands surrounding it. He didn't believe in spirits or ghosts, but he believed that if anyone could walk here safely in the dark, it was him. But that was not entirely true. It hadn't worked like this for his father.

Isaiah focused on pushing back branches and climbing faster up the slope. Alexia didn't know him as he was really, with all his foolish acts. He heard the weird calling again and stopped, remembering to flick his torch on to the power-save mode. His circle of light shrank.

He panted and called, panted and called, took a sip of the electrolytes liquid, and, disturbingly, threw it up. He must have come further than he thought, must be pushing himself too hard. He called again. Now he was sure he heard an answer. He stopped and took a reading of his co-ordinates using a compass, puffing, noting them on the small pad in his pocket with the stub of a pencil. What was Taylor thinking, coming in here with no gear, on his own? What would anyone be thinking?

When Isaiah was a child he was always the last to be found in hide and seek. When he was older, he was always first to find the prize in orienteering. He understood how to search and he understood how to find. And he understood how to hide in plain sight, a skill which had paid off. The noise sounded again a little way off in the bush. Isaiah should be coming out of the heavy trees soon, according to his calculations. He should be able to see how far he had come. But where he thought the bush would be clearing there was more level ground and denser foliage, which didn't make sense.

Still, he could walk now without using the tree roots to aid him. His headlamp faltered, which was not good, and then lit up again. He pushed on.

Taylor would be through the next stand of trees. He would be there, and Isaiah needed to prepare himself, because he might not be in a good way. He'd never found someone who was seriously injured. He might have to shoot a flare. The rescue teams would see it; he would stay by Taylor's side; they would all come out safely in the end. He called again and the voice answered. But now it sounded further away. Doubt crept into him, and the torch flickered again. He would not

but then it

this part of the mountain was tapu

He was getting tired. He stopped in a hole in the bush. He had to admit he was off course, not where he'd thought he would be. There were no views and no clear ridgeline. There was no sound of water or identifiable bird call. The pounamu was warm at last, it was warm. It was the only thing. But he was cold. He listened to the sound he had been following, thinking it was Taylor's voice, a weird hum with points in it, a cool descending call. It occurred to him that the thing that had called might not be alive in the usual sense. This caused him to feel such a blind panic that he found himself crouched down, head clasped between his hands.

Isaiah was raised as his father had been with the idea that he was special. When he grew older this thing he was meant for had not become immediately apparent. Instead he saw a world of wrongdoings that he could not engage in, that he was morally bound to oppose. How could anyone see what humans did to the world and not be in opposition? He'd always had the conviction that he was in the right. But what if he was mistaken, about this, about everything? The pounamu bounced against his chest as he moved, but at last it was warm. Perhaps his father had been used to it, so used to it he could not feel its weight.

The sound came again. Tapu. He'd learned from Polly that in the days before pākehā came the highest-ranking people were put to rest here, in locations so secret that no one knew where they were. Their bodies would be taken into the bush and placed high up. It was the greatest honour. His father would not have come here, not on purpose. Now Isaiah could see for himself how easy it was to go off course.

'Taylor!' his voice went out, and out, into the dark. He stood and ran a few steps, ran and then crashed into a tree. His body was hot but his hands and feet were suspiciously cold, now that he thought of it. 'Taylor!' There was a small needling answer, the same as before. It was not Taylor, or a bird. But it was there

if he had been wrong

a man's life was at stake, a man

if he was wrong in his convictions

perhaps he had been wrong to act

Isaiah was confused, that was all. He was mixing things up. He tripped and came to rest on his knees, one hand on a cool stone. When he closed his hand the stone came up with it: it was not a stone but longer and lighter. He could not see in the dark. He directed the head torch onto its cool length. It was a bone.

It was not a bone from a small animal. It was not a bird bone, or a pig or a rat bone. It was a part of something's leg, something big. Not large enough to be cattle. It shone up at him, pale in his brown hand

what if he had

done it on

A sound came out of his throat as he fell back, the bone falling from his hand. It was there, in the bone on the ground and all around him. It was the thing. And now it all went

why would someone go into the bush a

she said that they were happy

Distantly he heard himself retching. He tipped himself onto hands and knees and crawled back towards the bone. Maybe the other bones were here, too. Maybe he had found him finally, and all the old folk, the sainted folk. But that was wrong. He was looking for someone else. Perhaps the pressure had been too much: the pressure to save the pā, to restore it to a thriving place, to bring back wealth from the city, to rebuild. Or even, as Isaiah was trying to do, just to save it from further dissolution. Perhaps his father was the type to surrender after all

perhaps he just wanted it all to

error of judgement. I can understand

There. It was in his hand, the surface flush against his skin.

It was not a bone at all. It didn't even look much like a bone. It was a pale stick, a branch that had fallen long ago, bleached by the sun.

Isaiah stood and took a breath, and then another, quick and shallow. He pressed the light on his watch and read the time. He took out his compass and made notes. He took out his phone and turned it on and checked his GPS positioning. He activated the point A to point B route map he had programmed into his phone before leaving, overlaid onto the topographic maps he had saved on the hard drive. His position was a red dot in a wilderness of green, the line a red thread, but as long as he could find north he could roughly follow it.

He knew he might have been wrong. He had been so convinced. He kicked the white stick away with the toe of his boot, casually, watching it arc out of the light.

Before he turned back, he went down on his knees, took off his glasses, and cried.

49

At the part of the river known as Taniwha Bend, Alexia saw a dark shape in the water. She pointed, and even Sam jumped. They shuffled closer.

'It's a piece of wood, right?' Sam said. Then they were laughing, falling over each other like old friends. Of course it was a log! Only a log! They walked on.

Alexia tried to engross herself in the small details: a wet branch striking her face, the uneven ground. But she could hear them; there was no doubt about it any longer. It started as a low hum, in the left ear, not the right, piercing and intermittent. She knew with a deep conviction that it was not coming from inside her but was of this place. It came. It went. She was so scared she could hardly breathe. But they needed to keep calling.

'Ana!'

'Tama!'

To her ears their own voices sounded more and more remote, as if they were swimmers drifting out to sea. Alexia was sweating now. The whistles grew louder. Soon they took on distinct rhythms. It had happened to her twice before for sure, perhaps three times, when she had walked alone to her campsite after dark, past the urupā, through the bush. She stared at Sam's back in the dull light of the tower burning. They came in flares and bursts. Green. Gold, red. She quelled it. It was cold. She closed her ears. But still she heard them. She began to breathe unevenly. They seemed to be closing in, first on the left-hand side, then her right. But there was nothing there. Only bush only bush only bush sounds. Only birds. They were higher up in the forest now than Alexia had been before.

'They wouldn't have come up this far,' Alexia said.

'They wouldn't,' Sam agreed. But she seemed unsure. They looked up the path, towards the mountain. Sam checked her watch.

'We'll be pushing it to make it back for Polly's roll call,' she said.

'Shall we,' Alexia said, 'just to make sure.' But Sam was already walking up the path.

For some time the odd sounds receded. Alexia repeated old Greek rhymes in her mind. She had the idea that certain things worked against them as a charm: certain rhythms, words in her own language. She made herself invisible to them; she was untranslatable. Her hands were freezing cold. Sam was panting freely, still calling the children's names every so often. The lights danced, elusive, then there, in front of her, then far away again. They followed no regular pattern. Finally Alexia could not stand it.

'Can't you hear them?' she asked. She knew that she sounded crazy. But just then one sounded, close, then further away. They were being led up the mountain. 'I don't know, Sam. I don't know if we should go on. I think it's a trick. I don't think they like us.'

Sam flicked the torch at Alexia's face. 'Alexia, sit down.' She made her sit on a damp log. She gave her another thing out of her pocket: not seeds, but chocolate. Alexia loved Sam, she loved her. 'I think we'll just go a little further, ten minutes or so,' Sam said, 'and then we'll turn back, okay?' When she was speaking Alexia could not hear the odd notes. She wanted to hug Sam, wanted to kiss her. She was so calm and good. Sam pulled Alexia to her feet.

They went on for a while longer, still calling out. Then Sam spun around.

'Did you hear that?' she asked. She bent low to the ground. Alexia had only been listening to the odd squeaks and rustlings, the terribly organised notes. It reminded her of the nose instruments Māori used to play, but higher pitched. Even now it was hard to concentrate on what Sam was saying. 'They're there,' Sam said. 'They're over there!' She ran a few steps, to the edge of a little rise.

'Tama! Ana!' she yelled. And Alexia heard Ana's voice.

'Told you, stupid,' she said, just a little off the path. 'Wasn't the patupaiarehe. Was just them, coming to get us.'

'Ana!' Alexia was at the edge now, leaning out into the dark. Sam was already climbing down.

'Hello?' Tama called.

'Tama!' Alexia wanted to jump down and squeeze him. She heard a muffled growl: the stupid cat. She could not see well under the trees. She leaned forwards.

'You,' Sam said. 'Stay up there!' But she was too late.

It was not a long fall. Alexia winded herself on a tree root and landed a little above where they sat. When she moved her ankle she felt a sharp pain. Still, she was overwhelmed with joy. She reached out and felt Tama climb into her lap. Sam patted everyone and ascertained that they were all right. Tama put his arms around Alexia. He still had his baseball cap, turned backwards, as always.

'I didn't go on my own,' he said.

He was very, very cold. She put his hands inside her shirt. He was dressed in only a couple of layers. He had his cat. At least that was keeping him warm.

'He thought there were patupaiarehe singing in the forest.' Ana was talking fast. 'He thought they were coming for us. I told him no, they don't like little boys. We fell down here and I thought we should maybe sleep here if we had to. But we stayed close to the path.'

'You did the right thing, Ana. Now I'll tell you what we are going to do.' Sam was speaking softly, but she was all business.

'We are all going to climb up, and then we are going back, as fast as we can go. And Tama, when we get to the top you are leaving your cat behind.'

'No!' Tama said. 'No way!' Sam ignored him.

They started climbing up, but it proved difficult for Alexia to use her leg. Sam came up behind her. They gained the path.

'My ankle,' Alexia said. 'I don't think I can walk very fast.' She pulled Tama up the last bit. He was shaking. So was Ana.

Sam stood for a long moment, thinking. 'I'm going to have to leave you,' she said. 'I'm going to have to get these two back.'

'Not leaving my cat,' Tama said.

'You are leaving that bloody cat!' Sam said. It was this beyond anything else that told Alexia the situation was serious. 'I have to take the torch,' she said. 'I'm not happy about this. You must understand that this is very risky, splitting up. You have to stay here and not move, do you understand me? *Not move from here.*' She seemed furious. Alexia realised that she was afraid. 'Someone will come and get you,' she said.

Tama gave Alexia the cat. He was sobbing. The animal was warm in her arms, heavy and surprisingly solid. It tried to squirm back to Tama.

Sam spoke quickly into the radio. The voice at the other end was Mary's. Cheers broke out as those at the pā heard the kids were all right. Sam interrupted them.

'Alexia needs rescuing now,' she said.

She gave Alexia the radio, which she put in her pocket. The cat was still trying to get away. Then they went, Sam carrying Tama and almost running down the path, Ana rushing after them. Tama began to wail, complaining about leaving the cat behind. What about Alexia? She supposed he thought she could take care of herself. Before the sound of their voices died out, the music started up again.

Time passed. Tunes looped and overlapped in her head. She patted the cat, though it did not seem easy on her lap. At least it was a warmth in the large dark. The lights were overwhelming, coming at her from all directions now. She was crouched on the track, arms around her knees, too cool even in her jacket, ankle throbbing. She tried breathing them out, the odd, sickening notes. She looked for patterns, but this made it worse. Green, gold, green, gold, red. She stared at the canopy, faintly visible through the trees, pinched her own arm. But the sounds went loud and full and thin and faint and high and sharp and low and cool and green and gold, and red, and she could not block them. She had been here a very long time. Flash, fade. Flash, fade.

Then came the great approach. The bursts converged on a point not far from her face. Alexia was drawn in, the colours forming one giant sheet of sound. They were close. She could almost touch them. She stumbled up and forwards. Now the sheet went gold, all gold, and red. A metre from her face. A millimetre. They were deafening. The song grew high and fell down into her body. She knew she shouldn't go. She ran.

The blood had left her foot in a great rush with the sprain, and now was pooling back into it. The pain was sickening and sure, a needle, a needle, each step radiating points upwards. Now that she was moving the patupaiarehe receded a little. The radio was gone. She was cold. The scales she had used to practise played over and over in her head, descent, ascent, descent. His fingers on the frets of the bouzouki. It held them off and so as she walked and tripped and got colder she sifted through all the songs she had ever heard. But they were there. She was sure of it.

A branch slashed her face. Cat, where was it? Yes, still here, heavy in her arms. She had been immersed for hours, for days. It was a drowning. The dark was complete but for the bursts of light, which illuminated nothing, not being actually there. But they were there. How people could have lived here she didn't know. Isaiah was not afraid of the bush. He could listen to the birds' songs and identify them, he could tell which trees were good for shelter, which bark could be made into food, which fern to eat. Isaiah would be coming in. He would be coming down the path. Sam would have told him. He would find her.

But she wasn't on the path.

She stopped for a moment, confused, finding herself on her hands and knees. The branch

had struck her and

her mother struck her

fallen into this deep ditch. Beethoven's fifth. Isaiah was coming. It was cold it was cold. The cold was an actual pain. The fairies were mischievous, not evil, as in the stories. The flutes called and called. Gold, green. Rangi had said to stay away. They were meant to be friendly. But they weren't like the Irish pixies. Red. The cat scratched. It wasn't happy. They weren't little. They had white faces and red hair. Like the Englesika. Don't watch the lights. She pushed herself up with one hand but slipped and went down again. When had she lost the path? Vivaldi. Moumourakia. Under it they were there. The cat knew they were there. She was not dreaming. Smell was magnified, the death smell of soil under her nails. Gregorian chant. Damp. Everything, her hair, her clothes. It was like those nose flutes but coming all at once, from one direction now, off to her right. Gold. Deep in the

but she wasn't sure anymore what

and she couldn't get off her

Isaiah was coming, and she was being stupid. She put the cat down at last, and it went off with a hiss into the bush. Die Zauberflöte. She staggered up, walked forwards. The flutes sounded a way off. It was ridiculous. She was shaking. She was going to. Green. If she took off her clothes and left them in the bushes, hanging them there like little flags, then whoever was coming would find them and know that she had gone this way. Breadcrumbs in the wood. She pulled her shirt over her head and snagged it on a twig. Green flashes, gold. The treacherous things. So beautiful. The shaking was uncontrollable. It was breaking up. What? The flutes. Rangi had said. Not to go in alone. White crumbs. Violin concerto in A minor. They would follow. She began to walk again, took one step, two. Her white T-shirt glimmered faintly in the black, a silver flag. But wait. This was. She was going to step out of her skirt but the stepping hurt her. Needles. But then it

> kounia, bella

> omorfi kopella

occurred to her quite suddenly that this was counter-intuitive. Of course! She must put her T-shirt back on, immediately. How could she be so? The flutes. She turned and pulled the shirt back over her head. Her fingers wouldn't work very well. Rembitika. When she was very young Papou had pushed her on the swing, back, forth, back again, like the pain swaying up and down her leg. Kounia

> swing, bella

> beautiful little girl

but she needed to get back. The flutes were coming thick and fast, spanning a broader space behind her. She decided that that was the wrong way, quite certainly, and that she had to go somewhere else. It was no use just sitting here. Isaiah was coming. Bach. Wedding Cantato. Adagio. But the thing was the thing was

kounia, bella

omorfi kopella

little girl. The ground was cold and the plants cut at her like knives, but she couldn't feel it all that much except as heat. But there it was. She had made the wrong decision. She should have listened to Sam, who had tried to warn her. Flutes behind her. There it was: there was always a choice. She raised her head and pulled herself up the bank. It was easy. The nursery rhyme went on ahead of her. The flutes were close behind. Green red green gold green red gold. I mean, it's quite simple, I mean. Alexia. All you have to do is

second strings

she'd always had a lead to follow

She went on for quite some time. The pain came and went. At length the flutes began to recede, the sound of Papou's voice filling her head. A nursery rhyme. She cleared her mind of everything else, and followed it.

The grass of the open field was dewed and soft. It felt to her numb hands like candy floss. Her shudders had gone entirely. She had gone into a new place. The tunes had gone away too, all of them, all music of any kind. There were no flashes anymore. Behind the tower the sky was lightening into dawn. A man came at her with a flashlight.

'Who is it?' Bryce sounded afraid.

'Where's Isaiah?'

Bryce's eyes were tracking down her face and clothes. 'I don't know,' he said. 'You thought your boyfriend would save you?

What a touching gender-specific fairy tale.'

'He's not my boyfriend,' she said. Now she was pitching forwards. 'I got myself out.'

'You're ...' Bryce said. 'Alexia, are you ...?'

'Patupaiarehe,' she said.

The emergency services were there. It hadn't taken them so long to arrive after all. They were just over the fence now, cleaning up at Taylor's place. Alexia acquiesced to the men in uniform who took her pulse and shone lights into her eyes. She was pronounced all right but instructed to stay in bed and stay hydrated until the effects of the hypothermia had worn off. They bandaged her ankle firmly. It was not broken. She didn't tell them about the music in the forest.

By the time Bryce had carried her back to the pā, Taylor had been found. Search and Rescue teams had seen a shape high up on the ridge above the fracking land. He had been surprised at all the fuss, and reluctant to leave without having found his dogs.

The children had come in with Sam, and were apparently unharmed. But Isaiah had got it into his stupid head to mount his own special search. Search and Rescue had been organised to look for him as well. Polly had been beside herself.

When Isaiah had come in, an hour late, and tired, and hypothermic himself, Polly had refused to speak to him. But he'd gone and sat by her, Te Kahurangi told Alexia, until she took pity on him again. The one thing Te Kahurangi did not know was the condition of the guard who had been hurt in the explosion.

It was nearly daylight by the time the police officer interviewed Alexia. It was just for the record, he said.

He asked what time she had left to search for the children. He asked how many searchers had been sent into the bush. He asked what their instructions had been. She was tired, and her vision was beginning to blur. He asked a lot of things which afterwards she could not clearly recall. All she knew was that she was saturated in a thick relief. The children were safe, Isaiah was safe, even stupid Taylor was safe, and the fire in the tower was being described as 'stable'.

The officer was kind. He put a reassuring hand on hers. He took small, neat notes, and under his pen the events of the night acquired a sense of order. Why had she walked out of the bush alone? Didn't she know that was more dangerous than staying put? How well, exactly, did she know the terrain? How well did this other fellow know it, the one who had gone searching for Taylor, on his own?

She didn't have an answer to this, so she answered everything else. She had never been so happy to see a policeman in her life. She wanted to tell him this. She wanted, deeply, to put her head against his uniformed chest, and rest her head.

50

It was dawn. Isaiah was sitting on the porch of Polly's house. Polly was beside him, directing Te Kahurangi in how to rinse a tub of pūhā. A requirement of staying at Polly's was that they must all get up early. In the wake of the night of the explosion Polly had suggested Isaiah stay with her to recuperate, and he had agreed. It had been three days since the tower caught fire. There would be a large shared meal today, and a discussion of what action should be taken over the injured guard.

The burned tower was not visible from where Isaiah sat drinking his coffee. From Polly's porch you could see only a few metres into the dense bush. Her house was small and wooden and very old: one of the first in the settlement. Sitting here he could almost believe that none of it had happened: the rough stripping of the frack land just over the rise, the tower falling and the search afterwards, his great error of judgement.

Polly had done her waiata, her greeting of their tīpuna, in the hallway, as she did every morning. The sun was rising but it was cool. A tūī called, its *brrr bapp bap bap* going out a little way into the bush, soon falling into the decaying fronds of fern.

Polly was listening to the bird call. 'Something's wrong,' she said. The phone rang.

'So early!' said Te Kahurangi, and went to answer it. In her absence Isaiah ran the pūhā over his fingertips. It seemed an almost miraculous shade of green.

Te Kahurangi was running onto the porch, her pupils black

and full. Polly was standing up. Isaiah knocked over his coffee, spilling it on the wooden boards.

'That was the big house… ' Te Kahurangi said.

There was a man in the clearing with a gun. There were many men in the clearing with guns. They had semi-automatics of the kind used only by the Special Forces. Police? Army? SIS? They surrounded Polly, Te Kahurangi and Isaiah. His mind flitted through the house and out the back door, to where the path led towards the mountain. But the guns were aimed at them: there would be no breaking free.

'Come down with your … come down with your hands up … descend with your hands up …

'All remaining residents of the building come out unarmed with your … with your … come out with your …

'Lie on the ground … lie face down on the ground … lie down with your hands behind …

'Do not resist do not resist lie down lie down with your …

'Do not resist …'

The commands came in small, concentrated bursts. Polly grasped the tokotoko and heaved it upwards. Isaiah flung his hands up and stepped in front of her. He'd never been arrested like this, with an elderly woman and a young cousin.

The uniforms were black and unmarked. Behind him Polly was swinging her tokotoko. The hand of the young recruit in front of them twitched on the trigger – then he grabbed for Polly's tokotoko, but Te Kahurangi was already there, pressing the old lady back onto the porch.

'Machine guns, Aunty,' she hissed. 'They've got machine guns, for fuck's sake.'

'Why are you arresting us?' Isaiah called. 'Do you have a warrant?'

'Come out with your … lie face down do not resist …'

'Why are you arresting us?' The guns were trained on him.

He could count maybe twenty men in his direct line of vision –
the situation was clearly insane. 'Why are you –' They paid
Isaiah no attention. Three or four men thundered across the
porch and into the house.

'Clear!' one of them yelled.

'You have no right –' Polly said. Isaiah heard a sound; the
wrenching of fabric, he guessed. A cop in front of him gestured
downwards. They wanted him flat on his stomach on the
porch. He started to kneel. The rough grain bit at his knees.
'Have you got a warrant for searching the premises?' he asked.
'Your superiors …'

'There's your warrant,' one of the cops said. He came forwards and pinned it to the front door, where none of them
could read it.

'I am meant to sight it first, before you enter,' Isaiah said.
But the men were carrying Polly's pictures out onto the porch
and lining them up. They started to rip the portraits from their
frames. Polly cried out. Te Kahurangi held her down, swearing
softly in te reo. Isaiah tried again.

'What is the reason for this arrest?' he said. 'This is a
violation –'

'They said you would say that,' the young cop said. He
laughed, a short, odd laugh. He was breathing fast. 'They said
you'd try to tell us some crap about your rights. They said not
to listen.' The man behind him jabbed him in the back, and
he was quiet.

Polly refused to walk. Instead she fixed her watering eyes on
the porch where photographs of Isaiah's father and grandfather
fluttered in piles and went limp. The men began to drag her.
Her legs bumped over the uneven path to the pā. Isaiah was
cuffed aggressively, hands twisted up behind his back until
his shoulder sockets burned. No one was hit, even when Te
Kahurangi spat at one of the cop's feet.

They came into the light and saw the field. Isaiah felt several
things go through him at once: an odd kind of excitement,

and a clear, biting horror. He could see children sitting on the ground with their arms and legs crossed, as if they were at school and ready for instruction. The men with machine guns stood over them.

51

'Get out of the house … Get out of the house … Come out of the house with your hands up!'

Alexia woke. The sleeping bag was rucked around her waist. She was bare from the waist up and men's voices were shouting outside. Dimly she realised they were shouting for her. Where was she? She wasn't in her tent. But yes, no … she was in the little wooden house next to Lizzie's. She had been recuperating from the night on the mountain. Aidan and Hannah had been caring for her and were in the only other room.

Before she had her eyes open properly she had clothed herself in a T-shirt and was out of bed, her ankle twanging under its bandage.

'Come out with your hands up!'

Aidan and Hannah emerged into the dark hall, and together they all stumbled onto the porch. Black-clad figures. Too many of them. Ten? Twelve? All men. Their guns were trained on the house. What were her rights? Alexia had never been arrested before.

Alexia was cuffed with a kind of plastic cord. They were doing extraordinary things to the furniture. One of the men knifed open a chair and was pulling out the stuffing. She heard the sliding sound of coffee beans rattling onto the kitchen bench. They slit the upholstery of a couch beside her. The battery from Aidan's head torch was brought through and sealed in a bag. A man began photographing the residue on their cooking utensils. She had no idea what was going on. There was a queer smell in the air, which she realised after a moment was the smell of young men's sweat, made acrid by adrenalin.

She was pulled towards the path. Her ankle had almost healed, but still hurt. Thankfully she had spent almost two days sleeping, and the hypothermia had worn off. Hannah was speaking quietly to the cop dragging her – was that what he was, a cop? She could see her feet, the soles bare and vulnerable. Aidan was ahead. Suddenly he seemed to wake up, and started to scream. She could hear him thrashing around the bend in the path. They asked Alexia for her name, which she gave them. Behind them, all their gear was now being flung out of the house. Someone was photographing the contents of her pack: her meagre stash of reading material, her underwear. They put the law book in a large plastic bag and sealed that too. Now they were asking for her address.

'I don't have an address,' she said.

'You are required by law to give an address,' the man said.

'This is my address, then,' she said. 'This pā.'

'A hut in the bush is not an address,' the cop said. He had a gun in a holster on his hip, and a taser. He looked at a man ahead of them, presumably his superior.

'This is the only place I live,' she said, a little hopelessly.

'What is your occupation and date of birth?' asked the superior with the note pad. They wore black stab-proof vests and black guards over their faces. They had no IDs. They all had guns. There were no women.

'Law student,' she said. The superior officer laughed.

'You should know better then,' he said. 'Date of birth?'

She tried to make her breathing less ragged. Aidan was screaming about his rights, his status as an Irish international, the UN – screaming and screaming. It didn't seem to be helping. Hannah was still speaking quietly.

'You're somebody's son,' Hannah was saying. 'You're some-body's father. You're someone's brother.' It was like a litany.

'Date of birth?' Alexia asked. 'You can't ask a lady a question like that.' She judged herself almost old enough to make jokes of this kind. The superior officer hesitated, and then laughed. 'We've only just met, after all,' she went on. He had very white teeth. 'Could you loosen my hands?' she asked him. She let her smile linger, tipped her face up towards his. 'I'm bound too tight. It hurts.'

'Move the prisoner to position one,' he said.

When she came out into the broad expanse of the field she realised the extent of the operation. The space was full of black uniforms. Unmarked black vans were parked along the edge of the car park and they'd set up a road block. In looked like nothing so much as a day of athletics, with all the people performing almost comical physical feats: lining up, gesturing wildly, being made to lie flat on the earth. The iwi were arranged in a group in the centre of the field. Off in the distance, Taylor's land was free of cars. It was just the pā that was being locked down. She turned to the policeman beside her.

'Is this about the tower?' she asked.

He answered quietly. 'You're not obliged to speak without a lawyer present.'

'But I didn't tell you anything,' she said. She was aware suddenly of the keen attention of the man behind, and that the superior officer had gone quiet.

'The tower,' she said. 'I hope you don't think –'

'Who do you think it was?' asked a voice from behind a black balaclava. She didn't answer.

Up ahead, Aidan was still yelling. If they weren't police, who were they? But they must be police, of some description. 'Violation of me human rights! You bastards! I'll have you!'

She saw him struggle before being laid headfirst onto the ground. His boots flailed in the dirt. Now she could place half a dozen of the people lying down, but many more were being brought out of their houses, most coming quietly.

Alexia's cop let her go and gestured towards the ground. She did not want to lie face down.

The rest of the invaders fell back to guard the group. She didn't move.

'Are you arresting us?' she asked.

The cop who had held her arm gestured to the ground again with the tip of his gun. Hannah was lying down, and Aidan. Further down the line Melissa was a limp form on the grass. Kate was in a worse state, her arms twisted and cuffed behind her back. Sam was oddly quiet.

Alexia kept her voice clear. She was in a law exam, an oral, a presentation. She was authoritative.

'If you are not arresting us, then you cannot hold us, under law. If you are not arresting us, then you are obliged to let us go.' The whole group was listening. The voice of the senior guy came from behind her.

'I wouldn't be recommending that they offer resistance,' he said.

'Who are you, anyway?' Alexia asked. 'Can I see your ID?' He turned away without answering. She saw a dark, impossibly small figure being dragged towards the line.

'I will not,' Polly was saying. 'You cannot make me.' She spat into the face of one of the officers dragging her. He dropped her to the ground, but the other man still held her, her arm wrenched up crookedly. Polly yelled in te reo. It sounded like a challenge. Her limbs were frail, as slender as Papou's had been in his coffin: doll-like. She bit and kicked. Her slippered foot scraped up the grass, and the bright earth showed through, a shocking yellow. The slipper came off. Polly kicked up dust, and stood up again. Te Kahurangi, glaring, and Isaiah, already cuffed, walked towards them. His hair was ruffled. Even from a distance she could see that he was focused on her. She wanted to go to him. She was sure she could see tears in his eyes.

'You let me go,' said Polly. 'I will not lie down in this place.' She lunged and scratched at an officer's face, making two red marks. 'Why are we being gathered here?' she asked. Alexia saw a little way off the rounded river stone Aidan had shown her.

Polly spat again, and another officer backed away. There were five on her now. Alexia was still standing, forgotten. 'Don't you know what this spot marks?' Polly threw an arm out, struck a man in the face. If they knew the land's history, they did not show it. The senior guy went towards Polly to quieten her, but Polly would not be quietened.

'That's the place you killed him!' she yelled. 'That stone marks the place where the Crown murdered our last chief! This is where you killed my grandfather!'

But she was made to lie down.

The wrongness of it made the light go weird and full into Alexia's eyes. Suddenly the scene seemed backlit. Polly's elbows hit the dry ground. Polly was a rangatira in the whakapapa of this place. Isaiah's father would have been in the same line. She hadn't thought about it directly before. The colours were all too vivid, too real. The sky was a deep blue and the marae red and black against it, the people like actors playing at war. The green of the grass was a wall. She stepped forward to try and pierce it with her body but was grasped and held back. To enter, to halt. But there was only the untouchable tableau, all the figures apart from Polly frozen, their faces anguished, some pressed into the earth.

Alexia faced the cop nearest her. He moved his gun sideways with an almost casual gesture. She was to lie down as well.

She struck him. Then she was moving so quickly she did not know how she was hitting or where. When she found her feet, she was in the middle of a crowd of men in black, as Polly had been.

The baying started again.

'Get down down on the ground ... down on the get on your knees ... on your knees get ...'

She struggled in one of the cop's arms. Her face stung where another had struck her and there was a scratch on her arm.

'Kneel down now on the ground ... kneel ...'

It took a heavy blow to knock her down.

52

It terrified Isaiah to see Alexia like this. It was not so much the men restraining her that bothered him but more that he did not trust her to stay in control. He needed to run to her – free himself and pull the men off her. She was on the ground, still fighting. He admired it, but it scared him too. He took deep breaths in through his nose. The men of either side of him were holding his arms. He must not move. Alexia lay still.

Sam was calm. She lay between Aidan and Te Kahurangi, who had grown subdued as soon as they'd come close to the stone marker. She was prone and quiet, and when he met her eyes he realised she had been watching him. Everyone else was watching Alexia, but Sam was watching him. Te Kahurangi seemed dazed, as though she couldn't believe what was happening. The scar still showed on her temple.

Despite their uniforms Isaiah was sure they were police. Their movements and formations didn't suggest they belonged to the army, but rather to some elite force.

After everyone was brought out they were made to rise and walk in a semblance of a line, with a police accompaniment for almost every person.

'They asked me where me weapons was hid,' Aidan whispered from behind him.

They came to the front door of Lizzie's house, which was set a way off from the marae. It was surrounded. A piece of paper was pinned to the front door but the door was shut, and two policemen were banging on it and yelling. The line halted.

The men knocked and yelled. Still no one answered. Beside the front door was a ranchslider curtained with white nets. There was movement inside. The two cops at the door ran to the side and struck the glass. The pane shattered, exploding inwards.

'There are children in there!' Isaiah yelled. More police rushed towards the opening, guns raised and crouched low. Before they could enter, someone burst through the hole where the pane had been. It was a figure out of a movie, clad in camo gear and slashing at the air and swearing, holding in one hand a large knife, and in the other a hunting gun.

'Auē!' Rangi yelled. He surveyed the prisoners and their captors on the porch, the shattered ranchslider. 'It was unlocked the whole time,' he said. 'You could have just opened the bloody door.'

Then they were on him. Te Kahurangi yelled, and Polly, but it was no use. Within moments Rangi was being dragged along the ground towards them. Out came Lizzie, her hands up and calling to her children.

'They won't hurt you,' she called. 'Come, Ana, Tama. Come, Maitai. Just come and walk with Mama.'

The police swarmed around her and into the house. Ana and Tama came out. But Maitai would not come. Finally he was carried out by one of the men, kicking. In front of the house the men tried to make Lizzie lie face down.

'I'm hapū,' she said. The men around her took this for disobedience.

'She's pregnant,' Alexia said.

Lizzie was pushed onto her back and frisked in front of the crowd. Her eyes turned up in her head.

Now the police tried to lie Maitai on the ground, but he would not do it. He was calling for Aunty Polly. Polly called out that he should lie down, that he should try to calm himself. Even then Maitai kicked and fought. He could not help it. Eventually he was put on the ground with his arms above his head and searched. Ana began to cry. Maitai writhed. A policeman stood at his back and pointed his gun at him.

'He's only ten years old,' Rangi said. But the cop continued his search, hands moving all the way down Maitai's body. The line absorbed them and moved on.

53

They were led to a shearing shed at the edge of the pā.

'Are you kidding me?' Rangi asked, but they were led in anyway. When her body resisted at the door, Alexia felt the end of a gun pressing into her back. Inside it was cool, and there were no chairs, only a few bits of disused farm gear.

They sat on the floor. It was crowded. Alexia felt fear rise in her throat, now that the anger was gone. Someone shut the door. A few police were left to guard them. Matiu made to tidy things away, to make others comfortable, putting Polly on a horse blanket, settling the children on the straw. Polly seemed entirely unsurprised. Te Kahurangi was breathing in short, panicked breaths. Maitai was weeping ashamedly, hiding his nose and running eyes.

'You can't do this,' Isaiah said loudly. The police didn't answer.

There was one window. They sat on the floor and stayed quiet. For a long while nothing happened. She took Te Kahurangi's hand. She wanted to take Isaiah's, but he was on the other side of the shed and strangely distant. Through the small window she saw three pigeons land on a telephone line, land and leave, circling away and back. Sam was still, her head between her hands. But she was always so competent, so fierce. There was a dull expression in her eyes. It was Sam's silence that convinced her that what was happening wasn't normal. Alexia had read that all around Auschwitz the birds did not go near the camps, as though they knew what terrible things were happening there. This means we are okay, she thought. The birds are still here. Her breathing, like Te Kahurangi's, was laboured. She watched the pigeons circle and land.

After a long time Isaiah stood and walked towards the door. He was still cuffed. The police trained their guns on him. Even now he had something about him which made Alexia want to go forward and hold him. It was the line of his body and his dark eyes.

'You can't go that way,' one of the men said. There were seven of them in the shed with guns: why hadn't she counted before? She must get herself together. Outside there were four pigeons and one starling exactly, and one sparrow.

'Why not?' Isaiah said, a little grandly. 'By what authority are you holding me? I have not been arrested.' He put his shoulder to the door and shoved it hard.

They pushed him down. He thrashed, his face twisted into the hay. Maitai cried out and was hushed. They watched the officer kneel on Isaiah's back till his face went red. The barn smelled of offal and shit.

Time elapsed. They handcuffed Isaiah and put him in the corner on his own. Alexia tried to make eye contact, but Isaiah had gone away into himself.

'This woman needs water,' Matiu said, nodding at Lizzie. 'She's pregnant.'

The policemen looked at the officer closest to the door, who must be in charge. He was fair, moustached, youngish. Alexia's cheek throbbed where it had been grazed on the ground.

'How can you not give a pregnant woman water?' Matiu said.

Slowly the officer near the door nodded. One of the men left the room. Rangi tapped Lizzie on the back.

'You should pretend to go into labour,' he said, in a whisper the captives could hear. 'Give them something to freak out about.'

'I wouldn't do our baby the insult,' Lizzie said loudly. Polly's eyebrows went far up on her forehead.

More time elapsed, and they were brought water. Matiu demanded food at intervals, for the children. They were not brought any. Hannah began thanking the cops profusely. She thanked them for the water, she thanked them for doing their jobs, she thanked them for their common humanity. Alexia realised she was trying to get behind their masks and make them human. They remained unmoved. Polly had lost one slipper. Tama was bent beside her, holding Polly's dry brown foot in his small hands, chafing it to keep it warm.

Hannah began, slowly, to sing. It wasn't a song in te reo, but a long stream of other vowels and blurred consonants that Alexia recognised as Gaelic. Aidan must have taught it to her, but Aidan was resting with his head in his hands, his anger flared and spent. The song was lilting and a little dreary, silver and grey. In the next gap in the music, Alexia began to sing, a rhyme in Greek that awkwardly filled the space. Hers was a gaudy, almost trashy gold, the small notes flittering. They went back and forth, very low, only murmuring, but everyone listened. The tunes didn't work together, not really.

None of the others sang. Maitai sidled up to Isaiah. The cobbled-together song ended, and one by one they all turned to Polly, waiting for her to sing. But Polly just stared at her bare foot cradled in Tama's hands. Alexia held Maitai to her, and tried not to notice the tears that Maitai did not want her to see.

A long time passed. Sam, still, was oddly quiet.

'Come here, son,' Polly said to one of the young cops. 'All of you look like you sat on a bunch a pins. Except you,' she said, to the moustached man by the door. 'You musta sat on a cattle prod. A big one.'

Alexia felt pity for the officer, whose moustache twitched several times. He went over. Polly leaned in close to him.

'What are you doing holding an old woman like me?' she asked, her voice low. 'I'm just a grandmother. Let me go and get some food for the children. There's a good lad.'

The moustache twitched again. 'My grandmother doesn't

run quite such a militant operation as this,' the man said. He moved away.

Matiu was on the ground, fingers steepled together. The birds circled and fell. It had been many hours. They had asked for food and drink again and had received only water. Matiu rose.

'Everyone has the right to life, liberty and security of person.'

The cops did not stir.

'No one shall be held in slavery or servitude …'

'Oh for Christ's sake, Matiu, can't you see they don't give a shit?' Rangi said. Matiu took a breath and tried to go on. Rangi pulled him down.

'You're just embarrassing yourself, cuz,' he said.

'Where did you learn that?' Alexia asked.

'School,' Matiu said, suddenly sheepish.

'I was trying to remember it myself,' Alexia said. 'The Universal Declaration of Human Rights.'

'Everything you are doing is in violation of it,' Isaiah said to the police. They had let him sit up some time ago. None of them answered.

The air inside the shed was rank. Slowly Isaiah stood, and moved to Alexia's side. She made room for him. He sank down beside her. She could smell his unwashed hair, his sweat. She rested her head on his shoulder, no longer worried about who might see.

'They don't give a drunk rat's arse about our rights,' said Aidan.

One of the officers raised his eyebrows comically, as if in agreement.

PARÁBASIS

The first time I went in I was young. I wasn't all that big, for a boy of eighteen. Not like now. The tatts are armour.

I was in the front row. The cop opposite was young, not much older than I was then. Nineteen? Twenty? I could have grown up with him. I was yelling into a megaphone when he pushed me. I hit him. It was not graceful or nice or clean like in a video game. It was sweaty and imprecise. Then they were on me.

On the floor I was on the floor. They'd taken my watch and I didn't know the time. I'd never been in trouble before

I want my koro I want my

If this hurts the baby

He put his hands on me and I was on the ground. I didn't want it in front of everyone they let him I know he had a gun.

They made me strip. They made me crouch down. They promised someone would be along soon to do the body search. They told me when the time came not to resist. Resisting would make it worse. A man came in with a glove.

I told myself I'll learn my rights I'll learn my rights

*

288

I have been waiting for this time, e Pāpā, e Pāpā. You told me it would come. All I can do is comfort them. Oh, my anger. They have hemmed us in. Perhaps I have acted wrongly? They were watching us. All I can do is. But I can no longer speak. My anger. E Pāpā, why is it me who is always called on? You know I have always been the bad one, the least patient of us all!

I want my Da

When we get out I'm going to put this out over all the social networks they'll see what they have to contend with I'll put the pānui out to all the activist groups in the country the fascists thinking they can do this and have it pass unnoticed they'll have a revolution on their hands the first thing I'll do is ring the capital everyone needs to know we have to organise

The taniwha said that she would stop it

I'm sure they know. Is there a chance they weren't adequately briefed? Of course, they need to treat me the same or the others would suspect

I shouldn't have done it. They've had enough trouble

'Páter imón, o en tís ouranís.'
    'Again. Kneel.'
    We do our crosses three times over our hearts in an anti-clockwise direction. The candle burns away.
    I swear I swear I swear please if you are there God just let them not be angry anymore I won't ever be bad again

'Of course I wouldn't say something so bloody serious to a three-year-old. "Daddy's not coming back!"'

The dark room, the table, the candles on the cake.

'I wouldn't have said that,' she said, leaning forwards.

He pounamu, he pounamu, he pounamu.

'It was your father's. Now it's yours.' Cold around my neck.

'He would have wanted you to …'

'It's very old.'

'He hoped for you to …'

'He believed you were destined to do great things.'

'You know he carried the hopes of his people.'

'As if I'd say that to a three-year-old! What a well-developed sense of the dramatic you have, Isaiah. As if I would say something so ludicrous, "Daddy's not coming back!"'

She struck her. I couldn't. I can't be good enough.
If I could just

I'm thirsty

They can't seriously expect us to

If they lay their hands on me I will fight I will not let this happen

It was after the eels I really lost it. What else was I going to do? Nothing?

54

The senior officer entered the shed, flanked by other men, and began to question them.

'I want my cat.'

'This is unjust.'

'If you think I will talk, you have something wrong with your head. I'm a foreign national and you should be afraid of what's going to happen when this gets out. You're all fucking off ye heads, init? What cache? Think this is the Intifada? Think we're the bloody Sinn Fein? Oh wait, wait, I've got Bin Laden on the line. He wants his machine guns back.'

'Please, please just let us go.'

'What do you mean, what was the plan after the tower was brought down?'

'Death to the fascist pigs.'

'I never heard about any explosives.'

'You don't have to talk to them.'

'You should be ashamed, questioning children.'

'It was the taniwha that blowed it up. The taniwha.'

'Forces that you wouldn't understand are working in this land. Forces that are beyond you, officers. I've seen them at work. You should be afraid.'

'The patupaiarehe blew the tower up. It was the bush fairies.'

'I'm hapū, for god's sake. You have to let me out of here. I feel sick.'

'I have no legal obligation to answer any questions. And when this is over, I will be taking legal action.'

'Along the fence line? All the activity going on over there was pretty suspicious. They appear to be poisoning the land for commercial gain.'

'We already told you. It was the taniwha. It got that dumb tower, and it blowed it out its arse.'

'Let my children out. They need to go to the toilet. They need fresh air.'

'We need more water. I'm not talking to you till we get some more water. And some food.'

'One a yous did it. One a yous did it, so you could frame us. Or it was one a yous acting as us. We've seen it coming for months.'

'The spirits of the land are angry. We did nothing to the tower. Call it patupaiarehe, call it an accident, call it the taniwha. If you push the land too hard, the land takes care of itself.'

55

Rangi snapped. Isaiah had been wondering when it would happen. He heaved himself off the floor and at the nearest guard. He was still cuffed but his bulk was considerable and the young man nearly fell. In the end though they pushed him to the ground. Alexia flinched, seeing the two men kneeling on Rangi's back. They let him go.

Throughout their whole stay in the shed Sam had barely said a word. Melissa patted at her, and Kate sat beside her. But Sam was silent. What was going on in her head? Why had she given up now? He followed her gaze as it moved over the men's gear, their unlabelled uniforms. Like him, she would have been trying to place the force that was holding them. She would know, also, that everything happening was entirely irregular. Perhaps that was what he could see in Sam, something he'd never seen before. Fear.

The officers decided to take action, counting everyone off into two groups. They were to be separated. Isaiah let his eyes rest on Alexia. His number was even; so was hers. She would be in his group. Sam was in the other. He nodded to her reassuringly, but she just stared at him. They were led out the door. Rangi, Isaiah, Alexia and Polly were together. The children were left in the shed. Isaiah tasted old panic in his mouth, adrenalin, all the missed opportunities for escape.

56

She tried to calculate the hours. They'd been seized in the early morning, right after sunrise. She needed to memorise their exact movements, the passing of the time, for future legal action. How many people had been questioned without lawyers present? How many had been held without food? She felt light-headed.

All the black vehicles were still there, and men with guns were posted outside various houses. Alexia assumed the people she had seen pressed onto the earth were being held there. The rest were taken past the marae to the adjoining wharekai and hall. Many of the armed figures were passing in and out of the wharekai doors. The lock on the door had been smashed off. They were carrying boxes of material: folders and ledgers, records she recognised from the council appeals. A man passed her with a box of the zines that Melissa had scattered on a coffee table. Isaiah went on ahead. She missed his warmth beside her. She was prodded up the steps from behind. Isaiah stopped and Alexia ran into him. He pointed to a crate next to a box of papers.

'Avocados,' Isaiah said.

'They must think they're grenades,' Rangi said. He spoke to the officer about to lift the crate. 'They're avocados, man,' he said. The cop looked embarrassed, but picked it up anyway and walked away.

'I guess orders is orders,' Rangi said.

Before long it was night, and they were still being held in

the hall off the wharekai. No one had spoken for a long while. Alexia practised scales in her head, then more intricate pieces, and then she just stared at the wall. Rangi belched deliberately at intervals but failed to get a rise out of the police.

57

Isaiah asked to go to the bathroom. There was a complex series of nods before permission was granted, and then he was out, in the dim light of the moon. The pā looked as it always did at night: peaceful. He was escorted by three police to the ablutions block, where he studied himself in the fly-specked mirror. The day was not wearing on him too badly, not like it was on some of the others. But he could feel the tightness in his body from being cooped up for so long.

On his way back he was surprised to see the paddy wagon that had pulled up, the crowd of black uniforms, the open door.

'I'm arresting you,' the senior officer said. It was so unexpected that Isaiah laughed.

'You're arresting us now?' he asked. 'What do you think you'll get out of us that you haven't already got?' He stopped laughing. 'Who's going to look after the children if you arrest everyone?'

'That's no longer your concern,' the man said. He cuffed Isaiah and put him in the wagon. The floor was cold steel. The man gave him a large, surprising smile, brilliant in its directness, disturbing in its weird conviction. He shut the door.

STÁSIMON

The shining furrows. Year after year
the lightboned birds and beasts cling to cover,
lithe fish lighting their reaches of dim water,
the stormgrey sea. Earth, holy and inexcusable.

May the anarchic man find rest?
My thoughts are his thoughts.
O gold intelligence, when all the laws
are broken, what of your city then?

58

Isaiah had been locked in the room for around twenty-four hours. He had asked to call a lawyer, but his request had been declined. This was enough to convince him that he'd fallen out of the kind of story he knew and into a new one entirely.

The holding cell was lit by a fluorescent light that they had turned on very early in the morning. Judging by his tiredness it might have been evening, though he could not be sure. The room's perfectly square dimensions and slightly rounded corners were disorienting. It smelled slightly of fresh paint, and had a steel toilet with no seat. A wooden bench was the only feature, other than the bed. He'd been given a rough, grey blanket but hadn't used it. The room was stiflingly hot. The one window was high up and had enough wire embedded in the glass that he couldn't see out. He'd entered the station from the west and then been led on through smaller and smaller corridors, but he had no idea now which direction he was facing.

He hadn't expected the place to be so grim: that was a TV version of prison. The reality was both cleaner and more psychologically difficult. Isaiah could hear people yelling from down the hall, mingled voices in other holding cells raised in conversation or conflict. He assumed he was being kept on his own to break him down prior to questioning. This was worrying. It meant they thought he knew something important. The other possibility was that they'd put him in here for his own safety. Isaiah knew he looked young, but would the cops care enough about his welfare to keep him separate? He wasn't sure which was more concerning, this possibility or the first.

There was a relentless quality to the fluorescent lights and the lack of anything to focus on. He'd paced the floor: four and a half steps by four and a half steps. The window was one step wide but the ledge was too high to do pull-ups on. He'd tried last night, thinking that it would be hilarious for the guards he presumed were watching him through the surveillance camera in the corner with its unblinking red light. He'd done three and given up. Now he realised why there were all those movies with inmates exercising in their cells. If you didn't get the energy out of your body you would channel it into thought. Only one day in solitary and he'd started to think about how he could smash the camera's red light. The lens was present while he rested and while he shat in the morning, and even when he was trying to put any watching eyes out of his mind.

If he tried to smash the camera there would be nothing to smash it with but his bare hands. They'd stripped him of everything: wallet, watch, Sam's ring which he wore sporadically and had been wearing yesterday. They'd taken his pounamu. That alone he had cared about. He'd had to steel himself not to try and take it back from the box. If he smashed the camera, would that be further proof of his crime? 'See?' they would say in court. 'He couldn't even last a night in the cell without damaging something.'

After he'd eaten the toast and sausage they brought for lunch, the room gained a particular timelessness. Day stretched into afternoon. The other cells fell quiet. He fought the urge to scream or talk, just to make sound happen. Sound was as desirable as food. Isaiah discovered that he could make a noise, covertly, by rubbing his leg on the wooden bench. The sound of the clothes rustling was a feast. He repeated the motion subtly so the camera could not see, feeling distantly anxious for himself.

Almost as though the movement was a signal, a guard came to collect him.

*

The policeman sat behind a desk.

'You're in a lot of trouble, son,' he said.

Isaiah tried very hard, but he could not suppress a smile. How could he take this statement seriously, when he had seen so many cop dramas on TV?

'I'd take this a bit more seriously if I were you.'

Isaiah cleared his throat. He knew he was being fatuous, but he could not quite unbend his face. He supposed this was the good cop, the paternal one who he was supposed to tell all his secrets to. He positioned himself slightly on an angle towards the door: the bad cop must be arriving soon. The good cop looked up philosophically into the swinging light, as though he had a problem that was located in the bulb. He had a blue shirt and a moustache and thick brown hair. He pursed his lips in a fussy way and puffed out his cheeks. Isaiah was aware that he did not have to speak without a lawyer. He still had not been given his phone call. He decided not to make an issue of it just yet. Better to play dumb, perhaps, and let them think he didn't know his rights. He imagined that the others were being subjected to similar forms of persuasion right now. The others, who must be being held in individual cells too. He hoped Rangi would hold his tongue. Alexia would be so anxious, locked in a cell alone.

'Just between you and me, son, you're going to want to talk,' the cop said.

'I'm not your son,' Isaiah said, firmly and gently. The cop raised an eyebrow and nodded slightly. They were in accordance on this. There was no antagonism between them; rather, an almost pleased air of expectation, as though they were about to perform a song together, or conduct a business deal. The man had a lazy eye. It was flicking off slightly to the side, to a frame which, Isaiah assumed, held a photograph of his wife and kids. The cop picked up the photograph.

'I'm an ice skater, by trade,' he said. He turned the photograph towards Isaiah to reveal a photograph of himself, much younger and more slender than he was now, with slicked-back hair, dressed in spandex and an open shirt. The photo certainly seemed pre-Photoshop, which meant that the vague mist that hung around the man in the portrait was real smoke. The cop sighed. 'Got disillusioned with the industry in the nineties. So superficial.'

The door opened. The policeman who came in was weedy but unexpectedly handsome, like a miniature model.

'We're charging you with terrorism,' he said to Isaiah, with no preamble. 'We want you to tell us who else is in your cell. You give us their names, and we'll let you off the larger charges.'

Now Isaiah did laugh. The sound barked out of him. There was a small silence afterwards, in which the good cop stroked his fingernail along the edge of his ice-skating picture. No one said it was a joke, the terrorism, or the ice-skating business either. No one took anything back.

'We're charging you under the new law, with intent to commit a terrorist act, the intention to conspire with a group, and with operating illegal arms. Your bail application was automatically declined.' The younger cop was quite full of the specialness of his news. 'The maximum gaol stay for terrorism is twenty years.'

He certainly was the bad cop. He stood by the door like a student expecting a badge for good conduct. He seemed to notice the photograph that the good cop was holding.

'Can I move?' Isaiah asked. 'Can I stand up?' His hands were cuffed behind his back. He walked two steps towards the wall. He lifted his arms behind his back, as if to stretch. He attempted a yawn. Surely this sort of thing could not happen here? He turned around. The bad cop had moved to the good cop's side. There was an abbreviated struggle in which the bad cop attempted to wrench the photograph away. The good guy won, and put the photograph in a drawer.

'Sorry,' he said.

'Are you serious?' Isaiah asked the bad cop. The man's eye flicked. 'Terrorism?'

Layers of possibility unfurled in his mind. The photograph was a prop. He was meant to sympathise with this cop, he was meant to be surprised, then tricked into trusting him, he was meant to be disturbed by the juxtaposition of the man sitting there and the ice-skating youth, he was meant to be frightened by the word 'terrorism', he was meant to tell them everything. He continued to stand. He felt that being upright might give him some sort of grasp on the situation. But what was the situation exactly?

'Will you talk?' the bad cop asked.

The other cop muffled a laugh, turning it into a cough in a very obvious manner.

'What about the others?' Isaiah asked. The bad cop, the young model, seemed surprised.

'You mean, are they talking?' he asked, slowly. 'Are they being charged with terrorism?'

There was a weighted pause in which the bad cop widened his nostrils and then relaxed them again. The good cop interlaced his fingers and in one graceful and fluid move set his feet on his desk.

'When I left my career on the ice, they said I wouldn't make it in the force. Said I was too much of a sissy.' Isaiah sat down in his chair. 'Not the cops, mind you, the other dancers. They were the ones said I couldn't make the shift.' He took the picture out of the drawer again. 'The police never had a problem with my past. The most I got was some ribbings about my routines. I still practised then, when I was a recruit, just to keep my foot in, you know. When I came second in the New Zealand Junior Champs in 1989 they were all there with me, all my mates from the force. I came second and they were proud of me, that was all.' He stared at Isaiah intently. 'What I'm saying is, it was a different world, back then. It was an innocent world.'

There was a silence. The bad cop cleared his throat. 'Sir. Detective Inspector, sir ...'

'Not like now,' the detective inspector said. Abruptly he pulled his feet from the table and placed both hands on it.

'I want to speak with a lawyer,' Isaiah said.

All the air left the good cop in a large puff.

'Finally he says it,' he said. 'About bloody time.' He watched Isaiah with his good eye, then the bad. 'There's more than one way to skin a cat, as they say.'

'I see what you mean, sir,' the bad cop said, though plainly no one was sure which cat was being skinned, or why. The detective reached out and slowly pushed the picture of himself towards Isaiah, until it was unavoidable. Up close the ice skater was a figure of beauty, all light triangular torso and muscular legs. His hair was shaped in a full-bodied eighties cut. There seemed no sign of his lazy eye. For some reason all this was more terrifying than if he had been pushed around or hit.

'Gold, 1987. First division. There's nowhere to go to after you've won gold. The only direction you can go is down. But I was saying, those were different times! Back then, people were what they appeared to be.' He leaned back and waited, as though he'd made a good case for Isaiah giving up his story, and it would soon come out.

'Sir, the defendant has requested a lawyer,' the bad cop said. The older man ignored him.

'How many others did you arrest?' Isaiah asked. He had kept the images and sounds away, but now they came on relentlessly. Men in orange jumpsuits. Black hoods. Shaky footage of dim cells. Unlikely durations of time in gaol, with no trial pending. The older man suddenly seemed to lose patience.

'How many?' he asked. 'How many are there in your group? What would you say if I said we'd got all of them, Isaiah Tane Mahuta Brown, and that they've all already talked?' His pronunciation of Isaiah's name was chillingly impeccable, though the man was pākehā.

The bad cop turned on one heel. 'Sir, Detective Inspector, sir,' he said. 'Permission to exit with the prisoner.'

The detective inspector stirred and nodded vaguely.

'Yes, Constable, go ahead,' he said. 'But no lawyers. Not yet.'

In the corridor, the constable stopped him. Isaiah thought he was about to be hit. This was where it would begin, the muted blow in the quiet hall, followed by the walk to a smaller room, where other things would happen. But the constable reached around Isaiah's body, moving quickly, and then his hands were free. He rubbed his wrists where the steel had left an indentation.

'There you go, mate,' the constable said.

'I thought you were supposed to be the bad cop,' Isaiah said.

'Just between you and me, none of your mates are in here.' He spoke softly and Isaiah had to lean close. A door opened somewhere in the building. 'You're the only one. If I were you, I'd think carefully about my options. Twenty years is a long time.'

'But how can you charge me with terrorism if you think I'm working on my own?' Isaiah asked.

The constable seemed to consider this a theoretical question.

'Well, you do have your standard-issue suicide bomber, don't you? But you're right, we do have you on conspiracy charges.' He seemed unsure.

'I'll speak with my lawyer now,' Isaiah said.

The cop gave a shrug, and ignored him. He led Isaiah along the corridor and past the guard into the now familiar room with the wooden bench, the army blanket and the steel-rimmed toilet in one corner. He was locked in. The constable went away and Isaiah was left to turn the word 'terrorism' over and over in his mind, blocking out the pictures as best he could. Orange suit. Hooded figure. The images played on, until the sky outside the window turned black.

59

In the days following the raid people went to the marae, not to talk but just to be there. There were greater numbers eating communally than there had been for weeks. The locals needed to convene, to catch their breaths. Polly was not seen for the first few days: according to Te Kahurangi she was taking Isaiah's incarceration badly. People were strangely quiet. Alexia noticed that everyone, including her, put their hands on each other more. She would see Lizzie and pat her shoulder, stop herself from stroking the small bump on her stomach. Ana would come up and put an arm around her. Tama was almost attached to Alexia's waist. No one was angry: not yet. And Isaiah was gone.

He was the only one. Sam went about like a war hero herself, as if his absence conferred honour upon her. Alexia was still puzzled by Sam's strange passivity in the face of the police. Aidan was subdued, and Hannah was silent a lot of the time. The land and the houses were a mess – they had a lot to do before things would feel at least a little normal. Clothes to put back in drawers, smashed plates and confiscated items to replace. At the house Alexia was sharing, the stuffing still hung out of all the chairs, a scratchy reminder.

To Alexia's frustration, they could not manage to get any message to Isaiah. They knew he had been arrested, because Rangi had seen him taken away through the window of the marae. They knew he had been processed at the regional station in town, initially – the police confirmed the fact – but they would not confirm where he was being held. Isaiah was in remand somewhere, awaiting his first bail hearing. But the days went by with no call from him or from a lawyer, and Alexia had called so many people she was beginning to despair. They weren't following due process with this, and she could not believe it. She rang and rang, using her poshest phone manner, but it didn't work. They didn't know where he was.

Then news of the raid hit the media, and things got busy at the marae.

Alexia got a call.

'Are you okay? I saw the news, Alexia.'

'Katherine!' She was so happy to hear her voice. No one else from the Family had called, not that she had expected it. 'I'm all right. We're all right. Well, not really …' Her voice was breaking. 'My friend is in gaol.'

'Your friend? The guy they're talking about on the news?'

'Yes. My … friend.'

Katherine was quiet for a moment.

'I see,' she said. 'I'm at Yiayia's house, by the way. They've all forgiven me for leaving with you. She's in the other room, but she wants to talk to you.'

'How is she?'

'She's gone nuts,' Katherine said. She rushed on. 'The raid looked pretty serious. Don't you think maybe you should come home?'

Alexia ignored her. 'Tell me about Yiayia.'

'Or I can come up, Alexia.'

'You don't need to do that.'

Katherine sighed. 'Yiayia's throwing out all of Papou's things.'

'The bouzouki?' It was selfish. But it was the only thing she cared about. His aged hands on it.

'I don't know.' Katherine would hardly remember the bouzouki. By the time she was there he had grown older and ill. His friends didn't come so often, to argue and blow smoke all over Yiayia's furniture. After he began having heart attacks, he had hardly picked the instrument up.

'This morning I saw them loading the last of his clothes into the car. I'll check about the bouzouki.'

'It's only a bouzouki, after all. It's only an object.' The clouds crossed the grey sky. She saw in her mind the gold-edged frets, the painted key design. Last time she'd held its small rounded belly in her hands she had been on the roof of the house. After Stephen had left she'd gone back to the attic and brought it down and propped it on the windowsill with Papou's favourite things: his tobacco box, his throwing beads. She'd believed it was a temporary thing, putting the bouzouki down.

'You're not all right, are you, Alexia? It's only a few days till uni's over. Then I'll come up.'

But how could Katherine, with her dresses and make-up and shoes, come here, where her friends were anarchists and ex-convicts?

'I'll put Yiayia on,' said Katherine.

'Yia sou, Yiayia.'

'Alexia. I tell you something. I tell you, I leave my family too.' Yiayia had never been back to Greece, not once. 'I leave my mama. My baba. Katalavenis? You understand?' Alexia's silence was a complex thing. She hadn't heard any of their voices since the day she left.

'Now what is this I see on the television?'

'My friend's in gaol, Yiayia.' Why was she telling her this? She would just worry. 'We're trying to get him out.'

There followed a long excited passage in Greek. Alexia listened with all of her attention. But she couldn't understand all of the words. She pressed her ear to the receiver and turned the volume up, but it was no good. She caught something about the news, guns, the Māori, Neo Zealanthia. But the grammar slid over her ear like water. She could not make sense of it.

'Do you hear me, Alexia? I ask you a question.' Yiayia spoke in English now.

'Did you give away the bouzouki?' She heard her own voice, too free with what was inside of it.

'The bouzouki? Why? You want it? It's old. None of us use it anymore.'

'You haven't given it away?'

There was a long pause, in which Alexia heard her grandmother moving around.

'No. Is here. I give it to Katherine, she gives it to you. You sure you don't want me to buy you another one, a new one?'

Yiayia had not gone mad. She'd just cleaned the house, in her pragmatic, immigrant's way. Her act was not a random act of grief. Yiayia preferred modern houses to old, preferred clean lines to antique ones.

'No! The old bouzouki will be fine.' Her body flooded with relief. 'What did you want to ask me?'

There followed more words in Greek.

'I don't understand.' There was silence on the line.

'You somewhere noisy?' Yiayia asked. She went on in English. 'I think, where you are, they are Māori.'

'Yes.' There was a pause.

'Then why is everyone talking about them being tourists?'

It took Alexia a moment, then she began to laugh. She put her hand over the receiver but she could not stop.

'It's "terrorist", Yiayia mou.'

'Oh. Like the Palestinians, those people on the news with the bombs.'

Alexia stopped laughing. Katherine came back on the line. She wanted to know how Alexia was, how she really was. Alexia was fine, she was really fine.

She would not tell Katherine about this new thing, this hole like a lost tooth: the loss of her understanding. Perhaps her Greek would come back.

Katherine dragged the details of Isaiah's incarceration out of her.

'You haven't been able to see him,' Katherine said.

'No, I haven't,' Alexia said. Her own voice was impossibly casual. She was pressing both feet into her shoes, very hard. There was a silence on the line.

'I'm coming up on Saturday,' Katherine said. 'I'll text when I get in.' Alexia saw no further use in resisting.

Alexia was driving back from the city, from a meeting with lawyers which had been panicked and inconclusive. They were coming home – Matiu, Polly and her – jaded from the travel and from the unpromising recommendations of the lawyers. They were still not sure if Isaiah was being held in the local station or in a prison on remand, and had trouble getting the proper information. As they pulled up the road to the pā everyone reflexively looked at the burnt tower, which still hung there, dilapidated and black.

There was no police presence, and no extra supporters, but the media had begun to turn up. They wanted to interview the kaumātua, they wanted to talk to the elders, they wanted to hear the story of how Maitai had been searched at gunpoint and the children had been held in the shed. It was exhausting.

Alexia pulled into the car park next to a couple of media vans. Through it all the fracking had continued, for which Alexia was grateful. It must make a difference, she thought, that the journalists could see the towers and hear the drilling for themselves.

'You'd think it would make for good pictures,' Matiu said. Everyone thought of Isaiah's cameras, the pictures he'd taken. Surely his gear was still here somewhere, but Alexia doubted anyone would have the skills to use it. 'What about the land around it? The fallout, the ash and the waste. We can show people that.'

'Ka pai, Matiu,' Polly said. 'We've got to be good hosts, invite people to have a look around.'

It was Isaiah's dream, and he wasn't here to help them realise it. Alexia would have to get access to Isaiah's photos so she could give them to the press. He was so scrupulous that she knew he must have saved back-ups somewhere. Sam would know. But that would entail navigating the delicate space between her and Sam.

They got out of the car. Tinny music burst into the car park. The others were dispersing, but one or two of them stopped to watch the red hatchback arrive. It spewed loud music and then fell silent. Katherine got out of the car and ran to her, a tangle of scarves and lipstick scent and vanilla perfume and crystal necklaces. Alexia found that she was laughing, somewhere inside the circle of Katherine's clothes.

'I borrowed a car!' Katherine said. 'I drove here, by myself!' She opened her eyes wide in amazement at her own daring. 'Before I forget,' she said, and pulled a cloth-wrapped object from the back seat and handed it to Alexia.

She unwrapped the bouzouki and breathed in the smell of the metallic strings. The fretwork was brassy and needed a clean, and the red and black of the key-patterned strap had faded. But Alexia put the strap over her head and cradled the instrument, its rounded belly. The landscape blurred.

They walked to the wharekai, where everyone had convened for a cup of tea. Mary bustled around, adding sugar to a cup for Katherine and starting on some scones. Polly studied Alexia's sister for a long time, then brushed her cheek with her hand.

'You look like her,' she said. 'Too thin.'

Matiu was shy. Lizzie hugged her. Rangi hongied Katherine gladly, his large form nearly crushing her. Te Kahurangi blushed.

'Katherine, Te Kahurangi,' Alexia said. 'Te Kahurangi is a student too.'

'History and politics,' said Te Kahurangi, staring at the floor.

'Me too!' said Katherine. 'Politics, I mean.' Katherine gave Te Kahurangi what was perhaps a special smile.

Sam came into the room. She noticed Katherine, and then busied herself with wiping a bench. She boiled the jug and performed a series of important-looking tasks, before joining them.

'I'm Katherine, Alexia's sister,' Katherine said.

'This is Sam,' Alexia said.

'I'm sure you'll feel as welcome here as Alexia has,' Sam said, and subjected Katherine to her sunniest smile.

Katherine raised both eyebrows at Alexia: two groomed, matching arches of disbelief.

60

'**G**uard!' Isaiah called. The guard came, a man squeezed too tightly into his uniform. It seemed as though he'd been interrupted watching a TV programme he enjoyed. 'I want my phone call,' Isaiah said.

He'd been asking intermittently for three weeks, since the day he'd been arrested. He'd had no contact with a lawyer or anyone on the outside. They had started keeping the light on all night. The light was there whether he closed his eyes or not, fluorescent, harsh, centring everything in the room in on itself. He wasn't sure anymore of the rate of time's passing. He had been called in for questioning seven more times, and each time he'd told the detective inspector that he knew nothing, and each time the detective inspector told him some ice-skating-related tale. It would not be so disquieting if he had been given his rights. The night after they'd said the special word he'd worked himself up to yell and had continued yelling for hours. Usually the guards checked him in the middle of the night. This time, no one had come till morning.

'You want your phone call?' The guard sounded tired.

'I have a legal right,' Isaiah said. By now, his voice sounded thin.

'You have a legal right,' the guard said. He could have been repeating lines learnt by rote at school.

'If you don't get me in contact with a lawyer ...'

But what could he do? Alexia was there, somewhere on the outside. They would all be working, trying to get to him. They would be wondering why they had not been contacted. They would be doing all they could.

'You're to come with me anyway,' the guard said. 'May as well come now.' He let Isaiah out of the cell and escorted him to the office.

Every time Isaiah arrived the detective inspector was seated the same way, his feet up on the desk. Each time he was gazing philosophically at the photograph of his former self, rather than at Isaiah. Isaiah decided to start today's interview a different way.

'I'll complain to the Human Rights Commission,' he said. 'And the Board of Prisons. And the government. And the Police Review Authority. And the local council. If you don't let me see a lawyer.'

'We have you in here on a charge of terrorism,' the detective said. 'Don't you think those people already know about you?' He stared for some time at the photograph, then at the light that hung from the ceiling. 'You're here on a charge of *terrorism*,' he said again, drawing the word out slowly. 'This is quite different from our usual charges. It's new. You're new. Don't you know what this means? It means the normal rules don't really apply.'

Isaiah decided on silence. He felt his body relax entirely. It was a relief, in a way. He wouldn't have to be so insistent anymore. They would bring him food on a tray, they would light his room all hours. He did not have to fight for his rights: he had none.

'So do you have anything for me today?'

Much as Isaiah hated himself for it, he liked the detective inspector. It was the quality of his attention. Even while he looked at the light or the photograph Isaiah knew the man was observing him. He gathered his eyebrows together into a hunched caterpillar and squinted eagerly at Isaiah. His mouth puckered, and he blew air upwards so hard that his hair ruffled.

'Isaiah Tane Mahuta?' As always, the detective's pronunciation threw him.

'Not until you get me a lawyer.'

The surface of the desk between them was pockmarked. Perhaps it was all fake, this whole thing; these people just actors in some protracted, low-budget joke. It was possible he'd been transferred in the night, that they'd given him drugs, and that these were not police at all. He could be in an underground bunker. The window in his cell with its cyclical light and dark was just a light and a timer behind a screen.

The constable came in. He went to the detective's side and stood at attention, like an army officer.

'I want my phone call,' Isaiah said.

'Funny thing, dentistry,' the detective said.

Isaiah had eaten poorly that morning, thin oatmeal that could only be described as gruel. Sometimes they brought him reconstituted mashed potato with a piece of spam on top. Other days it was 'stew', or dry bread. There was a distinct lack of fresh vegetables. Last night he'd requested vegetarian meals, thinking this might get him better rations. His vegetarian dinner had arrived: a packet of unopened juice crystals in a bowl.

'They called me Pearly White,' the detective was saying, 'on account of my dazzling smile.' He turned the ice-skating photograph towards Isaiah with a flourish. 'Naturally gifted to me that smile was. Never had a filling till I was in my thirties. It's all downhill from there. It's inevitable, really. One day you're an athlete, shooting half-axels and spinning with the best of them, then, the next day, *boom*.' He struck the table, hard. Isaiah jumped, and so did the constable. 'You expire, son. Like over-ripe fruit.'

'I'm not your son,' Isaiah reminded him.

'Ahh, but you're someone's son, aren't you? You've had a lot to live up to, coming home, haven't you, Isaiah Tane Mahuta?'

'I want to speak to a lawyer,' Isaiah said.

'Tell me what you were planning to do next,' said the policeman. 'Tell me how you blew up the fracking well. Tell me who was involved. Where are you keeping the explosives? We know you were a key figure in the planning of the riot,' he said. Isaiah realised he meant the protest. 'We know you advised the development of various weapons caches. We know you were involved in facilitating the attack.'

Isaiah said nothing.

'You see, your comrades have already turned you in.'

The other cop stirred uncomfortably.

'Sir, I think we should let this man speak with a …'

'Terrible thing,' the detective said, 'when the people you thought were your comrades turn on you.'

Isaiah screamed.

It surprised him most of all. His scream went up and filled the air. It was a short scream, wordless, but he let the words go into it that he hadn't said. He flinched, as though someone else had screamed. It was a horrible sound. Panic crossed the constable's face. The detective was impressed.

'This has gone on long enough,' the constable said.

There was a silence.

'Permission to speak to a lawyer granted,' the detective said.

The young cop led Isaiah out.

'Is it true about the ice skating?' he asked.

The constable shrugged. 'I've seen old videos,' he said. 'That guy was magic on the ice.'

61

As the days wore on it became apparent that Isaiah would not be released. In the wharekai, Aidan told Alexia that things like this usually went one of two ways. If an injustice was bad enough, it could motivate people to act. But if energy was diverted into little petty litigious issues, you could expect people to become disenchanted. These sorts of charges could be very complex, he said. They could drag on for a long time.

Alexia could have reminded him that she had more than a passing knowledge of the legal system, but she didn't. The date of her bar exam had come and gone unmarked. She had noted it, and thought vaguely: next year. But that was before the raid. Often now she found there were things that she need not say. It was enough for her to try and serve the pā in some way, as more and more people around them began to drift away. It was enough that she was discovering a new feeling of commitment.

She'd had to tell Tama about leaving his cat in the bush. He had cried, then, typically, grown angry with her and stormed off. The next time she saw him he made noises about going to look for it. She took him straight to Polly, who forbade him. Tama listened to her.

Katherine was sleeping on the couch in the house where Alexia was staying with Aidan and Hannah. It was still leaking stuffing despite Alexia's attempts to mend it. The pillows she gave Katherine were old and lumpy, but at least there were a lot of blankets to go around since so many supporters had left.

The first time she showed Katherine into her shared lounge,

she watched as her sister let her bag drop from her shoulder. Katherine took in the chairs, knifed open and hastily stitched, the kitchen utensils still scattered across the floor that none of them had had time to sort. There were mattresses on the floor, where Aidan and Hannah were sleeping; their bed had been ripped open by the police. Papers covered the table. Alexia's printed lists of prison facilities where Isaiah might be. The last time Katherine had visited her, Alexia was living in a new apartment with Stephen. They'd had high ceilings and white walls, new appliances and house plants. Their music collection was alphabetised, and they had sets of matching crockery.

Katherine seemed untroubled by the change. She took a warm layer from her pack, a vintage coat with wool edging, put it on, and buttoned it resolutely. She went over to the table and touched the papers there as if they might burn her, scanning the words.

'You still don't know where they're keeping him?' she said. Alexia shook her head, no. 'You really like him, don't you?' This, Alexia didn't answer.

They went to sit on the porch. Her sister flopped onto the partly gutted couch.

'It's so pretty here, isn't it?' she said. There were five new towers that could be seen from the porch since Alexia had moved in. The burned tower hung in the sky like a threat. 'I can see why you like it.'

Alexia wondered how long it would take for her to get bored, to want to go back to the city and its bars and cafés. She watched in wonder as Katherine pitched in with the dishes and the cooking, though she baulked at small things: gutting the kina, picking fish off the bones. Polly seemed to accept Katherine's presence easily, as if she were an extension of Alexia. She got along with everyone, but everyone did not get along with her. In the first few meetings with Sam, Alexia could see the way Sam's eyes, and Melissa's, and Kate's, returned to Katherine's pretty dresses and careful lipstick. It wasn't as if they disapproved of her, exactly. It was more that they seemed confused to find such a creature in their midst. Alexia couldn't tell how aware Katherine was of their attention. She only smiled, the same warm smile she accorded eveyone.

Alexia had not been sleeping properly since the police had come. She wasn't seeing lights, not anymore, and she wasn't hearing music. Her days had begun to blend into each other: a long, repeating nightmare of calls to lawyers and police, never resulting in anything.

One morning Te Kahurangi came and sat with Alexia and Katherine at breakfast. Usually she didn't drift in until lunchtime. But here she was, in her hoody and jeans, clear-eyed over her porridge. Katherine sat beside her in a vintage dress. They ate quietly, going over the tasks of the day. Alexia was pretty sure that under the table, Te Kaurangi was holding her sister's hand.

That day a busload of family arrived from the city. Alexia's day became a blur of fetching beds and blankets for the guests, and sorting their koha in the wharekai. Polly greeted each of them formally, her formality quickly dissolving into hugs. Alexia marvelled at this change. It wasn't until she saw Polly seated at lunch, at the head of one of the long wooden tables, that she understood. These people didn't know Isaiah, but they knew who he was. They rubbed Polly's back and patted her shoulder as if she was recently bereaved. Until now, Alexia had regarded all of this, despite appearances, as a temporary situation. But none of these people did. They had lost one of their sons to the legal system, and they did not expect to get him back any time soon.

Sitting at the table, with Katherine on one side and Melissa on the other, a plate of pūhā and pork in front of her, Alexia wanted to throw up.

The next day Tama turned up on Alexia's porch. He was uncharacteristically quiet. Since the raid Alexia hadn't had much time with the children. She worried about Maitai, remembering his small body lying on the ground. They'd been sleeping in the wharenui because of their smashed ranchslider: the glass had been cleaned up, but the door hadn't yet been replaced.

Alexia sat down. Tama perched next to her. After a moment, sensing he needed it, she pulled him close.

'Maitai's going away, Mum said.'

Alexia squeezed him.

'Where? Is Lizzie … is your Mum going with him?'

Tama shook his head. 'Our baby's coming soon, she says. So she's staying here. Maitai's going to stay with our uncle. There's no room for us.'

Lizzie's stomach was round and tight under her T-shirt. Alexia thought she must be due in a month, maybe two. 'Why's Maitai going, Tama?'

'It's the nightmares,' Tama said. 'His wairua's all messed up. That's what Rangi said.' He spoke casually, but his body was taut under her arm.

'Does Lizzie think it's better for him to go away?' she asked, carefully.

'It's this place,' Tama said. He was furious now, and this reassured her. 'He keeps going weird every time we go past our place. And he can't go past the field where we sat down. Mama says it will just be a while.' Tears began to move down his face.

'It's okay.' She knew it wasn't.

'I'm not crying cos a that!' Tama said. 'I don't care about him! Just my cat. He hasn't come back. And none of you even cares!'

Where had the cat got to? Would it survive out there all alone?

Alexia tried to hold Tama closer. But he hurtled down the steps, and away.

What else did Maitai dream of? Men with batons? Smashing glass? Dead eels?

*

There were small, frantic bouts of communication with the authorities. Weeks passed. And in between phone calls, there was little to do. At these times Alexia began to teach herself how to play her grandfather's bouzouki. It was slow and painstaking, as the instrument required entirely different chords and fingerwork to a guitar. She started with YouTube videos but had to deal with the frustration of knowing nothing about an instrument that she felt she should automatically be able to play. This was, she realised, how Isaiah might feel about te reo. She took the bouzouki out into the field, wearing the winter coat that Katherine had brought for her, and played into the night. She played in full view of the mountain, but kept away from the bush. She was waiting for the notes and the lights, almost tempting them. They didn't come.

One night Ana and Tama found her in the field.

'What's that?' Ana asked. 'Can I play?'

Giving her the instrument was like entrusting her with some part of herself, but Alexia handed it over. She played a little rhythm, *a chink a chink a chink*, so different from the music her grandfather had played. The girl's song made little popping sparks in the air. How stupid she had been. By the time she had acquired her synaesthesia her grandfather had already been ill, the bouzouki stowed in the attic. She remembered his music from her childhood, but she had never seen his notes as she saw Ana's now. Now she never would.

But Ana and Tama were missing someone too.

'Have you heard from Maitai?' she asked.

'He's gone away,' Ana said, distractedly.

'I know.' She remembered Maitai's hand in hers in the shed, the way he tried to hide his tears.

'There's a lot of things you don't know, but,' Ana said, 'there are a lot of people leaving soon. People from here. It's all changing. We always hold the sports festival here, every year. And the kapa haka. But they chose another marae to do it at this year. Polly says it was the raid. People don't know what to 'think.' She handed the bouzouki back. Its strap felt so familiar around her neck. Ana looked across the field to where the burnt tower was visible.

'They think Uncle Isaiah did that?' she said. 'If he didn't do it, who did?'

Alexia felt a hot red flush spread across her cheeks, a hot thing rising in her throat. It was the thing no one was talking about.

Tama was watching the urupā as if listening, perhaps watching the lights that for some reason Alexia could no longer see. His eyes came to rest on hers, a deep brown, all-knowing in his young face.

62

There was a complicated process around the making of a phone call, involving the filling out of many forms. After weeks – he wasn't sure how many – Isaiah was led to a rough stall. Above the booth was a window through which he could see the courtyard in front of the station. He had not been drugged in the night and smuggled away after all. It was daylight outside. He watched a scatter of sparrows, their complex arrivals and departures. It was incredibly beautiful. He traced his finger over the lawyers' section in the phone book and picked a name at random, dialled. The lawyer was in the office. It seemed a small miracle.

'Terrorism,' Isaiah said, eventually.

'Terrorism?' the lawyer said. 'It's not my specialty.' He gave a small laugh. 'But then, I wouldn't say it was anyone's, not in this country.'

'I've been here for weeks,' Isaiah said. 'They've been keeping me in solitary. I've had no contact with anyone aside from you. I need to be bailed,' he said, aware of his own voice rising. 'You need to get me out on bail.'

The lawyer was silent. When he spoke again he seemed ruffled.

'I suppose, under the new Act, they could do that,' he said. 'But what do they think they're playing at? What on earth is it that they think you were doing?'

Isaiah thought it best not to speak.

When he hung up he didn't want to face the next few moments. He would walk back through the metal door with its reinforced glass into the corridor. He would be escorted back to his cell, where the light would continue to burn. The constable who had brought him was watching him intently.

'Want another call, mate?'

Isaiah could not stop his hand from jerking towards the phone.

'Go on. It's only you and me.'

'I need an unlisted number,' Isaiah said.

'I'll sort it.' He picked up the phone. 'Operator,' he said, 'we need a line to the pā, out west. You know the one.' He smiled and handed him the phone. 'That's the number you wanted, isn't it? Let them know you're all right.' Isaiah knew he should feel suspicious, but his fingers had already dialled. The phone was ringing. The constable moved away discreetly.

'Kia ora.' It was Rangi.

'It's Isaiah.' There was a silence. Then Rangi let out a great whoop, words in te reo streaming down the phone.

'He's on the line!' he called, presumably to the others in the room.

'Listen, Rangi, they haven't let me speak to a lawyer until today. Rangi …' But he could hear a great number of whistles and calls. He could pick out their voices: Melissa's shaky cry, Sam's yell, though the words were indistinct.

'We've been trying to find out where you are. What prison. They wouldn't tell us nothing. Tried to get someone in to see you, but they wouldn't authorise it. It's good to hear from you.'

The constable made a slicing motion across his neck. Steps were approaching in the hall.

'Rangi,' Isaiah said. 'I've got to go.' He could hear the others clamouring to get on the phone.

'They treating you well in there?' Rangi asked. Rangi had been in gaol himself. He knew how things worked.

'They're keeping me in solitary, Rangi,' he said. 'They won't turn out the light.'

Rangi was quiet.

'How many days have I been here?' Isaiah asked.

'Three weeks, five days, and this morning,' Rangi said. 'We're gonna get you out.'

The constable hung up the phone.

Isaiah was led away from the booth. Somewhere along the corridor, he and the constable took an unexpected turn. Isaiah found himself in a different grey room.

'What's this?' he asked.

'He requests a form for visitation rights,' the constable said to the guard. 'The prisoner would like to authorise a guest.'

The guard reached into a steel filing cabinet behind him and laid two forms on the desk side by side. Isaiah cast his eye over the authorisation form. How was he meant to spell her last name? It was long and Greek and complicated. He approached the desk but saw there was nothing to write with.

'Could I have a pen?' he asked. The guard didn't speak, but gestured calmly towards the other piece of paper on the desk.

'Application for a pen,' he said.

The constable stared at the wall. There were no pens anywhere in sight, not on the cabinet, not on the desk.

'Well,' he said. 'Can I borrow a pen, to fill out the application for a pen?'

'Pens are fifty cents,' the guard said.

'I don't have fifty cents,' Isaiah said.

'Pens are fifty cents,' the guard said again. The constable's face was still impeccably blank. It must be something they taught them to do in police school. The guard stirred himself in a grandmotherly way, as if he'd just had a too rich meal. 'Your money is kept in your account,' he said. 'You use the money in your account to buy the pen, to fill out the forms. Then you can apply to have a visitor.'

'How do I get money into my account?' Isaiah asked.

'Your visitors put it in for you,' the guard said.

'But my visitors don't know they need to do that until they visit,' Isaiah said. 'And they don't know they can visit until I call.'

The guard swung around on his swivel chair and got another piece of paper out of the drawers. He laid this carefully on the desk.

'Application to make a phone call,' he said.

'Come on, Keith,' the constable said. 'Give the prisoner a bloody pen.'

The guard popped open a drawer in the desk. It was filled with pens. He handed one to Isaiah and sighed.

'There's no guarantee the requests will be granted,' he said.

They came for him in the early morning before it was light. There was no explanation of where he was going. He had no possessions anyway, and went in the clothes he stood up in. The guard signing patted his back.

'Sad to see you go, Greenpeace,' he said, and the other guards laughed.

'Jeez, at least the other fellas in here, they got something for their trouble before they got caught.'

'Shut up. He's famous now. A star. You better not cross him or some hippies will protest outside.'

'Make you eat your veges, ha ha ha.'

Isaiah demanded that people be notified of his destination.

'Not the usual practice,' the guard said. 'Not even for a superstar.' They opened the van.

'Bye, Greenpeace. Go save a whale for us.'

'Go plant some trees. Good luck.'

The inside of the van was lined with steel cages, like crates of robust chicken wire. They uncuffed him, then opened one of the cages and locked him in. He quickly grew cold. The cage did not allow him to lie down, or to sit up fully. There was no seat. He had to crouch, holding his knees. One by one others were led into the transport and locked in. Eight of them, and one swinging bulb.

An hour in, someone had to go to the bathroom. He was

told he had to wait till the only stop, halfway down. He didn't make it.

Another hour in, Isaiah himself had the burning need. He meditated on a spot on the metal floor. The cages jolted and rattled, jolted and rattled. They had not been given breakfast.

Another hour in, one of the other inmates lost his composure. He screamed for water. He screamed that they were all bastards and treating them like animals in cages. They weren't given anything.

Another hour in, they stopped and got out at some tearooms. They were led through the rooms with shackled ankles. They all got sandwiches, the edges of which had been neatly trimmed of crusts.

On being locked in again, Isaiah closed his eyes. He would think of anything but this jolting. But his body was soon asking to be stretched. He'd never known anything like this: the hot pain in his knees, the cramps in his back, the inevitable limits of his body. He focused on the point on the floor, and became it. He was nothing, just a small blue dot. The dot became everything: the pā, the forest, the bone, Sam and all the mistakes he'd made, Alexia, who felt like she was of his body. Polly, and the cool proud angle of her neck.

It took a long while to reach their destination.

After he had slept in his new cell, alone, he asked the guards if he could call Alexia.

'I've approved her as a visitor,' Isaiah said.

'Not today,' the guard said. 'She has to apply to visit you.'

'I know that,' Isaiah said. 'But how is she meant to know?'

'I guess, if she really loves you, she'll know,' the guard said.

63

Alexia's court shoes clicked on the marble floor. The escalator she'd ridden many times before on her undergraduate placement rose before her. But the law book that she needed to revise for the bar exam languished in some police vault, labelled evidence. She wore the same clothes she would have worn on her work experience: a high white collared blouse, her black pencil skirt. Sam came after her, muttering about the state, and Melissa and Kate went on ahead, whispering fretfully. Isaiah had been denied bail twice in the six weeks that had passed since the raid.

She wished for Katherine's presence, but Katherine had gone home – to pick up some things, she said. To get into the building they had passed through a line of chanting supporters with banners and flags, and broken through the line of media. TV cameras had been thrust in Alexia's face. She had needed to push her way through, causing her heart to quicken uncomfortably. How much of Katherine's absence was a fear of violence, she wondered, and how much was a reticence about being on the news? The Family would be watching, of course. Katherine needed to maintain the appearance of neutrality if she wanted to be free to come and go, as Alexia no longer was.

Somewhere ahead of her was Isaiah's mother. She had turned up the night before, a flurry of long scarves and elaborate jewellery, explaining to everyone who she was, where she came from, how she had raised Isaiah, explaining and explaining, a big woman with a loud voice. When she entered the marae where the supporters were staying, Alexia had been surprised to see Polly rise and go to greet her. Hadn't there been some sort of rift? But Polly had stood immediately, and gone over to the woman, who'd stood with her bag in her hand, unsure of where to go. Polly took the bag from her and laid it down. She kissed Isaiah's mother on each cheek. The woman's face relaxed.

None of the supporters was dressed for court as Alexia was, or as the Family, with their immigrants' respect for decorum, would have been. Inside, most of people from the pā were circulating. Matiu was ahead of Alexia on the escalator, with Lizzie, who had left the kids behind. Behind her were Rangi and Sam. Alexia wore her best chain and gold rings on her fingers, given to her by the Family. She was buckled together with her tight belt and her jewellery. So much of what happened in the courtroom was costume and performance; didn't these people understand that? But then, why should Rangi change the way he appeared? This court was not his court.

The glassed roof opened up into a many-storeyed room, forcing whoever was ascending to look up into the bright space. What did Polly make of the crest above the entrance: a Māori woman and a white woman standing side by side in apparent harmony? Alexia imagined she knew exactly what Polly thought. The escalator progressed as if they were on a production line and about to be processed. Up there somewhere, in a holding cell in the depths of the building, was Isaiah.

If he was released, it would be through a doorway to the rear of the building. They had planned for this eventuality. Alexia and Sam would face the cameras outside, while Te Kahurangi and Rangi would collect him and take him away. The plan was for Isaiah to avoid as much media exposure as possible. Polly had chosen Alexia and Sam to be the face of the protest. Alexia had wondered at this. Should it not be a rangatira of their iwi who was chosen to speak? But the raid was being presented in the press as an indigenous issue. Polly would not give the press what they wanted quite so easily. Isaiah would be whisked away, probably under strict bail conditions. Alexia would see him tonight, at the marae where they were staying. Perhaps he would sleep next to her.

Her hand sat obediently on the moving escalator rail, travelling slightly faster than the rest of her body. A weird tension set itself up inside her, her thin brown wrist moving forwards, her feet in their smart court shoes remaining behind. The foyer carpet went beige at her, beige, beige. The room was oppressive under the lights. Alexia was back in the city she had studied in, but her flat with Stephen had gone. She didn't even know where Stephen was, if he had gone overseas as he had planned or not. She still guessed that he had. It did sting a little, now she was here. Across from the court was a great coffee shop, one where Stephen would pick her up a flat white before collecting her after work ... but it didn't matter. The memories were oddly distant, as if they were ten years and not less than a year ago.

She hadn't contacted her university friends. What would she have said? They were law students, graduates, young journalists or accountants, all of them working at various firms if they had not already gone overseas. She could not bring herself to make any calls. The word 'terrorist' was plastered over the newspapers. And here Alexia was, alongside the protestors with their tino rangitiratanga placards, and the activists with their patches, with Polly, Te Kahurangi, Matiu and Rangi, for whom the city was nothing and their poisoned corner of land everything. During her placement she would have studied them curiously, possibly taking notes on behalf of a senior lawyer, before going off after work to drink wine at a bar. She would have mentioned them in passing to her friends: the case that gripped the nation, etc. But they would have remained cut-outs.

'All right, sis?' Rangi asked. He clapped his hand across her shoulder. They sat together on the plastic seats facing the doors, which were shut. The court agenda was up but she knew already that the hearing started at ten.

Every morning she gave a briefing on the latest legal matters. Māori and pākehā supporters she didn't know circulated with instant coffee and cups of soup. But all the busyness and the continual updates and activity masked was that nothing was happening. Isaiah had been denied bail even when Alexia thought he would most likely be granted it. It was without precedent. But then, the whole thing was without precedent, a thing her legally trained mind failed to accept. This meant it would be hard to argue the case, either for or against. It was outrageous. If Isaiah lost this hearing he would remain in gaol while the state prepared its case against him, for however long that would take.

Sam approached with her customary briskness, clipboard in hand. Alexia felt wildly guilty, in a way that only a good Greek girl might feel. She hated this deeply entrenched guilt without the benefits that would have been conferred by faith. If she was truly Christian maybe the guilt would be worth it; she didn't know. Wasn't that the way it was meant to work? You sinned, and offered your apologies up to God, and he would wash you clean. It was a fair and symmetrical exchange: information for absolution. If only the justice system worked on a similar basis.

She was rendered culpable by Sam's presence. She wanted to excuse herself, to explain, no, it was only that one time. Nothing else happened. Her thoughts were written across her face, she was sure of it. Her feelings for Isaiah were just another divine rip-off, with all the disadvantages of a relationship without any of the pleasures.

'We need to have a talk,' Sam said.

They went to the far corner of the foyer. Alexia readied herself for a confrontation of some kind. But Sam suggested they might work out their key messages before facing the post-trial cameras. She talked about sound bites and how to phrase things to evade editing. The TV news would be wanting something that could be taken out of context.

'Don't you miss him?' Alexia said. All at once she needed everything to be real and true and out in the open. Sam's finger stopped on the page that she was scanning.

'You must realise,' she said, 'that this is what he is. That this was always going to happen.' She examined Alexia's face, then reached out to a passing volunteer and got them coffee. Alexia became aware that the space around them was charged and respectful. Everyone here knew who they were. Sam was the known campaigner and loving partner, bearing up bravely in the face of adversity, and Alexia was the group's unofficial legal adviser. The young volunteer who gave Sam the coffees dipped her head – she could almost have bowed. 'He's been preparing for this for years,' Sam went on. 'He knew that this might happen.'

'Being labelled a terrorist?' The coffee was scalding hot.

'He always knew we were being surveilled. And any activist who has ideas like Isaiah does is going to be caught eventually. You'd probably find he doesn't care that he's being "blamed", if it's drawing attention to the cause.'

'You talk about him like he's some kind of saint. How can you be so sure of what he's feeling?'

'Long association,' Sam said, and took a sip of coffee. She leaned forward then and tilted her head and spread her hands out wide in the air, much, Alexia realised, like Alexia herself. 'And who do *you* think sabotaged the fracking site, Alexia?' Alexia said nothing. Then Sam changed, sitting back, and swiftly becoming herself again, so that Alexia had to wonder if she had really sounded so mocking. 'I wouldn't waste my time feeling sorry for Isaiah, that's all. He's probably happy with what he's achieved.' She shook her head. 'I bet he's not having an easy time being locked up though.'

'I don't know how you do it,' Alexia said. 'Stay so calm.'

Sam shrugged.

Perhaps Sam did not feel Isaiah's continued imprisonment as keenly as Alexia did: as a constant stinging lack. Alexia thought of him when she woke up and when she went to sleep. His physical absence overlaid everything. It was a great irony, she thought, that she'd never really had him in the first place.

'You've lost weight,' Sam said. 'You should watch yourself.' This was what people under stress were meant to do, lose weight. It had never happened to her before. 'It's not going to help anyone if you let it all get to you,' Sam said.

Melissa and Kate were watching them from a distance.

'Doesn't it bother you that he might not come out?' Alexia asked.

'We're lucky,' Sam said. 'In other places, if you oppose the state, they come in the night and shoot you in the head.'

'That doesn't mean this is right,' Alexia said.

'I've never been able to hate you,' Sam said. She grasped Alexia's arm and Alexia tried not to flinch. 'I didn't mind him fucking other people. They were people we knew, usually, or random girls ... whatever. I could deal with that. And I had my own adventures. You hate the other woman, a little, just at first. It's biological. Then you see the hate and change it. It's a matter of overturning our ideas about private ownership. It's a matter of strength of will.'

Written on the clipboard between them was: *What happened to innocent till proven guilty?*

'But I couldn't properly hate you in the first place,' Sam said. 'You're too much like him for me to feel resentful towards you. You're too messed up.'

Alexia felt, keenly, the body she inhabited. What was it that Te Kahurangi had said of Sam, that day on the porch with Alexia in hot-pink heels? Stupid white girl.

Alexia wished she had something clever to say. But then she thought of Sam in the forest, handing her chocolate, and getting so angry when she had to leave Alexia alone.

'I guess only you and I and Isaiah know how messed up you really are,' Sam whispered.

The courtroom doors opened.

Alexia went in gladly. Polly sat to her right with her bottled lavender smell, and Te Kahurangi sat on her left. The layout of the court, its pomposity and decorum, was no great surprise to Alexia. For a moment, though, she saw it as Te Kahurangi might: a hierarchy of tiers. The supporters all sat in rows towards the back. The next rung up were the lawyers – Isaiah's, with his assistants on either side, and the Crown's. From this row forwards, everyone was white. This was common to most courtrooms that Alexia had been in. The lawyers' desks were covered with papers, and in front of them was a place where they would pace before the court. She tried to angle herself to see if she could read the documents, but she couldn't. At the highest desk of all sat the judge himself. Architecturally the room gathered itself up to him, a collection of inanimate, supplicating shapes.

'They actually wear wigs?' Te Kahurangi whispered. 'And dressing gowns? No shit.' Alexia could tell she was afraid.

Isaiah was led into the room by a bailiff. There were gasps, and calls of support. Melissa began to sob. Polly stirred, and Te Kahurangi half stood up and had to be pulled down again. Rangi called out a loud greeting.

'Order in the court. Any further disturbers of the peace will be held in contempt.' Alexia appreciated how keen the judge must be, given the numbers of protestors outside, to keep a lid on any disobedience.

'Kia kaha,' Rangi yelled, one last time.

Isaiah saw her. He waved to everyone, but his eyes stayed on her. She looked away, to the prosecutor's table, to the guards all around. They uncuffed him. He wore ill-fitting clothes. There was a sparseness to his face behind the new beard. She told herself to breathe deeply, not to blush. Sam was seated behind her, a little to the left. Perhaps he was searching for Sam's face in the crowd, not for hers. But no, he was looking at her.

Then the long talking began.

Alexia did not expect things to happen fast. She was not

surprised to find that they got through morning tea and into lunch without anything significant being said. After lunch the serious action started. It was the nature of a courtroom: the sonorous reading out of charges and counts, the methodical presentation of evidence, the ceremonious forms of address ('Your Honour,' 'Counsel'). In the past, it had made her feel a kind of satisfaction. But now every second was a small trauma of waiting; the collected seconds like a fist in her chest, while her body went torpid with inactivity. They had brought in character references for Isaiah – an old lecturer, a family friend, a man who had worked with him in an environmental NGO. She appreciated what they were doing, and tried to explain it all to Te Kahurangi: the Crown was making allegations about terrorist acts, and the first thing for his lawyer to show was that Isaiah was not an immediate threat to society. This shouldn't be too hard, she said.

Isaiah's last character witness sat back down.

'Permission to question the defendant.' The Crown's head lawyer was standing.

Alexia had hoped Isaiah would avoid this. Isaiah stood.

She hadn't managed to see him. She had got all the way through the first level of security at the gaol he was staying at now, before someone had come to say there was a mistake in her paperwork.

Polly grasped at Alexia's hand, though she seemed unaware of it. The Crown lawyer asked Isaiah's name and date of birth.

'You are pleading not guilty to all of your charges.'

'Yes.'

'You expect us to believe, that you, a seasoned activist with a criminal record ...'

'Objection. Prejudice –'

'Objection sustained.'

'You expect us to believe, that someone such as yourself, a man passionately committed, as we have heard, to environmental causes, who has a known record as a protestor and organiser of demonstrations, would return to his ancestral land to find it polluted and do nothing?'

'Well,' Isaiah said. 'I didn't exactly do nothing. We did organise a fundraiser –'

'You expect us,' the Crown lawyer went on, 'to believe that when your appeals to the council failed, and your protests did not draw attention, that you gave up?'

'Objection, Your Honour. Leading the witness.'

'Sustained.'

The torpor of the last few hours dropped away.

'We've been told,' said the Crown lawyer, 'that you are a fine upstanding citizen. One, we have been asked to believe, who does not pose a threat to his or to any community, or the general public. A fine, upstanding citizen, as your character witnesses said – ethical, intelligent, professional.'

'Yes,' Isaiah said into the gap the lawyer left.

The Crown lawyer turned theatrically to the court audience. 'A pacifist,' he said. 'An advocate for peace.'

'Yes,' Isaiah said. His eyes turned to Alexia, wide behind his glasses.

The Crown lawyer turned towards the judge. Now his voice was quiet. 'You're aware, Your Honour, that charges such as these have not been heard before in this country. You're aware of the importance of the Crown's allegations. You're aware that the police do not lay firearms or conspiracy charges lightly. The Crown has sufficient evidence to prove that, quite in contrast to Mr Brown's peaceful image, Mr Brown is in fact the leader of an organised terrorist cell.'

The word 'terrorist' fell on the court like a knell. The judge cleared his throat, but did not speak.

'Permission to present exhibit 2a, Your Honour.' Permission was granted.

The court attendants set up speakers at the front of the court. The Crown prosecutor seemed almost gleeful. Surveillance. They really had been listening all along.

'Play the recording from 3.42 minutes through, please,' the Crown lawyer said. He was brisk now, as if disgusted with the whole affair. The recording began.

'We'll need some lengths of pipe,' Isaiah's voice said.

'For locking on? We're planning an occupation, then?' a voice asked. Alexia recognised it as Rangi's.

'Not an occupation, an attack,' said Isaiah. 'An attack on their house of power: the courthouse. They attack us with their chemicals and trucks, ripping out trees, destroying the earth. So we attack them. Who could blame us? We'll slip the pipes up our sleeves, like batons.'

The recording clicked off. Then Isaiah's lawyer was up and objecting, and his assistants were scrambling through their papers, and the judge was telling everyone to quieten down.

'We are asked to believe,' the Crown lawyer said, 'that this man is of good character; law abiding, peaceful. He is accused of plotting terrorist acts, of sabotaging private property, of conspiracy with a group with the intent to cause violent harm. He says he is not guilty of these acts, and he asks us to take him at his word.'

Isaiah's bail was denied.

Kate went out of the courtroom doors screaming the news to the supporters waiting outside. There would be no speeches to the waiting cameras, no clever sound bites, no pithy interviews. There would be no Isaiah being led out the back door. Alexia watched the news go along the corridors of the court and out into the street through the towering glass windows. It went through the protestors outside like a ripple, bowing them. Then they started to wave their banners anew. She stood for a moment in front of the court doors, wordlessly.

'Get her out of here.' It was Rangi. He spoke over her head to Te Kahurangi and Polly. 'Get her out.' He touched her face and his hand came away wet.

And mercifully she was whisked from the front door to the back, out into someone's car, through the crowd around the courthouse and back to the city marae, and into a chair, where she was given a cup of tea. Polly sat near her.

'You expected something else?' she asked. She laughed. Alexia had never heard her laugh sound like that before. 'Really? You expected them to let the Māori terrorist go?'

Later that night Alexia found herself on a bench, alone. Everyone had gone to bed. Their meal had been subdued. The food was stale – the same donated bread and hummus that they'd eaten the night before. The marae was a popular space, used by many different iwi and hapū. The tukutuku patterns were done in pastels and the carvings were modern in design. Alexia felt homesick for the deep browns and reds of the home marae, the old pāua carvings. Was she homesick for the house that had been her house, Papou's house, with the olive tree out the front? She wasn't. She remembered Papou, breathing out cigarette smoke all those Sunday afternoons, playing his bouzouki.

She didn't miss the house because it was her: it had made her, and it would always be her. There was nothing, really, to miss.

Alexia had never smoked, perhaps sensing that hers was the kind of personality that would fall wholeheartedly into the habit. But right now, if she was offered a cigarette, she would smoke all of it, down to the nub. She would grind it out and ask for another. She would take all that sickness into her body, all that bitterness. She thought she understood the drive towards self-abnegation, the need for a thing that made you feel alive but that was also death.

She saw Polly's slight form outlined near the open door. She was smoking, of course, her long bone cigarette holder hanging from her hand. She watched the smoke curl around Polly's face, half-thinking she would ask for a drag, but when Polly came to crouch next to her on the ground, as gracefully as ever, the smoke hit at the back of Alexia's throat unpleasantly. She didn't want it after all.

'Don't know how long it will take to get him back, do we?' Polly had never appeared subservient, not to anyone. Her mana was unquestionable. Her old eyes were rimmed with tears. 'What do you think, Alexia? How long will an appeal take, and how likely is he to get out on bail?'

Alexia didn't know, and she said so. There was no blueprint, no source to turn to for information, no set procedures. There was no way of knowing how long such a trial would take, or if Isaiah would be declared guilty or freed. It struck Alexia that as hard as this was for her, Polly was in a different situation. How old was she? In her eighties, maybe. Polly did not have a great length of time to wait.

Polly's voice was loosed into the air. It was unintentional, It seemed the woman could not control it. The sound turned into a mourning song, like the one she had heard the morning the eels had died. Except as she followed the notes, distracted, their green and gold flashes fading against the night air, this song broke into sobs.

Now Polly was weeping. She reached out to Alexia, and Alexia, as surprised as if an idol had become animated, reached for Polly. Her frame was tiny. She felt the warm, unlikely tears against her collarbone. Polly was muttering into her shoulder. Alexia pulled away so she could hear.

'But he's only just come back home,' she said.

STÁSIMON

The next day, they released Rangi's tape.

TV One
    Morning Report
        and today a potential case of police brutality

        TV Three
A seventeen-year-old youth involved in a protest

                        Midday Report
            Someone's calling from the newspaper
                connected with the paramilitary raid on
    a small rural evening news you're here with

                Terrorist

        The nation is divided over claims that the police

        Someone needs to take this call. Someone needs to
        write something. Sam? Sam? Alexia?

            Local resident Rangi Tuhene says that the
                protestors were peaceful
                    Sam?

We were just protecting ourselves, he said.
We were just going in prepared

The girl involved in the incident has declined to

Māori are calling for investigation into the brutal
beating of a

Morning Report
One News
raid on a small rural community

I can come back if you need, Alexia. Alexia?

Black uniformed government forces entered the small rural
community

Midday Report

It's the legal team. Can you take this, Alexia?

Māori are calling for an apology

A local resident took this footage with his phone as he was caught up
in the

Six o'clock report

Terrorist

He said the group had been voicing their concerns for
quite some time before

The girl you see in the footage is seventeen

Morning Report

Alexia, the radio

*Following an incident with a gas exploration tower the small
rural community*

Midday Report

Terrorist

Footage of a young woman

Nationwide concern over the nature of the police response

Six o'clock news

Was the action justified?

*to protest fracking, a process by which the
land is fractured from underneath*

The accused is still being held after being denied bail

64

In court Alexia's face had grown flushed. Isaiah would have expected nothing less. He hadn't wanted to make her uncomfortable, but he had wanted to memorise her outline so it stayed with him, just in case. It was lucky that he had.

When his bail was denied he breathed deep into his stomach to keep his shoulders from slumping. What would it do for them, for Rangi and Matiu and Sam and all his supporters, if he seemed defeated by the judgement? He had been surprised to see his mother, waving and smiling unconvincingly as he entered the dock. When the judgement was read she turned to Alexia, as if for confirmation. He pulled his shoulders back. His mother started talking but he couldn't hear anything amidst the protestors' calls. Shame, they called to the judge, to the prosecution. Shame.

Rangi yelled some words from the local haka. Isaiah tried to catch his mother's eye, to send her some strength, to convey that he would be all right. She had raised him to be a leader, to resist. Was this what she'd had in mind? Beside her (strange, they were sitting close to one another) Polly sat with her customary composure. She looked at him along her nose, much as she had done on the day they met. And as on that day, the tears were moving down her face as naturally as the movement of the river. She lifted her chin, very slightly, tipping it upwards, and glared at him.

He understood. This was the latest in a long series of injustices Polly had seen. He was to stand tall, to withstand it.

The glare was for the people who had put him here, but also for him. Don't you dare, Isaiah. Don't you dare give up.

Next to her, Alexia was a mess of tears. She didn't seem to realise she was crying. He tried to meet her eyes but the guard pulled him out of the dock, and then she was lost in the crowd.

It wasn't until he got back to the cell that he let his shoulders relax and his head hang down. Everything felt speedy and off-key. He recognised the adrenalin comedown but he hadn't expected to feel so physically sick. Of course: he had not eaten breakfast, unable to stomach it. Here were four walls around him, a cold metallic bench, here was the floor. What were they doing now outside the court?

They would be issuing press releases, maybe, doing interviews. Alexia's face had been anguished, unpretty. She would be unfit to deal with the press. At least in all this people might hear about the fracking. Four walls, a metallic bench … He was to remain in gaol for an indeterminate time. He hadn't seen the detective inspector and the constable since he had been put in the transport. He almost missed them.

When the guard came in to say that the van was there to take him back to the remand prison, he jumped. Every time he was processed the fear came back: a slick, uncontrollable fear. Each time they asked him to hand in his belongings. He would need to submit to a quick search. Each time he held his breath, waiting for the window of possibility to be over. He was on his knees, naked, he was on his knees.

It didn't happen this time.

Back in his new cell he began to kick the wall, one, two, three, in a rhythm repeating over and over. Alexia's face, red and wet with tears. Polly, lifting her chin. His mother scattering words away from her like beads. She was like a child who had been playing happily until her toy had rolled away across the floor. His toes felt bruised but he kept on kicking. This and this and this moment. How else was he to mark the time inside this horrible luxury of enclosed moments? This moment, this moment. His toes were sore and full of pain. He was here, for the duration.

I won't let it happen ag—

You're going to want to talk, son.

What had he done?

65

The journey back to the pā was subdued. They'd hired a bus and were accompanied by a convoy of cars. On the way to the trial they had sung and done a lot of hopeful talking. Alexia had even been asked to play the bouzouki, and had agreed to mixed response. But the trip back was quiet.

When they got to the pā, they saw that the burned tower was gone. It was a smart move by the fracking company, this removal of evidence. Taylor had notified the people ahead of time, but still the absence of the black shape was a shock. As if the tower, and the explosion, had never been.

There was no welcome home. Everyone had come to the court. The land was as cruelly beautiful as ever, and the sun was shining. It was still winter, but the day was clear and bright. Polly disembarked and walked a few steps into the green field. Alexia went after her. When she'd come here it was spring, and she was planning on studying for her bar exam. It seemed she had absconded from her own life. She waited beside her, but Polly did not sing or speak. Instead she walked towards the marae, stooped slightly, unlike her usual self.

Alexia turned back towards the bus. There were voices, car doors slamming, many voices speaking at once. Where before there had been a couple of vanloads of journalists, now the car park was full. The media had properly arrived.

She searched the car park for another car: a small red hatchback. It was there. Katherine had returned.

In the days that followed Alexia presented her files of carefully curated fracking information which had been accumulating over the months of their stay. She had Isaiah's images. She had a collection of reports that she'd written for all of their submissions to the council and to the government. Finally, it seemed, there was a willing audience.

The media filled the pā with unfamiliar faces. The journalists, most of them, wore expensive walking shoes, new khaki-coloured shirts and functional pants, as if they were going on safari. The ones who spoke in front of the cameras sometimes wore ties and shirts while the cameras shot from the belt up so as not to capture their khaki shorts. Isaiah would have approved of the functional attire. With their rigorous attention to detail, their possibly genuine concern, and their meticulousness, they reminded her of him.

But then everything reminded her of him.

The media came, and the story blew up, for a little while.

Isaiah was still in gaol.

Mostly the media wanted to talk to Te Kahurangi who, now that she was seated in front of TV cameras, grew embarrassed and withdrawn. Until someone asked her about the trauma directly, about how it had felt to be held down and kicked and beaten by three adult policemen, Te Kahurangi had worn the incident like a badge of honour. A very nice journalist from Māori TV asked whether the line across Te Kahurangi's forehead would scar. Alexia, watching Te Kahurangi from the sidelines, saw an unexpected fear in the girl's face, as though it hadn't yet occurred to her that a scar from a police beating might be an undesirable thing for a young girl to have.

Which was better? The falsely tough Te Kahurangi who was proud of the altercation? Or this vulnerable young person who the media wanted to make out to be an innocent child? Alexia remembered the shiv and her own deft confiscation of it.

Katherine waited quietly while Te Kahurangi did the interviews. Te Kahurangi seemed to relax afterwards as Katherine led her away.

The fracking activity was a constant backdrop. The guard who had been injured in the tower explosion was approached by the media, but he would not comment. He had a meeting with Polly that lasted late into the night. In the days that followed Alexia heard pieces of the story: the guard had a teenage daughter he wanted to send to a school in the city. He had been offered a payout by the company to not talk about the accident. Alexia didn't know how Polly felt about this. Rangi and Matiu had an argument about it, one that they quickly censored when she entered the room. She had seen Polly hongi the guard in farewell.

The media found it difficult to gain entrance to the fracking site or to obtain any of their own footage.

The days unfolded at a frantic pace, with the visitors needing to be fed and housed, putting financial pressure on the locals, who were already stretched with the court-related travel. Mary and Polly convened late at night, bent in conversation. Alexia, who knew how low their funds were, didn't understand how their money could be made to go further. Rangi and Matiu began to go to town every day to receive the fisheries handouts: generally by-catch and things that couldn't be sold elsewhere. Mary wrangled this into meals. And people from other marae began to come with donations. Often they had little time to give, and would arrive, have a cup of tea and go, always leaving contributions of sacks of potatoes, flour or their local produce. Somehow, there was enough.

Alexia was either helping Mary run the wharekai, or answering calls, or photocopying fact sheets for the press. Rangi and Matiu grumbled at the work but went about the chores with a certain grim elation. Isaiah might be in gaol, but at least, finally, their concerns about the fracking were being heard.

For some reason the pākehā protestors were not doing so well. Melissa had not been seen to cry, aside from at the outcome of the trial, which Alexia considered a sign that she was actually stressed. Kate was oddly silent at meetings. They excelled at doing whatever was asked of them, but they both had an odd listlessness that Alexia could not fathom. One day she was clearing dishes when she saw the two standing close together, watching the many journalists circulating in the hall. Melissa was wringing her hands and Kate had a dazed expression. Perhaps Alexia understood. For so many years they had believed themselves to be surveilled by the police, to be the centre of so much important activity. They had longed for media attention, for the storm that was occurring now, but when it came, they were like those people who won the lottery and then went bankrupt the next year. They did not know how to welcome what they had thought they wanted.

Aidan had been behaving strangely since the tower caught fire. He and Hannah seemed snappish and short with each other. Taylor hung around like someone's lost dog, volunteering to do the most menial tasks, and Bryce had been banished again. Taylor gave many interviews, in which, unfortunately, he came across as some kind of environmental zealot. Despite his fervour, he was not well liked. Lizzie was very pregnant. Though she'd been determined to stay, to not be 'kicked out of her home', as she'd put it, she was considering moving herself and Tama and Ana away. Maitai's absence left a space. Alexia remembered him stroking her arm, the night of the fundraiser, his gap-toothed grin as he pulled her onto the stage. Te Kahurangi told Alexia that everyone was growing concerned for Tama, who had been seeing a lot more than friendly taniwha in his dreams. Lizzie wanted to take him north to be trained by an elder, by someone who would teach him how to use his powers, and also how to live in the world. Tama's wasn't the only case of paranoia, though. In the rush and the bustle of managing the visitors, Alexia caught odd looks between them all, small silences. No one addressed the question that Mary had asked the night the tower burned. Which of you has done this?

In contrast to the others, Sam seemed to be on form. She was running things again. She seemed, almost, to enjoy it.

Rangi and Katherine had struck up a friendship. Alexia was surprised to realise she felt slightly jealous. One night the three of them sat on her porch and watched the sky fade over the fracking towers. Rangi noted that three new towers had gone up, even with the media present. Music came from the wharekai behind them, and for a few moments Alexia let herself slip into watching the small notes flash and burst. Since the raid she had seen no more disembodied lights. Every synaesthesia-like flash she saw had a musical accompaniment. Perhaps whatever it was she'd seen had expended itself that night in the forest.

Te Kahurangi passed them, with Polly. Katherine waved. Rangi nodded to himself.

'Just like ya sister, aren't ya? Getting right into the local issues.' Katherine did not seem put out.

'I love it here,' Katherine said. 'But I do have to go back sometime. By the end of the holidays, at least. What about you, Alexia?'

Alexia opened her mouth, and closed it again.

'Ahh, but it's difficult for her now,' Rangi said. 'She has commitments.'

'That's it,' Katherine said to Rangi. 'Tell me what the deal is with her and Isaiah. I can't get anything out of her. She just clams up.' She smiled sweetly and patted Alexia's leg.

'When I got here he was with Sam,' Alexia said. 'It was complicated.'

'And Isaiah's important round here. We've been waiting for him.' Alexia was surprised. Usually Rangi ribbed Isaiah mercilessly, but this time he was sincere. 'He had bigger fish to fry.'

'What's he like, this Isaiah?' Katherine asked.

'Kinda like his dad. Quiet. Clever,' Rangi said. 'Less full of himself. But something's going on in Isaiah all the time, and you can never be sure what it is.'

Matiu was standing behind them. 'It's like, the whole time he's around, you're kind of waiting for him to snap,' he said.

Rangi, Katherine and Alexia were silent. He backed away, hands raised in defence. 'Jeez, I'm just stating the obvious!' he said. 'I know he's our great long-lost leader and everything, but he does have this thing about him. He's pretty intense.'

Melissa came out of the building behind them, with Kate. Sam followed them. Aidan and Hannah walked away across the field.

'You could say that about a lot of people,' Rangi said. 'You could say that about all of us.'

Katherine studied him. Nothing more was said.

The next day, the phone rang, interrupting a meeting. Kate answered.

'Isaiah's on the phone. Alexia?'

Alexia stood and crossed the floor. She felt Sam watching her. She tried to stand straight, not to rush. She tried not to smile too obviously. She picked up the phone.

'You're on my approved list,' Isaiah said. Katherine, too, was watching her from across the room. Everyone was watching her.

'Do you need anything?' she asked.

'Cigarettes,' he said. 'No, really. I need them to trade for other things. I could do with another pen, and some toothpaste.'

'Right,' she said. 'Isaiah, you should know, we're all over the news. We released a tape with Te Kahurangi on it, at the protest. The media are packing out the marae right now. They're covering it all: the fracking run-off, the eels, Polly's water, the gardens, everything. They're doing another special tonight.'

'Great!' Isaiah said. 'But I won't get to see it. You could write to me about it all? Or try and remember the details, when you visit?'

Of course, No smartphones, no internet, no emailing, no TV. Isaiah was in a vacuum. She could read unpleasant things in his voice. Long hours in grey rooms. Walks down bright corridors. Small humiliations.

'Right!' she said, cheerily. 'Yes, I will!' But she didn't feel cheery at all.

66

Isaiah began to journey. It was not difficult to transport himself away from the bed with the light swinging over it, the rough blanket, the smell of his own body and the prison-issue soap he'd had to buy. He used to do it as a child. It was easy: a deep breath or two, and he could be elsewhere, examining the detail of a copse of trees or a riverbank in his mind. He had used to do this after studying the maps of his father's lands. He would study a thin blue line, or the demarcation of a ridge, and then take a deep breath, and see the land.

He journeyed sometimes to places he didn't want to go.

His mother. A cold room, darker than it should be. Why was it so dark? The light was off because it was his birthday. How old was he? Three years old.

'Blow them out! Big breath!'

Three candles on the cake.

But the house is lonely, the house is newly quiet. The house is wrong, full of emptiness and his mother making choking sounds behind the door.

'Big breath!'

He had wondered then. About his father.

'As if I would say that to a three-year-old, Isaiah! "Daddy's not coming home!"'

He would come out, travel elsewhere.

There was that night, of course, which he returned to again and again. Her, moving over him. The lack of stars. It was a twice-imagined thing, a thrice-imagined thing, because as it had happened he'd needed to imagine her face above him. And when he thought of it now, he liked to imagine something nicer, softer, something that made it seem like she cared. Again and again, the darkness, the bush, the oddness after. Her challenge.

What else was there to do in a small room with a blanket and a bed? What else was there to do with all the moments.

He began to bite his nails again. The days passed with a disconcerting regularity. There were three meals each day, if you could call them that. They didn't question him anymore. He almost wished for it. His only reading material was approved books and letters. Alexia sent him an awkward letter. It was about patupaiarehe and the taniwha, about Tama's stories, and how she was teaching the kids to play the bouzouki. She had drawn fairies stealing keys around the edge. He read it again and again. Sam sent him a guide to the development of debt in the free world, a new book on climate change and a couple of local newspapers, but he was only allowed to read one thing at a time.

Where else did he travel?

To the night the tower caught fire, the night he had understood te reo. He remembered understanding instinctively, not the individual words but the general meaning of what had been said. He hadn't been around anyone who'd spoken te reo since the raid. He wondered if his new knowledge would stick.

He travelled. He thought of the bush on the slope, his body running hard upwards towards the ridgeline. He thought of the white bone in his hand, and how it was not really a bone.

He had gone home. And he had found that it was so easy to get lost.

67

The media began to leave. The lawyers said not to hold out too much hope for further appeals. The public outrage that had occurred in the wake of the release of Rangi's tape made conditions more favourable, they said. But Isaiah was in on serious charges, and there was no time in the foreseeable future when he might be freed.

One day Alexia and Tama were sitting on her porch when they heard a high call from the trees nearby.

'My cat!' Tama leapt up. The call came again.

'Tama, it's just a bird.'

He would not be satisfied until they searched the treeline. The cat did not appear.

'Do you think it's dead?' he asked her.

'It's a wild cat,' Alexia said. 'It's going to be all right. But Tama, it's probably not coming back.' He stomped away. Again.

The next time she saw him, he climbed into her lap, as though he was grateful she had told him the truth.

Alexia scheduled a visit to the facility where Isaiah was being held. It had taken many weeks, much faxing of paperwork and even some personal calls to former associates. He had placed her on his list of people to see, of course, but at the last minute there was still always some reason given for a visit being denied. Tomorrow, she had been assured by various authorities, she had permission. She was going to see him.

Polly was down by the river. Since she had cried on Alexia's shoulder after the trial she had softened towards Alexia, but the woman's favour was a fickle thing, which might be withdrawn. Polly was showing the last of the journalists the part of the river that had recently been found to contain gas. Like the water in her kitchen, they had found that if they put fire to it, the water would explode into flame.

There was the bridge where the eels had died. She was struck by the muddiness of the water, its unprecedented cloudiness. Today there were no writhing bodies, only the Gortex jackets of the journalists, grey and black against the water, and the slick shine of their camera equipment. Polly was standing in the middle of the river, as she'd stood now many times for many different camera crews. She was up to her thighs in the flow, the water murked and orange at the edges with fracking run-off. She stood in the water even though the wind sent the cold thrilling through Alexia, who was dressed in layers of thermals. Polly's skirt swirled in the flow. Her feet must be so cold. The wind came down off the mountain. It was true winter, and the air had the smell of snow in it. Polly was speaking to the cameras, holding up a lighter. She would be giving them information about the toxicity of the water, before she rewarded them with the visual they were waiting to record.

Polly bent and held her lighter to the flow. A plume of flame hit the air, much larger than the one Alexia had seen in Polly's kitchen. Polly stepped back, away from it, and it almost obscured her. She kept talking through the gasps of the journalists. There was a flurry of small, concentrated movements as the camera people jockeyed for better angles and adjusted their settings. Almost proudly, Polly flourished the lighter aloft.

Alexia left them all bent towards the unnatural flame. There was triumph on Polly's face, an intensity that had been missing in the weeks since Isaiah's incarceration. After all that had happened to her people, she was finally being allowed to speak. She would be featured that night on the news, and in the show afterwards, where issues were more intensively discussed. She would get to voice her concerns about the fracking, about its impact on the people of the land.

Alexia moved away towards her house. Just before she went inside, she looked back. Polly was bent over the orange light, which from a distance seemed like one of Alexia's own private visions. It was as though the flame originated from Polly, as though she was the bearer of it. Alexia tried to be pleased for her. But beyond the few days when the media would discuss what was happening in this place, Alexia wasn't sure if, in the long run, anyone really cared.

EPÍLOGOS

Three Months Later

It was routine to her now, the convoluted process of checking in, the jumping through hoops, but it was never ordinary. The prison reared up ahead of her, a grey block in a green landscape. At the first hoop she passed through the automated steel doors and into the cool, air-conditioned room. At the second she was required to relate her name, date of birth and occupation. At the third she needed to hand over her visitor's code and her wallet and keys and bag. Finally, she was required to give them an X-ray image of her body. This image would prove she was carrying nothing inside herself that Isaiah might use to escape. She imagined what the guard could see of her: all the bones revealed, as innocent as anyone else's bones, in the end.

Then she was claimed by the space, having left her identity at the door. She moved awkwardly along the pathways with the other visitors, unescorted, following the signs. The first time she had come she'd been hot with nerves, and this moment, the moment when the last steel door slid soundlessly closed behind her, was then and now the worst. She was locked in.

But he was there, slightly ridiculous in a bright orange boiler suit and with hair longer than the former Isaiah would have permitted. His eyes creased at the corners when her saw her. He started forwards and then dropped back, perhaps ashamed of his lack of control. They each moved towards the round table.

357

It had chairs attached to it that could not be moved. There was no screen between them, but on the first day when they'd tried to embrace, the guard had gestured at them to stand apart. The rules were: no handholding, no hugging. There was to be no touching at all.

'Lizzie had her baby!' she called across the space between them. Everyone else ceased to exist: the prisoners milling about, equally intent on their visitors, the guards lined up like toy soldiers along the walls. 'She had a little boy. Tama's decided he believes in Jesus. He asked him for a brother.'

'That's awesome,' Isaiah said. 'Is Rangi proud?'

'You should see him,' she said. 'No one can shut him up.'

'Any news about my appeal?'

Alexia shook her head. Isaiah had still been having trouble getting messages from his lawyer. 'Nothing's happened. I guess they're still sifting through the paperwork. Oh, and they are saying it's sabotage, what happened to the tower. The police found something that they think was used to blow it up.'

Isaiah nodded slowly. 'Have the documentary team left?'

'They've gone.'

So had Kate and Melissa and, finally, Sam, who had held on stubbornly, righteously, fighting for a cause that had turned into Isaiah.

Bryce had lingered for a while around the edges of the pā. Then it had come out that his wife Steph was the police informant. One day she disappeared from the campsite with the combi van. An activist from town had called them, suspicious, after seeing her visiting the police station. It hadn't taken long to work out that she had been the plant. Alexia hadn't thought she could feel sorry for Bryce. But she couldn't help it. How long had he been married to this woman? Bryce left, in apparent disgust. She couldn't imagine what it would have been like for the policewoman, living in that van through the winter, carrying on with her nudity and her bike mechanics and her female partner as she sent back her reports. There were many theories about who might have been working with her.

Alexia had wanted to believe the informant was Sam. There was a small, pathetic part of herself that would have enjoyed that. But she'd had to face it. Sam, and all her principles, all her political motivation, was entirely for real.

Even Aidan and Hannah had gone to the city to raise funds for the legal battle. After the last bail hearing most of the pākehā seemed to have finally had enough. The police had unwittingly made a hero of Isaiah for a little while. But everyone had drifted off, back to their lives. Katherine, though, was still at the pā. She had taken time off uni. She had discovered a love of animals and was learning how to milk cows. Te Kahurangi stayed too. Someone had to care for the sheep, she said, with Matiu balls-deep in legal applications and Rangi going gaga over his baby.

'The security guard who was injured,' Alexia told Isaiah. 'He's fully recovered now. And he managed to send his girl away to study.'

'That's great,' Isaiah said. 'But why are you so happy? You did throw rocks at him, remember?' He tried to smile. So did she, but they both failed.

They talked for a time about the people on the marae, and the fracking development, which continued. Isaiah glanced at the clock.

'How's Maitai?' he asked. Visits were twenty minutes long. 'Has he come back?' He was speaking too fast.

'Maitai won't come back,' Alexia said. 'He's staying with his aunty.' She would not tell Isaiah about Tama's bad dreams, or about how Ana cried often now, like a younger child. She would not tell him about how quiet Polly was all the time, how tired. Or about the panic that she felt grasp her own chest when she used her phone, convinced she could hear clicking on the line.

'I suppose you'll leave too, one of these days,' he said.

Three months of polite visits had come to a point. Alexia

found herself staring at him. Her hands were working at each other; she stopped them. The guard called that it would soon be time to go.

'Polly's asked me to be a music teacher here,' she said. 'At the kōhanga.' She had already said yes.

He laughed suddenly. It was a sound she realised she'd missed. His beard had grown in, and his skin was tanned from all the hours in the courtyard. He'd told her that their outside time was rationed. He spent as much time as he could out there, doing extra work so he could see some foliage, glimpse the sparse trees around the prison grounds. Did he take photos in his head, the same way that she heard music? She had started hearing tunes in her mind again sometime after he'd been transferred closer to the pā. It had been this more than anything else that had convinced her she should stay.

'What do your family think of that, then?'

'They're not talking to me. It's probably a good thing. I did talk to Yiayia. I suppose they all think I'm corrupting Katherine, that I've coerced her into staying here. I didn't want to tell them that Katherine's doing a good job of that herself.'

'But when will you sit your bar exam?'

'If I enrol in next year's test, I'll have time out here to study. I've decided I do want to be a lawyer.'

'Good. It would have been a waste otherwise. I would have felt terrible if all this had distracted you.'

'A distraction? This is our lives.' She had said it without thinking. Now it lay on the metal table between them. 'I shall be a defender of the innocents,' she said.

'I hope so,' he said. He leaned forward. 'I know you must want to talk, after everything that's happened.'

'But we can't talk,' she said. There were cameras in the room, and guards. 'Not any time soon.'

'Alexia,' he said. 'What do you think my sentence would be, if I was found guilty? They can't expect me to just stay here, can they, until they're ready to put me on trial? I'm in stasis. This waiting is a trial in itself.' He grabbed her hand. A guard near the door stirred.

Stasis, from the Greek; a standing still. The liturgia sung in her church was broken into kathismata, seats. After each seat came the stasis, the pause. Mama would chant, while Alexia would kneel, watching the rising of the lights.

'No touching,' the guard called out.

'You're the lawyer. How long do you think this legal stuff is going to take?'

'It appears …' She did not know what to say. 'It appears that it may take a long time.'

'Well, until we can talk, I guess you're just going to have to trust me,' he said.

His thoughtful eyes behind the glasses, his long hands, his earnest face.

'You're just going to have to trust me too,' she said.

The guard called time. Inmates began to leave.

'It's funny, isn't it?' Isaiah asked. 'We might have sabotaged ourselves. I thought myself that we could have been mistaken.'

'That night, in the bush?' she asked. 'It was stupid and impulsive, yes. It could possibly have ruined everything.'

'I'd like to think that we knew what we were doing,' Isaiah said, 'even if we rushed into it. Even if it didn't turn out very well.' The colour rose in his face.

She stood to go. She smoothed her hands over her dress. They were sweating. He stood, a bearded man in an orange suit, tired-looking, thin, possibly hers. The guards shepherded the visitors towards the door, and the leaving siren sounded.

'You can always choose whether to throw the stone or not, right?' she said.

Then he was against her, the coarse fabric of his suit next to her skin, his hand in hers. Alexia looked into his eyes for one second, two, before the guard came and pulled him away.

ÉXODOS

I cannot say of any condition of human life,
'This is fixed, this is clearly good, or bad.'
Fate raises up, and Fate casts down
the happy and unhappy alike.

A river east of the sea. From an eel's teeth
there sprang the ancestors of the nobility.
No man can foretell his Fate.
A spring on Mount Taranaki.

NOTES

The Párodos (πάροδος) in the theatre of ancient Greece can refer to the first song sung by the chorus. This Párodos is adapted from a translation of Sophocles' *Antigone, An English Version* by Dudley Fitts and Robert Fitzgerald (Harcourt, Brace & Company: 1939).

The Parábasis (παράβασις) in ancient Greek comedy is the point in the play when all of the actors leave the stage, and the chorus is left to address the audience directly.

The Stásimon (στάσιμον) in ancient Greek tragedy is a song composed of strophes and antistrophes and performed by the chorus. This Stásimon is adapted from *Antigone, An English Version*.

The Éxodos (ἔξοδος) is the exit point of the story in ancient Greek theatre. This Éxodos is adapted from *Antigone, An English Version*, including an adaptation of the editors' note 14: 'A river east of Thebes. From a dragon's teeth (sown near the river) there sprang men who became the ancestors of the Theban nobility,' and the editors' note 15: 'A spring on Mountain Parnassos'.

Antigone follows the events of *Oedipus at Colonus*. Antigone and her sister decide to return to Thebes in order to help their brothers. But upon her arrival in Thebes, Antigone learns her brothers are dead. Antigone's uncle has banned the burial of Polyneices, who he thinks was a traitor. Antigone defies the law, buries her brother and is caught. When she is locked in prison, she kills herself.

Māori spellings are from the online Te Aka Māori-English English-Māori Dictionary.

This novel is set at an imaginary pā. The atmosphere of this pā is reminiscent of the rural Māori community of Parihaka, but it is not Parihaka. The events in this novel reference the events of the 'Terror Raids' that occurred in Aotearoa in 2007. No figures here are representations of real people.

ACKNOWLEDGEMENTS

This novel has been made possible by the support of a Victoria University of Wellington Doctoral Assistantship from 2009–2013 and a Doctoral Completion Scholarship in 2013. I am indebted to Paul and Diane Beatson for the use of the Foxton Writer's Cottage. Parts of this novel were first conceived of at the Robert Lord Writer's Cottage in Dunedin in 2008.

Thank you to Bill Manhire for his wild suggestions. To Mark Williams, for reassuring me. To Damien Wilkins, for his astute novelist's eye. To Mary McCallum and Paul Stewart at Mākaro Press, and Sarah Laing for her cover – ευχαριστώ πολύ! To my te reo proofreader, Rangi Kemara, kia ora rawa atu. And thanks to Jane Parkin for proofing the English text, and my team of Greek proofreaders.

To Emily Perkins, Kathryn Walls and Nicholas Wright, for a pleasant conversation. To Katie Hardwick-Smith and Clare Moleta at the IIML, for practical support. To my classmates from 2009–2013: Pip Adam, Lawrence Patchett, Tina Makereti, Laurence Fearnley, Maxine Alterio, Marian Evans, Lynn Jenner, Christine Leunens, Stephanie de Montalk, Airini Beautrais, Hannah McKenzie Doornebosch, Gigi Fenster, Helen Heath, Sue Orr, David Fleming, Angela Andrews, Stephen Toussaint and others. To my MA class, Pip Desmond, Sarah Jane Barnett, Therese Lloyd, Rebecca Lancashire, Amanda Samuel, Nick Stanley, Amy Brown, Rachel Schmidt and Rob Egan. What a class! To the Greek community of Wellington. To my Bailey whānau, aroha nui. To friends who informed this work, Jack Trolove and Wai Ho. To my Ho whānau, we will eat dumplings. To Amy Ross, Kelly McNelly, Rosie Whinray and

Roxborough Street for being stalwart in the face of the storm. To all those who were raided under the Terrorism Suppression Act in 2007, my sympathies. To the New Zealand Police, for confiscating a box of avocados. To Gary Cranston, who informed Aidan's character, apologies. To Shomi Yoon, for her story about the Korean protestors. To Penny Leach, many golden ponies. To the community of politically aware people of Aotearoa working for justice in all its forms. To my sons, Niko and Ahirangi, and my partner, Ira, σε αγαπώ.